The Law of Liquidated Damages in Massachusetts

1ST EDITION 2013

Gary L. Monserud

2130575B01—1st Edition 2013

Printed in the United States of America

This publication should be cited: *Law of Liquidated Damages in Massachusetts* (MCLE, Inc. 2013)

Library of Congress Control Number: 2013947009
ISBN: 1-57589-793-8

All of Massachusetts Continuing Legal Education, Inc.'s ("MCLE's") products, services, and communications ("MCLE Products") are offered solely as an aid to developing and maintaining professional competence. The statements and other content in MCLE Products may not apply to your circumstances and no legal, tax, accounting, or other professional advice is being rendered by MCLE or its trustees, officers, sponsors, or staff, or by its authors, speakers, or other contributors. No attorney-client relationship is formed by the purchase, receipt, custody, or use of MCLE Products. The statements and other content in MCLE Products do not reflect a position of and are not ratified, endorsed, or verified by MCLE or its trustees, officers, sponsors, or staff. Contributors of statements and other content in MCLE Products are third-party contributors and are not agents of MCLE. No agency relationship, either express, implied, inherent or apparent, exists between MCLE and any third-party contributor to MCLE Products.

Due to the rapidly changing nature of the law, the statements and other content in MCLE Products may become outdated. Attorneys using MCLE Products should research original and current sources of authority. Nonattorneys using MCLE Products are encouraged to seek the legal advice of a qualified attorney.

By using MCLE Products, the user thereof agrees to the terms and conditions set forth herein, which are severable in the event that any provision is deemed unlawful, unenforceable, or void. To the fullest extent permitted by applicable law, MCLE Products are provided on an "As Is," "As Available" basis and no warranties or representations of any kind, express or implied, with respect to MCLE Products are made by MCLE or its trustees, officers, sponsors, or staff, individually or jointly. To the fullest extent permitted by applicable law, neither MCLE nor its trustees, officers, sponsors, or staff are responsible for the statements and other content in MCLE Products or liable for any claim, loss, injury, or damages of any kind (including, without limitations, attorney fees and costs) arising from or involving the use of MCLE Products.

Failure to enforce any provision of these terms and conditions will not be deemed a waiver of that provision or any other provision. These terms and conditions will be governed by the laws of the Commonwealth of Massachusetts, notwithstanding any principles of conflicts of law. These terms and conditions may be changed from time to time without notice. Continued use of MCLE Products following any such change constitutes acceptance of the change.

IRS Circular 230 Notice: Any U.S. tax advice found to be included in MCLE Products (including any attachments) is not intended or written to be used, and cannot be used, for the purpose of avoiding U.S. tax penalties or for promoting, marketing, or recommending to another party any tax-related matter or any other transaction or matter addressed therein.

Massachusetts Continuing Legal Education, Inc.
Ten Winter Place, Boston, MA 02108-4751
800-966-6253 | Fax 617-482-9498 | www.mcle.org

DEDICATION

For Ann Jones, my wife, confidante, and editor;
and for our three daughters, Josephine Elizabeth Monserud,
Eleanor Margaret Monserud, and Ingrid Justine Monserud,
whose challenges and achievements give joy and purpose to my labors.

PREFACE

Several factors motivated me to write a book about liquidated damages.

First, as a young lawyer in Rapid City, South Dakota, I was assigned many cases where contractors were fighting to avoid liquidated damages for delays in construction and owners were fighting to deduct damages assessed for delays. This aspect of the practice drew me into a study of the case law on the topic. Second, each time my wife and I bought a home, I was hesitant about signing a purchase and sale agreement designating a substantial sum as liquidated damages; I realized the impact of losing our deposit (which amounted to most of our savings) if we did not consummate the transaction. Third, having taught Contracts for the past twenty-five years, I am well aware that the topic of liquidated damages is usually allotted only one session. Such a brief introduction affords students minimal academic exposure to a topic that will bear upon virtually every contract agreement they will encounter in the future, either as practicing lawyers or as home buyers. Finally, I came to realize that the case law across the country is split regarding liquidated damages; about one-half of the jurisdictions require a single look, meaning that a judge must evaluate a liquidated damages clause from the vantage point of formation only. The other half of the country's jurisdictions allow a second look, meaning that a judge should consider postbreach economic realities in evaluating a clause. In 1999, the Supreme Judicial Court chose the single look rule, and this has been a choice with many implications. After 1999, decisions of the Supreme Judicial Court have refined the law pertaining to liquidated damages so that such clauses are very difficult to challenge, especially in contracts for the sale or lease of real estate. In light of the foregoing, I thought that a book summarizing the development of the law of liquidated damages could be useful to practitioners and judges.

Much of this book is descriptive, and by this, I mean that it is simply a case-by-case history of judicial treatment of liquidated damages clauses that begins with English antecedents and some of the earliest reported cases in Massachusetts. Naturally, given the abundance of case law, it would not be possible to cover each case and still write a book of manageable length: I had to select decisions that I found to be both important and representative. In the event that I have omitted to cite an important case, I would be grateful for any reader's feedback. Moreover, I found some opinions—especially some of the eighteenth century English opinions and early nineteenth century Massachusetts opinions—difficult to interpret. If any reader believes I have misinterpreted any opinion, I would be most grateful for his or her insights and corrections.

The concluding chapters of this book are prescriptive. I take issue with certain jurisprudential choices the Supreme Judicial Court has made in recent cases, and more especially with the long-term implications of those choices for the future of the law of liquidated damages in this jurisdiction. With respect to the prescriptive parts of this book, I understand that reasonable people may justifiably differ in their opinions. I invite views contrary to my own with this hope—that contrary views will be rooted in an understanding of our legal history and an appreciation of the values that stand to be either thwarted or advanced by different judicial approaches to liquidated damages clauses.

While the topic of liquidated damages may seem mundane, the law bearing upon liquidated damages clauses has many consequences. Like it or not, the enforcement or nonenforcement of liquidated damages clauses often has a significant impact on buyers and sellers, lessors and lessees, and many other economic players and, of course, on the lawyers who draft contracts and litigate when a breach occurs and one party claims damages as liquidated by agreement.

AUTHOR'S ACKNOWLEDGMENTS

I acknowledge with gratitude the support of Dean John F. O'Brien and the Board of Trustees of New England Law | Boston, for making possible a sabbatical semester during which I was able to do much of the research that provided a foundation for this book; I also acknowledge the diligence and excellence of the law students who provided research assistance, namely, Geoffrey Petis (class of 2009), Melissa Levine (class of 2011), Elizabeth Driscoll (class of 2011), Erik Hagen (class of 2014), and Zachary Heller (class of 2014).

I am ever grateful for the support and editorial work of my wife, Ann Jones; for the suggestions of Professor Paul Teich, long-time colleague at New England Law | Boston; and for the expertise, patience, and good humor of Maryanne Jensen and the editorial staff at MCLE.

MCLE'S ACKNOWLEDGMENTS

MCLE acknowledges and thanks Professor Gary L. Monserud for the pleasure of working with him on this book, and we are proud to offer this unprecedented analysis of liquidated damages as the latest addition to our collection of monographs for civil litigators. Professor Monserud's generosity in sharing his intellectual property with our organization is much appreciated.

We thank as well MCLE's board of trustees for its ongoing and enthusiastic support of the publishing program.

Finally, we thank the MCLE staff who shared their publishing expertise in the production of these pages.

John M. Reilly, Esq.	Maryanne G. Jensen, Esq.
Publisher	Editor-in-Chief
	August 2013

ABOUT THE AUTHOR

GARY L. MONSERUD is a Professor at New England Law | Boston, where he has taught Contracts and Commercial Law courses for more than twenty-five years. He earned his J.D. at the University of South Dakota School of Law in 1976, and an LL.M. in Corporation Law at the New York University School of Law in 1985. After earning his J.D. he clerked for two years for a federal trial judge, the Honorable Andrew W. Bogue of the United States District Court for the District of South Dakota. For eight years after his clerkship, Professor Monserud was in private practice with a firm in Rapid City, South Dakota. Professor Monserud has served as a visiting professor at the Vermont Law School and as a visiting member of the law faculty at the University of Bucharest, Romania.

TABLE OF CONTENTS

Chapter 1   Introduction

Chapter 2   The Uses and Decline of Penal Bonds in Commerce

Chapter 3   Extending the Compensatory Principle Beyond Penal Bonds

Chapter 4   Stipulated Damages in Contracts for Services and Sales: 1836 Through the Era of Justice Holmes

Chapter 5   Claims to Deposits: Deposits Fixing the Limits of Damages and the Parallel Law of Forfeiture

Chapter 6   The *Restatement of Contracts* (1932): A Two-Prong Test Replaces the Quest for the Intent of the Contracting Parties

Chapter 7   The Rise of the "Second Look Rule" in Real Estate Sales

Chapter 8   The Demise of the Second Look Rule

Chapter 9   An Evaluation of *Kelly v. Marx*: Strengths, Weaknesses, and the Need for Exceptions to the Single Look Rule

Chapter 10   The Extension of the Single Look Rule to Leases and Licenses: The Question of Mitigation

Chapter 11   An Evaluation of the Law in the Wake of *Cummings* and *Minihane*: How Can the Court Avoid Marginalizing or Submerging the Compensatory Principle?

Chapter 12   An Argument for a Limiting Principle on the Use of Acceleration Clauses in Leases and Licenses

Chapter 13   What's at Stake? A Collision of Jurisprudential Views

Chapter 14   The Challenge: Recharting the Law of Liquidated Damages in Massachusetts

CHAPTER 1

Introduction

Gary L. Monserud, Esq.
New England Law | Boston

§ 1.1   The Meaning of Liquidated Damages: The Purposes
        of this Book 1–1

§ 1.2   Current Case Law on Liquidated Damages Clauses 1–3

        § 1.2.1   The Prospective Nature of Judicial Review 1–3

        § 1.2.2   Burden of Proof 1–4

        § 1.2.3   Specific Performance 1–4

        § 1.2.4   Acceleration Clauses Enforced as Liquidated
                  Damages Clauses 1–5

        § 1.2.5   Evidence of Mitigation 1–5

        § 1.2.6   Economic Ramifications 1–6

§ 1.3   Objectives Served by Liquidated Damages Clauses.......... 1–6

        § 1.3.1   Freedom of Contract 1–7

        § 1.3.2   Predictability 1–7

        § 1.3.3   Efficiency 1–8

        § 1.3.4   Adhering to the Compensatory Principle............. 1–8

§ 1.4   Tension Between Freedom of Contract
        and the Compensatory Principle 1–9

CHAPTER 1

Introduction

Gary L. Monserud, Esq.
New England Law | Boston

Scope Note

This chapter provides an introduction to the concept of liquidated damages and a review of recent case law bearing upon the topic. The author discusses the purposes that liquidated damages clauses can serve and concludes with a discussion of the tension that exists between freedom of contract and the compensatory principle which has long served as a limit on liquidated damages clauses.

§ 1.1   THE MEANING OF LIQUIDATED DAMAGES: THE PURPOSES OF THIS BOOK

When parties enter into written contracts, they commonly include a stipulation for an agreed-upon sum, or a formula for computing a sum, that will constitute damages for the aggrieved party in the event of breach. Such a stipulation is commonly called a "liquidated damages clause" or a "liquidated damages provision." *Black's Law Dictionary* (9th ed.). Such clauses are often the subject of judicial review when there is litigation after a breach. If a liquidated damages clause survives judicial scrutiny, it will be enforced. If not, it will be void, and the party aggrieved will have the burden of proving actual damages, if any.

Practice Note

The term "liquidated damages" is defined in *Black's Law Dictionary* (9th ed.) as "an amount contractually stipulated as a reasonable estimation of actual damages to be recovered by one party if the other breaches." The terms "stipulated damages" and "estimated damages" are offered by Black's as synonyms. Black's defines a liquidated damages clause as "a contractual provision that determines in advance the measure of damages if a party breaches the agreement." Case law in Massachusetts is in accord. *See, e.g., Factory Realty Corp. v. Corbin-Holmes Shoe Co.*, 312 Mass. 325, 674 (1942) ("Liquidated damages . . . is a sum fixed as an estimate made by the parties at the time when the contract is entered into, of the extent of the injury which a breach of the contract will cause.") (quoting 3 Williston, *Contracts* § 776 (rev. ed.).

The possibility of nonenforcement gives rise to an argument for limiting the term "liquidated damages" to clauses that are enforced, using the broader term "stipulated damages" for agreed-upon clauses which may or may not be enforceable on judicial review. For example, Professor Farnsworth tended to use the term "stipulated damages" as a general description term, referring to stipulated damages that are judicially approved as "liquidated damages" and those that do not survive scrutiny as "penalties." E. Allan Farnsworth, *Contracts* § 12.18 at 811–20 (4th ed.).

A type of contract in which parties routinely stipulate damages for breach is a purchase and sale agreement for real estate, either residential or commercial. A common practice is as follows: a buyer makes an offer, for example, $500,000 on a house and includes a check for $1,000 as earnest money. If the seller accepts the offer, the parties later sign a purchase and sale agreement, at which time the buyer writes a check for $24,000, making buyer's total deposit $25,000, or 5 percent of the agreed-upon purchase price. The deposit may be held by the seller, or placed in escrow with a third party, such as a listing realtor or seller's lawyer. A clause in the purchase and sale agreement will often state that if the buyer fails to perform, the seller may retain the deposit as damages, and that this deposit will be the seller's sole and exclusive remedy for the buyer's breach. The amount chosen is not always 5 percent. Agreements may require more than 5 percent, or less; the parties are free to set the amount so long as it does not constitute a penalty. *See* E. Allan Farnsworth, *Contracts* (4th ed.); 24 Williston, *A Treatise on the Law of Contracts* §§ 65.1–65.35 at 211–372 (4th ed. by Richard A. Lord); 11 *Corbin on Contracts* §§ 58.1–58.22 at 395–533 (rev. ed. by Joseph M. Perillo); John E. Murray, Jr., *Murray on Contracts* § 125 at 812–25 (4th ed.). *See also* Joseph M. Perillo, *Calamari and Perillo on Contracts* §§ 14.31–14.35 at 530–36 (hornbook series, 6th ed.). Stipulated damages clauses are also common in real estate leases, *see, e.g.*, *Cummings Props., LLC v. Nat'l Communications Corp.*, 449 Mass. 490 (2007), construction contracts, *see, e.g.*, *Space Master Intern., Inc. v. City of Worcester*, 940 F.2d 16 (1st Cir. 1991) (applying Massachusetts law), and employment contracts, *see, e.g. Kroeger v. Stop & Shop*, 13 Mass. App. Ct. 310 (1982); *Wassenaar v. Panos*, 331 N.W.2d 357 (Wis. 1983).

The law governing liquidated damages clauses in Massachusetts is mostly case law, which is abundant, rich in detail, and spans more than two centuries. However, within a decade, from 1999 through 2008, the Supreme Judicial Court decided five cases that in combination defined and recharted the law pertaining to liquidated damages clauses more significantly than any five cases in the history of this jurisdiction. These cases merit careful scrutiny in light of our legal history and the competing value judgments currently being directed at liquidated damages clauses. My purposes are to tell the story of the evolution of the law of liquidated damages in Massachusetts, going deep into the roots, and then to subject current case law to a critical evaluation in light of that story. Gaining a good sense of the history is a tedious business, but ultimately worthwhile, perhaps necessary, in order to assess our current situation. But first, to provide a sense of issues recently addressed, consider the following five abbreviated fact patterns.

Practice Note

The U.C.C. has two provisions governing liquidated damages clauses. Section 2-718(1) sets forth a rule for clauses in contracts for sales of goods governed by Article 2, and Section 2A-504(1)(2) governs liquidated damages clauses in contracts for the lease of goods. To date neither section has been recognized and applied in any decisions by an appellate court in Massachusetts.

§ 1.2   CURRENT CASE LAW ON LIQUIDATED DAMAGES CLAUSES

Below are some examples illustrating current case law on liquidated damages clauses.

§ 1.2.1   The Prospective Nature of Judicial Review

Steve and Merrill (sellers) agreed to sell a house in Worcester to John and Pamela (buyers) for $355,000. The buyers made a deposit of $17,750 which was agreed upon as liquidated damages if buyers defaulted. A few weeks after signing the purchase and sale agreement, before the agreed-upon closing date, the buyers advised they would not go forward with the purchase. Within a few weeks, the sellers resold to another buyer for $360,000. Question: Are the buyers entitled to return of their deposit? Held: the sellers are entitled to retain the $17,750 as liquidated damages because

- damages in the event of the buyers' default were uncertain at the time of contracting, and

- 5 percent was a reasonable forecast of the sellers' damages in the event of the buyers' breach. *Kelly v. Marx*, 428 Mass. 877 (1999).

The Supreme Judicial Court decided that trial judges shall not take a "second look" to see whether or not there were any actual damages at the time of breach.

This holding reversed a decision of the Massachusetts Appeals Court which had required a "second look," meaning that a trial judge had been required to take account of evidence showing actual damages or the lack thereof. *See Kelly v. Marx*, 44 Mass. App. Ct. 825 (1998). Judicial review must be prospective, not retrospective; or ex ante, not ex post, as the jargon is currently used in case law and articles.

§ 1.2.2   Burden of Proof

A financial services corporation (lessor) leased equipment to a consulting company (lessee) for a term of years, and the lessee defaulted. The lease agreement contained a stipulated damages clause designating a percentage of unpaid rent as liquidated damages if the lessee breached; the contract was breached by the lessee. Question: Who had the burden of proof? Did the lessor need to prove that the clause was enforceable or did the lessee need to prove that it failed as a valid liquidation of damages and was *not* enforceable? Held: the burden was on the lessee; the party *challenging* enforcement of the liquidated damages clause has the burden of proving that it was not enforceable when viewed from the vantage point of formation. *See TAL Fin. Corp. v. CSC Consulting, Inc.*, 446 Mass. 442 (2006).

Practice Note

This case could have been decided under U.C.C. § 2A-504, but the parties litigated at the trial court on the assumption that *Kelly v. Marx*, 428 Mass. 877 (1999) was controlling. *Kelly v. Marx* became the law of the case. Since Section 2A-504 does not allocate the burden of proof, there is no reason to conclude that the application of that section would have changed the result.

§ 1.2.3   Specific Performance

Paul (seller) entered into an agreement to sell to Joseph (buyer) a property in Boston for the agreed-upon price of $2,250,000. Joseph made a deposit of $150,000 designated in the agreement as liquidated damages if he (Joseph) defaulted. Closing did not occur on the stipulated date, and each asserted that the other was in breach. Joseph commenced an action for breach of contract. Paul counterclaimed, and by motion sought specific performance which a trial judge granted. In addition to gaining the purchase price, Paul sought to retain Joseph's $150,000 deposit. Question: If a seller is allowed specific performance and thereby obtains the agreed-upon purchase price, may seller also enforce a liquidated damages clause if it passes the ex ante test for enforceability? Held: Specific performance precludes a claim for liquidated damages even if the stipulated damages clause would have been enforceable if there had not been specific performance. *Perroncello v. Donahue,* 448 Mass. 199 (2007).

§ 1.2.4 Acceleration Clauses Enforced as Liquidated Damages Clauses

Cummings (lessor) leased commercial real property to Communications Corporation (lessee) for a term of years. *Cummings Props., LLC v. Nat'l Communications Corp.,* 449 Mass. 490, (2007). The lease contained a rent acceleration clause pursuant to which all rent for the term could be declared immediately, payable as liquidated damages upon lessee's breach of any of several obligations which included payment of rent, payment of a security deposit, payments of taxes, or any substantial invoice for goods or services. The lessee failed to pay the rent on schedule. The lessor accelerated the rent, and demanded more than $525,000 for thirty-two months remaining on the lease. Question: If the accelerated rent was disproportionate to the lessor's estimated losses from lesser breaches, but was (arguably) proportionate to losses the lessor would incur on failure to pay the rent, was the clause enforceable? Held: It will be *presumed* that the parties intended the rent acceleration clause to apply only to *significant breaches* for which it might properly be enforced; hence, the rent acceleration clause was enforceable. *Cummings Props., LLC v. Nat'l Communications Corp.,* 2004 Mass. App. Div.112

§ 1.2.5 Evidence of Mitigation

Paul (licensee) licensed two luxury seats in Gillette Stadium from the developer (licensor) for the price of $3,750 per seat annually. The term of the license was ten years. The license agreement contained a clause designating as liquidated damages the accelerated total of all unpaid license fees for the term in the event of Paul's default. After paying a security deposit of $7,500, and $2,000 toward the first year's fee, Paul defaulted. The licensor demanded accelerated fees of $65,500 for the remainder of the ten year term Question one: Was the acceleration clause enforceable as a liquidated damages clause? Held: It was enforceable because the licensee failed to prove that at the time of formation, it was *not* a reasonable forecast of damages difficult to estimate at that time. Question two: Is evidence of mitigation admissible? Held: When the parties have entered into an enforceable liquidated damages clause, evidence of mitigation is not admissible. *NPS, LLC v. Minihane,* 451 Mass. 417 (2008)

Practice Note
The court had avoided the mitigation question *in Cummings Properties, LLC v. National Communications Corporation,* because the parties

had not rightly preserved the issue on the appeal. While the parties did not brief the mitigation issue on the appeal to the Supreme Judicial Court in *NPS, LLC v. Minihane,* it was raised by the pleadings and the court apparently thought it was prudent to decide the issue.

§ 1.2.6   Economic Ramifications

As is evident from the fact patterns, transactions involving interests in real property have featured prominently in the recent case law. Two of the foregoing cases arose from contracts for the sale of real estate: one from a rental of commercial real estate, and one from a license for stadium seats. While liquidated damages clauses can be inserted into any type of contract, the law of liquidated damages in relation to contracts involving interests in real estate (whether sales, rentals, or licenses) is important to sellers, buyers, lenders, brokers, and anyone else who has an economic interest in such transactions, given the hefty sums often involved. Consequently, the recharting of the law in these five recent decisions may have a serious economic impact on many people. It is worthwhile inquiring about the values underlying these decisions, the objectives the Supreme Judicial Court has sought to advance, and whether or not the holdings—if followed without exception and logically extended—will achieve the objectives enunciated by the court.

§ 1.3   OBJECTIVES SERVED BY LIQUIDATED DAMAGES CLAUSES

The courts in Massachusetts have articulated four objectives to be served by properly drafted liquidated damages clauses. These objectives have been either explicitly or implicitly approved by the Supreme Judicial Court, as the citations following will establish. These judicially enunciated objectives can serve as guidelines for deliberating about which clauses should be enforced and which should not be enforced. The objectives are:

- preserving freedom of contract;

- providing predictability thereby fostering security and peace of mind;

- promoting efficiency for the parties and the courts; and

- adhering to the compensatory principle, meaning that damages should compensate the party aggrieved rather than punish the party in breach.

I will anchor these statements about objectives with references to selected cases from recent decades.

§ 1.3.1   Freedom of Contract

Freedom of contract is a bedrock principle of private law. *See* U.S. Const. art I. § 10; U.S. Const. amend. XIV; U.S. Const. amend. XV. In *Lynch v. Andrew*, 20 Mass. App. Ct. 623 (1985), the Massachusetts Appeals Court upheld a liquidated damages clause in a real estate sales contract, and in so doing, acknowledged the importance of allowing private parties wide discretion in fixing their own remedies. Writing for the court, Justice Kass recalled the observation of Justice Holmes that, "so far as precedent permits the proper course is . . . not to undertake to be wiser than the parties." *Lynch v. Andrew*, 20 Mass App. Ct. 623 (1985) (citing *Guerin v. Stacey,* 175 Mass. 595 (1900)). More recently, in *Cummings Properties, LLC v. National Communications Corporation,* 449 Mass. 490 (2007), Justice Cordy noted a trend favoring freedom of contract with respect to stipulated damages provisions "as long as they do not clearly disregard the principle of compensation." *Cummings Props., LLC v. Nat'l Communications Corp.,* 449 Mass. at 495 (citing 3 E.A. Farnsworth, *Contracts* § 12.18 (3d ed. 2004); 24 S. Williston, *Contracts* § 65:30 (4th ed. 2002)). In fixing the terms of any bargain (considerations to be exchanged), parties are generally free to make their own deals, wise or foolish as any deal may be for one or both parties. Likewise, albeit to a lesser degree, liquidated damages clauses may be freely agreed-upon. As a baseline rule, the courts will respect the parties' freedom to bargain.

Practice Note
In *Lynch,* Justice Kass also advised that the court was "disinclined to tamper with a well-established solution" to the problem of fixing damages for breach in contracts for the sale of real estate, the solution being the parties agreed-upon stipulated damages clause.

§ 1.3.2   Predictability

Predictability leads to security and peace of mind; the latter flow naturally from predictability, which is simply a high degree of confidence in what a court will decide if called upon to evaluate a liquidated damages clause. Strong language in support of predictability appears in *Kelly v. Marx*, 428 Mass. 887 (1999), wherein the Supreme Judicial Court defended a single look rule, as opposed to allowance of a second look, confident that the latter would undermine predictability and peace of mind. The court touted the single look rule as one that will reduce challenges to liquidated damages clauses, thereby eliminating uncertainty, "making it unnecessary to wait until actual damages from a breach are proved." The desire for predictability is an understandable yearning, rooted in common sense. Lawyers and businesspeople reasonably expect that they should be able to know at the time of contracting whether or not their stipulated damages agreements will survive a judicial challenge. Ad hoc decisions in this area will serve nobody's best interests. Hence, a test for evaluating clauses should be straightforward, and enforceability or non-enforceability should be reasonably predictable.

> **Practice Note**
> "By reducing challenges to a liquidated damages clause, the 'single look' approach eliminates uncertainty and tends to prevent costly future litigation. The 'second look,' by contrast, undermines the peace of mind and certainty of result . . . the parties sought when they contracted for liquidated damages. It increases the potential for litigation by inviting the aggrieved party to attempt to show evidence of damage when the contract is breached, or, more accurately, evidence of damage flowing from the breach but occurring sometime afterward." *Kelly v. Marx*, 428 Mass. at 881.

§ 1.3.3   Efficiency

"Efficiency" is an elastic term. One accepted meaning of its adjective form, "efficient," is "acting or producing effectively with a minimum of waste, expense, or unnecessary effort." *The American Heritage Dictionary of the English Language* (4th ed.). Resolving disputes *efficiently* means keeping costs and time investments to a minimum. Efficiency has both private and public dimensions. On the private side, advancing efficiency means avoiding the costs of a lawsuit, if possible, and if litigation cannot be avoided, resolving a lawsuit with the minimal costs practicable. On the public side, efficiency means avoiding unnecessary judicial business, and saving the time of public servants in the courthouse, all supported by tax dollars or filing fees. The Supreme Judicial Court partly justified its single look decision with an eye to efficiency saying that "[i]n addition to meeting the parties' expectations, the 'single look' approach helps resolve disputes efficiently by making it unnecessary to wait until actual damages from a breach are proved." *Kelly v. Marx*, 705 N.E. at 881.

§ 1.3.4   Adhering to the Compensatory Principle

Adhering to the compensatory principle means that a stipulated sum should approximate the aggrieved party's lost expectation (benefit of the bargain). The compensatory principle was strongly endorsed in *Perroncello v. Donahue*, 448 Mass. 199 (2007), when the Supreme Judicial Court rebuffed the seller's attempt to retain a deposit as liquidated damages after receiving the full contract price pursuant to a decree for specific performance. Justifying the court's decision, Justice Cordy wrote that "[t]he law of contracts is intended to give an injured party the *benefit of the bargain*, not the benefit of the bargain and a windfall." *Perroncello v. Donahue*, 448 Mass. 199 (2007) (citing *Situation Mgt. Sys., Inc. v. Malouf, Inc.*, 430 Mass. 875, 880 (2000)) (emphasis added). Conversely, the purpose of remedies for breach of contract is *not* to punish the party in breach nor to deter breach by holding a party in terrorem fearing draconian consequences should a breach occur.

Practice Note

Protecting an aggrieved party's lost expectancy is an objective recognized in the Restatement (Second) of the Law of Contracts. *See* Restatement (Second) of Contracts §§ 344, 347–348. Of course, there are cases wherein the expectancy interest may yield to the reliance or restitution interests as recognized in § 344. But, the latter two interests play little, if any, role in the analysis of liquidated damages clauses.

§ 1.4 TENSION BETWEEN FREEDOM OF CONTRACT AND THE COMPENSATORY PRINCIPLE

To some extent the objectives discussed above can be applied harmoniously. However, the first and fourth objectives are often in tension. These principles collide whenever parties freely agree to a liquidated damages clause that by design or inadvertence substantially overshoots compensatory damages reasonably attributable to a breach. Writing in the Montana Law Review, Daniel Browder, Esq., a critic of the Montana Supreme Court's recent decisions on liquidated damages clauses, described these competing principles as "tectonic principles of law" that have created a "thrust fault" at the points of collision. Daniel Browder, "Liquidated Damages in Montana," 67 *Mont. L. Rev.* 361, 362 (2006). Mr. Browder observed: "[t]hese two principles have piled up against each other for centuries; the collision has created a notoriously inconsistent body of law." Daniel Browder, "Liquidated Damages in Montana", 67 *Mont. L. Rev.* at 362 (citing *Jaquith v. Hudson,* 5 Mich. 123 (1858)).

Practice Note

It is worth noting, however, that the Michigan Supreme Court in *Jaquith* took a fairly positive view of the case law (though apparently conflicting) in its review of a liquidated damages clause pertaining to breach of a covenant not to compete. The court stated: "We shall not attempt here to analyze all the decided cases upon the subject, which were read and cited upon the argument, and which, with others, have been examined. It is not to be denied that there is some conflict, and *more* confusion, in the cases; judges have been long and constantly complaining of the confusion and want of harmony in the decisions upon this subject. But, while no one can fail to discover a very great amount of *apparent* conflict, still it will be found, on examination, that most of the cases, however conflicting in appearance, have yet been decided according to the justice and equity of the particular case."

To change the imagery, the law of liquidated damages resembles a cable tightly strung between two poles: one pole is freedom of contract, and the other is the compensatory principle. Sometimes the poles are straight; sometimes one pole or the other tends to exert a harder pull bending it out of plumb and making the cable between uneven and unsteady.

The thesis defended in this book is that the Supreme Judicial Court in the five recent cases summarized above has created a set of rules that pull the law too far away from the compensatory principle and too far toward freedom of contract, with the result that *unreasonable forfeitures* from the breaching party to the aggrieved party will become common, unless limiting principles and exceptions are adopted. I am not arguing for a reversal of any of the five cases summarized above, each of which can (arguably) be justified on the facts of those cases. Rather, I am arguing that the Supreme Judicial Court should be open to adopting limiting principles, and that exceptions should be carved out, to prevent unreasonable forfeitures in future extensions of the law. My aim will be to articulate and justify limiting principles and exceptions in light of the long history of liquidated damages law in Massachusetts and jurisprudential considerations consistent with the objectives enunciated by the Massachusetts courts. My arguments will be developed with an eye to real estate transactions; however, because the law of liquidated damages has developed largely without limitation to any subject matter, I will of necessity be discussing many cases involving services, goods, and covenants not to compete. My purpose, however, is to suggest and justify a possible future for the law of liquidated damages in contracts for the sale, rental, and license of interests in real estate that is consistent with the objectives of such clauses.

CHAPTER 2

The Uses and Decline of Penal Bonds in Commerce

Gary L. Monserud, Esq.
New England Law | Boston

§ 2.1   **English Origins** 2–1

§ 2.2   **Penal Bonds in Nineteenth Century Massachusetts Case Law** 2–3

CHAPTER 2

The Uses and Decline of Penal Bonds in Commerce

Gary L. Monserud, Esq.
New England Law | Boston

Scope Note

Beginning with a discussion of the English origins of the penal bond as a form of liquidated damages in commercial practice, this chapter goes on to outline nineteenth-century Massachusetts' use of penal bonds.

§ 2.1   ENGLISH ORIGINS

Many legal historians are agreed that our law pertaining to liquidated damages has deep roots in English case law. *See* Kevin M. Teeven, *A History of the Anglo-American Common Law of Contract* at 157–74 (Greenwood Press, 1990); A.W.B. Simpson, *A History of the Common Law of Contract* at 90–115 (Clarendon Press—Oxford, 1987); William H. Lloyd, "Penalties and Forfeitures," XXIX *Harv. L. Rev.* 117 (1915). *See also* Morton J. Horwitz, "The Historical Foundations of Modern Contract Law," 87 *Harv. L. Rev.* 917 (1974). The law of liquidated damages developed against a background of the longstanding use of penal bonds in commerce. The historian A.W.B. Simpson used two characters, Hugo and Robert, to illustrate common uses of penal bonds. A.W.B. Simpson, *A History of the Common Law of Contract* at 97–115 (Clarendon Press—Oxford, 1987). Suppose that in the year 1500, Hugo agreed to lend Robert 100 pounds. The practice was for Robert to execute a bond in favor of Hugo binding himself to pay a higher sum, usually 200 pounds, on a fixed day, subject to defeasance if Robert timely repaid. The bond was instantly null and void if Robert timely repaid his loan. On the other hand, if Robert failed to repay on time, Hugo had an immediate claim to 200 pounds. Thus, the execution and enforcement of penal bonds provided a powerful incentive for timely payment of agreed debts.

The same technique was commonly employed in other commercial settings, such as agreements for sales of real property. For example, if Hugo agreed to sell Blackacre to Robert for the agreed price of 1,000 pounds, Hugo could execute a bond binding himself to pay Robert 2,000 pounds on a fixed date, subject to the condition that the bond became void if Hugo in fact made the conveyance as promised. Simultaneously, Robert could similarly bind himself to pay 2,000 pounds, double the purchase price, if he failed to close and pay for Blackacre as promised. Instead of real property, the subject matter might have been (and often was) a commodity, such as wool. Whatever the underlying agreement, penal bonds served as an inducement to performance and, in the event of breach, provided a reward for the party aggrieved.

The procedural law in relation to bonds was simple, but topsy-turvy from a modern vantage point. *See* A.W.B. Simpson, *A History of the Common Law of Contract* at 112–13(Clarendon Press—Oxford, 1987). An obligee needed only to produce the bond in court to make out a prima facie case. To be discharged, the burden was on the obligor to prove that the conditions on which defeasance depended had in fact occurred. The law pertaining to penal bonds had teeth, making breach perilous because the results were punitive if an obligor failed to prove the occurrence of conditions that caused the bond to become void. However, penal bonds were indisputably popular for many generations. They were akin to a pledge. Instead of tendering a hostage or personal property, a person bound himself to a performance of such gravity as to induce confidence of performance in the other party. Accordingly to Professor Simpson, "[t]he widespread use of the conditioned bond, both in England and upon the Continent, is only explicable upon the ground that it provided what the commercial community wanted." A.W.B. Simpson, *A History of the Common Law of Contract* at 113 (Clarendon Press—Oxford, 1987).

The use of penal bonds declined as the courts in England, beginning with the Court of Chancery, intervened to preclude forfeitures deemed unjust. The intervention happened incrementally in the seventeenth and eighteenth centuries for many reasons. A.W.B. Simpson, *A History of the Common Law of Contract* at 118–25 (Clarendon Press—Oxford, 1987). Some claims were brought on very old bonds. Even though no statute of limitations prevented the actions, enforcement was deemed inequitable due to lapse of time. Sometimes a defeasance was dependent on the occurrence of multiple conditions. Suppose nine of ten conditions occurred, but one did not. The question arose as to whether an obligee should collect the full penal sum for failure of one condition on a list of several. Chancellors, and later common law judges, adopted the practice of setting aside the bonds, and allowing only compensatory damages, when the penal sum was deemed inequitable. As this development was generalized, the *compensatory principle* was established as a limitation on damages whenever the stipulated sum was deemed punitive. Courts thereby moved toward our modern notion that a party aggrieved by a breach should be awarded the benefit of the bargain, by being put economically in the place where he or she would have been if the contract had been fully performed. *See* A.W.B. Simpson, *A History of the Common Law of Contract* at 123 (Clarendon Press—Oxford, 1987) ("[t]his development involves a recognition of the notion that a contracting party should only be permitted to recover compensation for loss actually suffered through default"). *Compare Restatement (Second) of Contracts* § 344(a) (defining the expectation interest). The rule developed that if a penal bond overshot the compensatory principle, it was not enforced.

§ 2.2   PENAL BONDS IN NINETEENTH CENTURY MASSACHUSETTS CASE LAW

The rule against penal sums in bonds given for breach of private obligations appeared in *Merrill v. Merrill*, 15 Mass. 448 (1819), a quaint Massachusetts case. John Merrill bound himself "to pay Charles Merrill or order, 50 dollars, on demand . . . ." providing that "if John Merrill shall permit Charles Merrill the free use of the washroom and hoghouse with himself, so long as the same shall stand, then the above note to be void." *Merrill v. Merrill*, 15 Mass. at 488. Apparently John did not allow Charles free use of the washroom or hoghouse. Charles sued demanding fifty dollars. The case went to a jury under a trial judge's instructions that the sum of fifty dollars was in the nature of a penalty, and that the jury should award only actual damages incurred. The jury awarded twelve dollars. On appeal, the Supreme Judicial Court upheld the award. The trial judge had rightly considered fifty dollars to be a penal sum, which was not allowable. Thus, as early as 1819, penal bonds were not allowed if the result was to overshoot the compensatory principle.

Despite judicial scrutiny, the use of penal bonds lingered long in Massachusetts. An example can be found in *Shute v. Taylor*, 46 Mass. 61 (1842). Taylor agreed in writing to convey a carefully described lot in Lowell to Shute, and also signed a penal bond in the sum of $500, payable to Shute if the conveyance as described did not occur. Taylor conveyed by a deed, but the property conveyed was less than described in the agreement because municipal officials had changed the width of the adjoining street, thereby taking some of the property. Shute sued on the bond claiming $500. The case went to the Supreme Judicial Court on agreed facts. The court held that the bond was unenforceable. Writing for the court, Chief Justice Shaw explained that the sum in the bond had been agreed upon for an entire breach (nonconveyance); Shute had received some of the consideration promised (albeit less than bargained for), so the bond was unenforceable as a penalty. The fact that the $500 was characterized in the bond as liquidated damages was not controlling. Shute, however, had a just claim for compensatory damages. *Shute v. Taylor*, 46 Mass. 61 (1842).

Practice Note

Chief Justice Shaw's more complete explanation was as follows: "It is not always the calling of a sum, to be paid for breach of contract, liquidated damages, which makes it so. In general, it is the tendency and preference of the law, to regard a sum, stated to be payable if a contract is not fulfilled, as a penalty, and not as liquidated damages; because then it may be apportioned to the loss actually sustained. But, without going at large into the subject, one consideration, we think, is decisive, against recovering the sum as liquidated damages, namely, that here there has been part performance, and an acceptance of such part performance. If the parties intended the sum named to be liquidated damages for the breach of contract therein expressed, it was for an entire breach. Whether divisible in its nature or not, it was divided by an offer and acceptance of part performance . . . . Conformably to the agreement of the parties, an assessor may be appointed to assess the actual damages sustained by the plaintiff." *Shute v. Taylor*, 46 Mass. at 66–67.

Another mid-nineteenth century example of an unenforceable penal bond can be found in *Fisk v. Gray*, 93 Mass. 132 (1865). Initially, Gray merely bought real estate subject to a mortgage, but thereafter signed a penal bond to avoid foreclosure. When the case came to the Supreme Judicial Court, the justices invalidated the bond because it covered obligations for breach of which the monetary consequences were readily measurable. As in prior cases, the inclusion of the words "liquidated damages" in the bond did not make the obligation contained therein enforceable. *Fisk v. Gray*, 93 Mass. at 133.

There were cases with contrary results, as is illustrated by *Chase v. Allen*, 79 Mass. 42 (1869), decided by the Supreme Judicial Court. Ethan Allen made plans to build a hotel in Worcester. To finance his project, Allen took $11,000 cash from one group of subscribers, and subsequently $9,000 in promissory notes from a second group. Allen promised refunds of the cash with interest, and cancellation of the notes, if his hotel were not constructed as planned. Additionally, Allen signed a bond deposited with Chase, promising $20,000 as liquidated damages *for the benefit of* all subscribers should his project fail. The hotel was never built, so Chase sued Allen on the bond for the benefit of the subscribers. Allen defended, claiming the sum agreed upon was a penalty. The case report says that "the case was submitted to the decision of [the Supreme Judicial Court] . . . upon a statement of facts." The court determined that the sum agreed upon was not a penalty, but rather a proper liquidation of damages, because the actual damages were "peculiarly uncertain and difficult of estimation in money." *Chase v. Allen*, 79 Mass. at 46

Hence, prior to 1870, two interwoven principles are observable. First, if damages were uncertain or difficult to estimate, the courts tended to find a stipulation to be compensatory, not punitive. The courts *presumed (inferred) an intent to liquidate damages,* not to punish. Conversely, if actual damages were subject to an exacting or reasonably accurate estimation, the courts *would tend to infer an intent to punish* and would tend to hold a bond unenforceable, especially if it appeared to overshoot compensatory damages. *See also Henry v. Davis,* 123 Mass. 345 (1877) (court refused to enforce the bond, finding "nothing in the bond . . . justif[ied] the inference of an intention that such sum should be treated as the stipulated and ascertained damages for a breach"). The *presumed intent* of the parties trumped the form in which any obligation was embedded. *See Guerin v. Stacey,* 175 Mass. 595 (1900). Whether the sum agreed upon appeared to be compensatory or punitive *in the facts of the case* was determinative. In due course, cases arising from penal bonds were generally treated as cases involving liquidated damages clauses. *See, e.g., Guerin v. Stacey,* 56 N.E. 892 (Mass. 1900).

Practice Note

This has been the case with respect to penal bonds into the twenty-first century. In the twentieth century the compensatory/punitive dividing line for penal bonds was adopted by the American Law Institute in § 339(2) of the first *Restatement of the Law of Contracts* wherein it stated "[a]n undertaking in a penal bond to pay a sum of money as a penalty for non-performance of the condition of the bond is enforceable only to the extent of the harm proved to have been suffered by reason of such non-performance . . . ." The same principle was included in the *Restatement (Second) of the Law of Contracts* § 356(2), which states "[a] term in a bond providing for an amount of money as a penalty for non-occurrence of the condition of the bond is unenforceable on grounds of public policy to the extent that the amount exceeds the loss caused by such non-occurrence."

CHAPTER 3

Extending the Compensatory Principle Beyond Penal Bonds

Gary L. Monserud, Esq.
New England Law | Boston

§ 3.1   **English Precedents** 3–1

§ 3.2   **Early Massachusetts Cases Involving Liquidated Damages: Covenants Not to Compete** 3–4

   § 3.2.1   *Pierce v. Fuller*, 8 Mass. 223 (1811) 3–4

   § 3.2.2   *Perkins v. Lyman*, 11 Mass. 76 (1814) 3–5

   § 3.2.3   *Stearns v. Barrett*, 18 Mass. 443(1823) 3–6

   § 3.2.4   Summation 3–7

CHAPTER 3

Extending the Compensatory Principle Beyond Penal Bonds

Gary L. Monserud, Esq.
New England Law | Boston

Scope Note

This chapter discusses the extension of the compensatory principle beyond penal bonds as a limitation on stipulated damages in English law. It then discusses three early Massachusetts cases illustrating the compensatory principle as a limitation on stipulated damages clauses included in noncompete agreements.

§ 3.1   ENGLISH PRECEDENTS

The compensatory principle migrated from the penal bond cases to stipulated damages clauses included in contracts covering differing subject matter. By the time of Lord Mansfield's tenure as Chief Justice of the Court of King's Bench, *see* C.H.S. Fifoot, *Lord Mansfield* (Oxford, at the Clarendon Press, 1936), this court was deciding whether provisions on agreed damages were compensatory, and therefore enforceable, or punitive, hence unenforceable. A case illustrating the dividing line was *Lowe v. Peers* decided in 1768, in which Peers promised Catherine Lowe, "I will not marry with any person besides herself: if I do I agree to pay the said Catherine Lowe 1,000 pounds within three months next after I shall marry anybody else." After a lapse of ten years, Peers married Elizabeth Gardiner instead of Catherine, whereupon Catherine sued. Could the stipulated sum of 1,000 pounds survive judicial scrutiny? Lord Mansfield thought the sum was a rightful liquidation of damages. *See Lowe v. Peers*, 98 R.R. at 164.

Practice Note

Chief Justice Mansfield in relevant part stated: "I think what passed at trial was perfectly right; that the measure of damages was the 1,000 pounds . . . ." *Lowe v. Peers*, 98 R.R. at 164. While the opinions in this case are confusing for a modern reader, *Lowe v. Peers* came to stand for the proposition that a liquidated sum for breach of a

single promise where damages were difficult to estimate could withstand judicial scrutiny. *See, e.g., Kemble v. Farren,* 130 E.R. 1234,
1236 (Court of Common Pleas, 1829).

More enlightening for current issues are two cases arising from employment
contracts: *Astley v. Weldon,* 126 E.R. 1318 (Court of Common Pleas, 1801), and
Kemble v. Farren, 130 E.R. 1234 (Court of Common Pleas, 1829). *Astley* arose
from a three-year employment contract between an actress (Weldon) and a theater owner (Astley) by the terms of which Weldon agreed to act in Astley's theaters in London and elsewhere for an agreed consideration, and agreed to abide
by the rules of the theaters where she acted. By the express terms of her contract,
Weldon also subjected herself to a schedule of fines and forfeitures for various
infractions. Furthermore, it was agreed "that either of them neglecting to perform
that agreement according to the tenor and effect and the true intent and meaning
thereof should pay to the other of them the full sum of 200 pounds of lawful money of Great Britain to be recovered in any of his Majesty's courts of record at
Westminster." *Astley v. Weldon,* 126 E.R. at 1321.

Astley sued Weldon for breach of contract and won a verdict of twenty pounds
in a jury trial. The judge allowed him the liberty to claim the 200 pounds as stipulated, if the sum agreed upon could survive judicial scrutiny as a true liquidated
damages clause. The Court of Common Pleas held that the stipulated 200 pounds
was a penalty, hence, unenforceable. Justice Heath shed light on the case, stating
"[w]here articles contain covenants for the performance of several things, and
then one large sum is stated at the end to be paid upon breach of performance,
that must be considered a penalty." *Astley v. Weldon,* 126 E.R. at 1323. Since the
reported case contains four opinions, it is difficult to definitively elaborate upon
the exact reasoning behind the decision, but the tendency of the justices is clear.
Since multiple breaches were possible, and many were compensable according
to the agreed-upon schedule of fines, allowing a clause where a large lump sum
could be claimed for any breach went too far; it outran the compensatory principle
and had a punitive effect.

Kemble v. Farren, 130 E.R. 1234 (Court of Common Pleas, 1829), was very
nearly a replay of *Astley v. Weldon.* Kemble, as manager of Covent Garden, entered into a contract with Farren to act as a comedian for four seasons. The contract set forth the considerations exchanged, including Farren's fee for each nightly
appearance, and the requirement of Farren's adherence to the rules of the theater.
There was a clause stating that "[i]f either of the parties should neglect or refuse
to fulfill the said agreement, or any part thereof, or any stipulation therein contained, such party should pay to the other the sum of 1,000 pounds . . . ." *Kemble
v. Farren,* 130 E.R. at 1235. The parties expressly agreed that the sum stipulated
was intended as a liquidation of damages, not as a penalty.

Farren breached by refusing to perform during the second season. A jury award-ed Kemble 750 pounds in actual damages, subject to an increase to the stipulated 1,000 pounds on a judicial determination that the sum was a valid liquidation, not a penalty. Counsel for Farren argued on the basis of *Astley v. Weldon* that the clause was a penalty, since the same sum pertained to multiple possible breach-es, some of greater significance, some of lesser significance. Counsel for Kem-ble countered that the inquiry should be only about *intent*: "In all cases the rule is, to collect the intention of the parties from the language of the agreement, and not to decide what is reasonable or unreasonable, for on that no two persons would be found to agree." *Kemble v. Farren*, 130 E.R. at 1237. Despite the stipulation that expressly designated the sum of 1,000 pounds as liquidated damages and not a penalty, *Astley v. Weldon* was deemed controlling, and the clause was held to be unenforceable. Henceforth, where a single sum was stipulated as damages for multiple possible breaches of varied significance, the clause was flawed; it was deemed punitive *if it would be punitive as to some breaches to which it could be applied. Kemble v. Farren* and *Astley v. Weldon* were both influential in Massa-chusetts courts.

Practice Note

The rationale as set forth by Chief Justice Tindall in *Kemble v. Far-ren* showed the court's willingness to go beyond the expressed in-tent of the parties. He stated: "[i]t is, undoubtedly, difficult to suppose any words more precise or explicit than those used in the agree-ment; the same declaring not only affirmatively that the sum of 1,000 pounds should be taken as liquidated damages, but negatively also that it should not be considered a penalty, or in the nature thereof. And, if the clause had been limited to breaches which were of an uncertain nature or amount, we should have thought it would have had the effect of ascertaining the damages upon any such breach at 1,000 pounds. For we see nothing illegal or unreasonable in the par-ties, by their mutual agreement, settling the amount of damages, uncertain in their nature, at any sum upon which they may agree. In many cases such an agreement fixes that which is almost impossi-ble to be ascertained; and in all cases, it saves the expense and dif-ficulty of bringing witnesses to that point . . . [w]e cannot, therefore, distinguish this case, in principle, from that of *Astley v. Weldon*, in which it was stipulated, that either of the parties neglecting to per-form the agreement should pay to the other of the full sum of 200 pounds, to be recovered in his Majesty's court at Westminster." *Kemble v. Farren*, 130 E.R. at 1239.

Practice Note

An example of the influence of *Astley v. Weldon* and *Kemble v. Farren* is *Heard v. Bowers*, 40 Mass. 455 (1839). The case arose from a contract for the sale of land. Under the contract, buyers were required to give the seller notice by a date certain of their election to go forward with the purchase. The buyers breached by failing to give timely notice, and the seller sued for damages. When the matter came before the Supreme Judicial Court, the justices seemed mystified by the terms of the contract, and rightly so: the purchase price was $6,343 and the sum of $300 was fixed as liquidated damages for certain enumerated breaches, including failure to give timely notice of the election to purchase. Then, as an appendix of sorts, the contract stated: "to the true and faithful performance of each and every [of] the covenants, promises, and agreements aforesaid, each of the parties binds himself to the other in the sum of $1,000, as liquidated damages agreed upon between the said parties for breach of either of the said covenants." *Heard v. Bowers*, 40 Mass. at 455. In an opinion by Justice Wilde, citing both *Astley v. Weldon* and *Kemble v. Farren*, with special reliance on the latter, the court struck down the $1,000 stipulations as a penalty, allowing $300 to stand as a valid liquidation of damages.

§ 3.2   EARLY MASSACHUSETTS CASES INVOLVING LIQUIDATED DAMAGES: COVENANTS NOT TO COMPETE

In the early decades of the nineteenth century, the dividing line between liquidated damages and penalties (in nonbond cases) in Massachusetts was most evident in cases that arose from noncompete covenants for breach of which the parties had stipulated damages. English cases commonly served as precedent. I have selected three illustrative cases.

§ 3.2.1   *Pierce v. Fuller*, 8 Mass. 223 (1811)

Stephen Fuller ran a stage coach line between Boston and Providence. Since Joseph Pierce wanted to run a stage line on the same route, and did not want Fuller in competition, Pierce agreed to pay Fuller $290 for his old stage coach, a horse, and Fuller's covenant not to run any competing coaches. For breach of this covenant, the parties stipulated that Fuller would owe Pierce $290 (the total sum paid by Pierce). Pierce sued, alleging violation of the covenant for which he claimed the sum stipulated. Pierce's declaration met with three defenses, the last of which was that the sum stipulated was a penalty. *Pierce v. Fuller*, 8 Mass. 223, 225 (1811). On trial to a jury, the plaintiff prevailed. On appeal, the Supreme Judicial Court affirmed that the stipulation of $290 for breach was an enforceable liquidation of damages, notwithstanding the fact that the agreement characterized the sum as a penalty for breach. The nature of the covenant was an important factor. Damages for breach of a noncompete covenant are difficult to estimate. The result was consistent with the compensatory principle.

Practice Note

Judge Sedgwick, writing for the court, stated in relevant part as follows: "The contract in the present case is not in the form of a bond with a penalty, but although unskillfully drawn, it is to be considered as a covenant with the damages liquidated by the parties, as a compensation for the breach, if the defendant were to choose again to run a rival stage. The parties were competent in law to make a contract imposing a limited restraint on the defendant's trade for the plaintiff's benefit, and without injury to the public. They were competent to consider on what consideration it should be made, and to liquidate the damages if it should be broken." *Pierce v. Fuller*, 8 Mass. at 228.

§ 3.2.2 *Perkins v. Lyman*, 11 Mass. 76 (1814)

Theodore Lyman agreed to sell James and Thomas Perkins a ship named the *Vancouver*, then-anchored in Boston Harbor, for the price of $8,000. The contract included a covenant not to compete whereby Lyman (seller) promised not to compete, directly or indirectly, for seven years in voyages to, or trade with, natives in a specified region in North America. For breach of this covenant, Lyman obligated himself to pay Perkins $8,000 (the price of the ship). *Perkins v. Lyman*, 11 Mass. 76, 77 (1814). Perkins sued in two counts, claiming that Lyman had breached the covenant by outfitting and having an interest in two competing ships, the *Hamilton* and the *Lydia*, allegations which Lyman contested. A jury decided in favor of plaintiffs (Perkins) on both counts. On these verdicts, plaintiffs sought damages in the stipulated sum of $8,000 plus interest thereon. The issue on appeal was whether the $8,000 was a valid liquidated damages clause or a penalty. Perkins' lawyers argued that the sum stipulated was an enforceable liquidation of damages, and in support thereof, cited English cases running back to *Lowe v. Peers*, and stressed the holding in *Pierce v. Fuller*, arguing "[t]he case of *Pierce v. Fuller* is extremely similar to the case at bar and there the penalty was considered as the damages liquidated by the parties." *Perkins v. Lyman*, 11 Mass. at 79–81.

The court did not accept the analogy to *Pierce v. Fuller*. The court opined per curiam that the proper result turned upon ascertaining the meaning ascribed by the parties to the language agreed upon, an ascertainment the court could best make by looking to the subject matter of the contract and the situation of the parties. *Perkins v. Lyman*, 11 Mass. at 81. On examining the record, the court determined that the parties had stipulated to a penalty, because the single sum of $8,000 was fixed as the sum owing for one instance of interference (one breach of the covenant) and likewise for one thousand interferences. Accordingly, "[e]xamined in this view, we see nothing that gives this contract any other determinate meaning than that of a penalty." *Perkins v. Lyman*, 11 Mass. at 82. The court allowed a hearing for a determination of actual damages. *See Perkins v. Lyman*, 11 Mass. at 83.

§ 3.2.3   *Stearns v. Barrett*, 18 Mass. 443(1823)

Stearns and Barrett each claimed patent rights for two machines used for drying and dying silks. They made an agreement in the form of a market division, the terms of which allowed Barrett exclusive rights to the use and sale of the machines in Massachusetts and Rhode Island while Stearns had equivalent rights in other states. Each agreed not to compete in the territories allotted to the other. The agreement contained a stipulation that for a beach of their covenant, the party in breach would be liable to the other for $1,000 per machine. According to Stearns's allegations, Barrett breached by making and using fifteen machines on Staten Island in the State of New York, for which he sought $15,000 as liquidated damages. An issue that eventually came to the Supreme Judicial Court was whether the $1,000 stipulated for any unauthorized sale or use of a machine constituted a penalty or liquidated damages. The court had no difficulty in determining that the stipulation of $1,000 per machine ($15,000 for the asserted violations) was a penalty because the express terms of the contract permitted Barrett to use the machines in New York, as he had done, if he paid the contractually agreed-upon price of $500 for the privilege. The terms of the contract made the penal intention, and the penal effect, plain to the court. *Stearns v. Barrett*, 18 Mass. 443, 458–59 (1823).

Practice Note

Barrett's and Stearns' contract included a provision specifically allowing Barrett to enter New York state without subjecting himself to liability for the agreed $1,000 sum, provided that he first give notice to Stearns of his intention to do so, and within an agreed time paid $500 for the privilege of using or selling machines in New York City ($300 for the same privilege elsewhere in the state). Indeed, Barrett gave the requisite notice of his intention to use or sell machines on Staten Island, and may have intended to pay the agreed-upon fee, but failed to plead this contractual privilege as a defense.

§ 3.2.4   Summation

From these cases involving covenants not to compete, and the precedents relied upon, several interrelated principles can be extracted for dividing liquidated damages from penalties. First, the enunciated guiding principle was the *parties' intent*. Second, the justices were not literalists, but rather looked carefully into the facts of the cases to discern intent. The use of the words "penalty" and "liquidated damages" in the contracts was not determinative. Rather, the justices used the text, the context, and the subject matter of the agreements to infer intent. Third, intent was often inferred from the consequences, or probable consequences, of breaches that occurred or might occur. Fourth, as in English precedents, if there were multiple covenants and breach of lesser covenants (causing less damage than the sum agreed upon) triggered a claim to the sum corresponding to the consequences of a more significant breach, the court inferred an intent to penalize, a point that may account for the appearance of inconsistency between *Pierce v. Fuller* and *Perkins v. Lyman* (see practice note below). Fifth, the subject matter of a contract weighed heavily when justices made inferences of intent. When the subject matter made damages for breach difficult to ascertain, the justices were inclined to find an intent to liquidate damages rather than an intent to inflict a penalty. Conversely, when damages were relatively easy to ascertain, given the subject matter, the courts were inclined to view stipulated sums as penalties. *See, e.g., Kellogg v. Curtis*, 26 Mass. 534 (1830). Finally, there was a preference and tendency to regard stipulated sums as penalties, suggesting that courts were suspicious of such clauses. *See, e.g., Cushing v. Drew*, 97 Mass. 445 (1867). The reports show tedious arguments, careful review of precedents, and insightful probing into the facts of cases to discern probable intent, but there was no angst as to whether judicial intervention was appropriate when a clause was deemed punitive. The justices were confident of their role in policing clauses for stipulated damages. If the justices sniffed out a penalty, they struck it down without qualms and allowed a hearing on actual damages.

Practice Note

This may explain why the covenant not to compete withstood scrutiny in *Pierce v. Fuller* and failed in *Perkins v. Lyman*. The cases were similar in this respect: the total contract price in the purchase and sale agreements were the sums stipulated as agreed damages for breach of the covenant not to compete. Yet, the context was vastly different. In *Pierce*, the only conduct sought to be prevented was running a competing stage between Boston and Providence. In *Perkins*, the possible breaches by competing vessels were virtually limitless and differing breaches might have wildly differing consequences. Hence, in *Perkins* there was a real possibility that the $8,000 sum agreed upon (the price of the vessel) might be claimed for a minor infraction.

CHAPTER 4

Stipulated Damages in Contracts for Services and Sales: 1836 Through the Era of Justice Holmes

Gary L. Monserud, Esq.
New England Law | Boston

§ **4.1**   **Selected Cases Prior to the Civil War**................................. **4–1**

    § 4.1.1   *Curtis v. Brewer*, 34 Mass. 513 (1836).................. 4–2

    § 4.1.2   *Higginson v. Weld*, 80 Mass. 165 (1859).............. 4–2

    § 4.1.3   *Lynde v. Thompson*, 84 Mass. 456 (1861)............ 4–3

§ **4.2**   **Justice Holmes and His Legacy: Greater Deference to Contracting Parties**.. **4–5**

    § 4.2.1   *Smith v. Brown*, 164 Mass. 584 (1895).................. 4–5

    § 4.2.2   *Guerin v. Stacey*, 175 Mass. 595 (1900)............... 4–7

    § 4.2.3   *Garst v. Harris*, 177 Mass. 72, 58 N.E. 174 (1900)... 4–8

    § 4.2.4   *Morrison v. Richardson*, 194 Mass. 370 (1907).... 4–8

    § 4.2.5   Summation 4–10

CHAPTER 4

Stipulated Damages in Contracts for Services and Sales: 1836 Through the Era of Justice Holmes

Gary L. Monserud, Esq.
New England Law | Boston

Scope Note

This chapter provides a history of the use of stipulated damages clauses in a variety of contracts from the pre-Civil War era into the early twentieth century. The chapter concludes with a survey of the contributions of Justice Holmes and his immediate successors, stressing that in the Holmes era there was a deference to manifestations of the intentions of contracting parties without abandoning the limits imposed by the compensatory principle.

§ 4.1   SELECTED CASES PRIOR TO THE CIVIL WAR

Alongside case law arising from noncompete covenants, there arose a series of cases involving varied subject matter in which the Supreme Judicial Court employed one or more of the principles discussed earlier, *see Law of Liquidated Damages in Massachusetts* § 1.3 (MCLE, Inc. 2013), either to uphold or invalidate stipulated damages clauses. Throughout the nineteenth century, the art of judging in these cases involved a very close examination of the fact situations. The three cases following, which arose from contracts involving sales or services, illustrate the manner in which the Supreme Judicial Court employed the agreed-upon principles to decide such cases in this era.

§ 4.1.1   *Curtis v. Brewer*, 34 Mass. 513 (1836)

The defendant in *Curtis v. Brewer*, 34 Mass. 513 (1836), promised Curtis that he would build a hull for a schooner within a stipulated time. The agreement provided that the vessel should "be built, caulked, finished, and ready for the rigger to complete his work, launched and delivered afloat in the harbor" on or before June 1, 1833. *Curtis v. Brewer*, 34 Mass. at 513. It was further stipulated that Brewer would be liable at the rate of $1.50 per ton per month for delay in completion. Brewer fell behind schedule, and Curtis claimed damages. A jury allowed damages in accord with the clause for delay attributable to Brewer, and the judgment withstood judicial review. The court noted that delay damages consisted of the loss of use, something difficult to ascertain. Moreover, the sum Curtis could claim was enlarged day by day, indicating an intent to correlate the severity of breach with the amount that could be claimed. Hence, an intent to liquidate damages rather than to penalize could be readily inferred.

§ 4.1.2   *Higginson v. Weld*, 80 Mass. 165 (1859)

The contract underlying *Higginson v. Weld*, 80 Mass. 165 (1859) was for carriage of goods from Calcutta to Boston. Higginson agreed to furnish 150 tons of goods in Calcutta for shipment to Boston for the price of $14.50 per ton, and Weld (the ship owner) agreed to provide carriage. The parties fixed the sum of $2,200 as the sum either party would owe the other for nonperformance. Weld's ship captain, in violation of orders, sailed from Australia to New York, refusing to call at Calcutta for freight. When Weld found out what had occurred, he offered to arrange substitute carriage which Higginson's successor (Codman) declined. *Higginson v. Weld*, 80 Mass. at 166. Weld was found liable at the trial court. When the case came to the Supreme Judicial Court on stipulated facts, the court ruled that the $2,200 stipulation should not be enforced for two main reasons: first, the single sum applied to a variety of breaches, some serious, some not. This was in sharp contrast to *Curtis v. Brewer* where the damages grew by each day of delay. Second, the parties, who were sophisticated businessmen, had adopted the word *penalty* to characterize the agreed-upon clause. In this case, the parties' word choice counted, *Higginson v. Weld*, 80 Mass. at 173, while in earlier cases the negative implications of the term had been discounted. *See, e.g., Pierce v. Fuller*, 8 Mass. 223 (1811). Given the facts of the case, it is doubtful that a designation of "liquidated damages" would have saved the clause. The court allowed actual damages of $600 calculated by a comparison of the agreed-upon rate of $14.50 per ton with the market rate when shipment was scheduled, thereby protecting the aggrieved party's lost expectation interest. *Higginson v. Weld*, 80 Mass. at 173.

§ 4.1.3 *Lynde v. Thompson*, 84 Mass. 456 (1861)

Due to its clarity and incisive phrasing, *Lynde v. Thompson*, 84 Mass. 456 (1861) is one of the finest nineteenth century opinions bearing upon liquidated damages. Lynde agreed to sell his business to Thompson, including good will and all of his stock and tools used in manufacturing tin ware, for an agreed-upon price. The written contract for sale contained the following clause: "[i]t is also hereby agreed between the parties that, in case either party shall fail to comply with the terms of this agreement, the party so failing shall forfeit to the other party the sum of three hundred dollars, which shall be paid in full. . . ." *Lynde v. Thompson*, 84 Mass. at 456. When Thompson (buyer) did not go through with his promised purchase, Lynde sued to recover the agreed-upon $300. At a trial in Superior Court, the judge instructed the jury that the $300 agreed upon was a penalty, not to be awarded, and that Lynde was only entitled to actual damages sustained. The jury returned a verdict for nominal damages. Lynde appealed.

The Supreme Judicial Court reversed. The opinion, authored by Chief Justice Bigelow, clearly articulated the dividing line between liquidated damages and penalties. Chief Justice Bigelow first observed that "[t]here was only one object contemplated by the parties . . . . It was not a contract for the performance of divers acts of different degrees of importance." *Lynde v. Thompson*, 84 Mass. at 460. It was a straightforward contract for the sale of a business wherein the seller promised to deliver and the buyer promised to pay.

Practice Note

In 2013 this case might be resolved under the rules of Article 2 of the Uniform Commercial Code. See U.C.C. § 2-102 and § 2-105(1), which are the primary scope sections for Article 2. Mixed contracts (contracts involving goods and nongoods components) will either be included or excluded from § 2's scope based on the predominant factor test as adopted and explained in *White v. Peabody Construction Co.*, 386 Mass. 121 (1982).

The case therefore came within the rule that applied when only a single specific act (taking delivery and paying) is required, and there was "no adequate means furnished by the contract or otherwise of ascertaining the precise damage . . . from the failure of the defendant (buyer) to fulfill his part of the agreement." *Lynde v. Thompson*, 84 Mass. at 460. Damages were difficult to estimate because of the subject matter of the contract, namely, the sale of a business.

The care and thoroughness of Chief Justice Bigelow's analysis are apparent:

> If the contract had been to pay a certain sum of money, or to purchase specific items of merchandise, the

value of which as between vendor and vendee could have been ascertained without difficulty, the measure of damages arising from a breach would have been certain and readily fixed, and the intent of the parties to stipulate for a penalty only would have been fairly inferrible [sic]. But such is not the nature of the present contract. It is the agreement for the sale of an entire stock in trade, and all the tools used by the plaintiffs in carrying on the manufacturing business. A transaction of such nature, involving the transfer and surrender of the business and good will connected with the trade and manufacture in which plaintiffs had been engaged, differs essentially from an ordinary agreement for the sale of goods or the payment of money. It is impossible to estimate with accuracy, or to measure by any definite or precise rule, the extent of damage which either party might sustain by reason of the breach of the contract. The necessity of taking an account of the stock, the consequent interruption of business, the preparation to relinquish an old occupation and to engage in a new one, and other similar elements, would necessarily enter into the contemplation of the parties in making an agreement like that which is the subject of the present action. But the impossibility of placing any estimate of money on the damage which might result from such causes is obvious, and leads to the reasonable inference that the parties intended to fix the amount of compensation in the event of a breach by inserting a sum to be taken as liquidated damages in the literal sense of that term.

Lynde v. Thompson, 84 Mass. at 460.

This language, and the opinions of a similar style, illustrates what Karl Llewellyn in a later era would describe as the *grand style* in American legal history. Karl Llewellyn, *The Common Law Tradition—Deciding Appeals* at 62–120 (Little, Brown and Company, 1960). *See also* Grant Gilmore, *The Ages of American Law* at 19–40 (Yale University Press, 1977). The principles guided the courts but the results were not dictated by a mechanical application of the principles. The justices made a careful examination of the facts, and the type of situation presented, e.g., sale of a business, a service contract requiring time for performance, or a covenant not to compete. They exhibited that sense of the cases that Professor

Llewellyn would later characterize as *situation sense,* Karl Llewellyn, *The Common Law Tradition—Deciding Appeals* at 121–32; 268–87 (Little Brown and Company, 1960), and thereby fashioned a body of case law that made sense, was readable, and yet gave due deference to precedent. While discernment of intent behind the stipulated damages clauses was a continuing theme, with attention to the facts in the opinions, it is clear that intent was inferred again and again from the probable or demonstrable results of breach, given the nature of the case.

Nearly 150 years later, *Lynde v. Thompson* will be read as supporting the view that a court should only make a prospective or ex ante analysis, meaning the court should only focus upon the time of formation to determine whether a clause is a valid liquidation of damages or a penalty. *See* Mark D. Robbins, Esq., "Another Look at the 'Second Look' Doctrine: Enforcing Liquidated Damages Clauses Without Hindsight," 44 *Boston Bar. J.* 8 (2000). One can read the case to support that view, but in 1861 Chief Justice Bigelow was not thinking in those terms. His analysis was limited neither to a prospective estimate of damages nor a retrospective look at actual consequences. His stress was *upon the nature of the case*, the probable consequences of breach, and the analysis was fact-driven.

§ 4.2 JUSTICE HOLMES AND HIS LEGACY: GREATER DEFERENCE TO CONTRACTING PARTIES

While selections could be made from many opinions in the latter half of the nineteenth century, heaping up opinions in the wake of *Lynde v. Thompson* would be of little benefit. Consequently, the focus now shifts to four opinions from the late nineteenth century and the beginning of the twentieth century, three authored by Justice Oliver Wendell Holmes, and one by Justice Morton wherein he relied upon Justice Holmes's opinions. I focus upon Justice Holmes, in part because his opinions on stipulated damages clauses have often been cited, but also because his views on this topic have been slightly misused, making him into an advocate for unfettered liberty in fixing remedies by contract. His opinions may, indeed, signal a slight shift of emphasis, but in the main he follows the approach made evident in *Lynde v. Thompson*; something short of a libertarian deference to private stipulations, as the first case selected will clearly illustrate.

§ 4.2.1 *Smith v. Brown*, 164 Mass. 584 (1895)

In *Smith v. Brown*, 164 Mass. 584 (1895), Brown made a contract to sell his apothecary business to Smith, agreeing to assign the lease of his shop, and to sell the personal property therein, as well as good will. The contract provided that Brown would not compete directly or indirectly in any drug business within two miles of the apothecary shop without Smith's written consent. *Smith v. Brown*, 164 Mass. at 585. Further, Brown agreed to be "under penalty of one thousand dollars . . . to be forfeited and paid said Smith or his legal representatives" in the event of breach. Brown subsequently participated in setting up a competing shop within the geographic limits fixed by the agreement, whereupon Smith sought an injunction and damages. The trial judge denied an injunction on grounds of laches, and awarded actual damages instead of the stipulated $1,000, believing that the stipulated sum was a penalty.

The Supreme Judicial Court sustained the trial judge's denial of equitable relief, *Smith v. Brown*, 164 Mass. at 585–86, and deferred to the trial judge's decision that the $1,000 provision was an unenforceable penalty. Justice Holmes's explanation shows his deference to the trial judge's findings and his regard for precedent. He stated:

> We assume in favor of the plaintiff that the words "under a penalty" are not conclusive against the sum named being regarded as liquidated damages, *Lynde v. Thompson*, 84 Mass. 451 (1861) (citing inter alia) . . . we agree that the event secured is one, in a certain sense, and we do not need to controvert what sometimes has been said, that in this class of cases the courts incline to treat the sum named as liquidated damages. *Ropes v. Upton*, 125 Mass. 258, 260; 1 Sedgw. Dam. § 418 (8th ed.). On the other hand, the breach might vary in gravity very much according to the degree of defendant's share in helping competition. . . . We cannot say that no view of the circumstances would warrant the judge in regarding this as being a "penalty" as it is called in the contract. Even if the use of the word is not conclusive, it has been declared by the court and by others that, very strong evidence would be required to authorize them to say that the parties' own words do not express their intent in this respect. The intention [stated] to liquidate damages may not prevail in all cases, but, if the intent expressed is to impose a penalty, the court cannot give the words a larger scope.

Smith v. Brown, 164 Mass at 586–87.

Much legal history is packed into this language. According to Justice Holmes, while word choices were not conclusive, they were objective evidence of intent that weighed in the judicial balance. If a scrivener chose the word "penalty," the word would have weight in a subsequent judicial review. The case-type (a covenant not to compete) tugged in the other direction, toward a liquidation of damages because damages for breach are usually difficult to estimate. This was counterbalanced by the fact that a single sum was stipulated for a possible range of breaches. At the end of the day, there were solid grounds on which to sustain the trial judge's decision; the clause was an unenforceable penalty.

§ 4.2.2   *Guerin v. Stacey*, 175 Mass. 595 (1900)

Although *Guerin v. Stacey*, 175 Mass. 595 (1900) is the Holmes opinion most often quoted in recent appellate opinions, the exceptionally sparse fact pattern makes it difficult to interpret, as the reader must fill in the gaps by reasonable inferences. This much is clear: a lessee (Stacey) entered into a sublease with Guerin, who was in a retail business. There is a reference to "the loss of plaintiff's stand and the general inconvenience of moving." *Guerin v. Stacey*, 175 Mass. at 597 In this context, Stacey (lessee) signed a bond obligating himself to pay Guerin (sublessee) the sum of $2,500 as liquidated damages if, on account of the lessee's actions, the lease was terminated or the sublessee ousted before the agreed expiration date. It was implied that if the sublessee enjoyed his full term undisturbed, the obligation would be void. A year before the expiration date, the owner terminated the lease and would only recognize the sublessee as a month-to-month tenant. The sublessee (Guerin), no doubt feeling insecure, vacated the premises and sued Stacey. A trial judge found in Guerin's favor as to liability but ruled that the bond was void as a penalty. No actual damages were proved.

The single issue to come before the Supreme Judicial Court was whether the stipulated $2,500 was a penalty or liquidated damages. As to the use of the words "liquidated damages," Justice Holmes advised that "[t]here is no doubt that a sum which is to be paid upon the breach of a primary undertaking may be treated as a penalty in some cases, notwithstanding the fact that it is called 'liquidated damages' in the contract." *Guerin v. Stacey*, 175 Mass. at 597 (citing *Fisk v. Gray*, 93 Mass. 132 (1865)). As to the case at hand, Justice Holmes thought that $2,500 was a valid liquidation, saying "[b]ut we heartily agree with the court of appeals in England that, so far as precedent permits, the proper course is to enforce contracts according to their plain meaning, and not to undertake to be wiser than the parties, and therefore that in general, when parties say that a sum is payable as liquidated damages, they will be taken to mean what they say, and will be held to their word." *Guerin v. Stacey*, 175 Mass. at 597 (citing *Wallis v. Smith*, 21 Ch. Div. 243; *Atkyns v. Kinnier*, 4 Exch. 776). However, the contractual expressions of the parties were only one factor. Justice Holmes was also attentive to the probable losses suffered by the party aggrieved, in this case the loss of the plaintiff's stand and the general inconvenience of moving or risking a stay upon an uncertain future. *Guerin v. Stacey*, 175 Mass. at 597. Justice Holmes had no qualms about looking at the actual damages found by a trial judge, and found the small verdict in no way disturbing, "because the plaintiff probably relied upon his claim for the whole sum stipulated, and put in no evidence of actual damage." *Guerin v. Stacey*, 175 Mass. at 598. Situation sense prevailed, and the clause was found to be enforceable.

§ 4.2.3   *Garst v. Harris*, 177 Mass. 72, 58 N.E. 174 (1900)

Although not as quotable as *Guerin v. Stacey*, *Garst v. Harris*, 177 Mass. 72, (1900) bolsters my conclusions about Justice Holmes's approach to stipulated damages clauses. The opinion takes up scarcely one page in the reports, but it does set forth the basic facts of a contract for the sale of goods. The plaintiff (Garst) sold defendant Harris a proprietary medicine, intending that Harris would resell it, presumably at a profit. Harris promised not to sell the medicine below a stipulated price, and agreed to twenty-one dollars as liquidated damages for breach of the resale restriction. Harris breached by selling below the stipulated minimum, whereupon Garst sued for twenty-one dollars. A superior court judge, to whom the case was submitted on stipulated facts, ruled in favor of Garst (seller). On appeal, Harris argued that the stipulation of twenty-one dollars as damages for resale below the agreed price was a penalty. *Garst v. Harris*, 177 Mass. at 74. This argument got short shrift, as Justice Holmes stated "[b]ut it is admitted in the agreed facts that the damages are substantial and difficult to estimate, and it was recognized in the contract that they would be so. It has been decided recently that parties are to be held to their words upon this question, except in exceptional cases where there are special reasons for a different decision." *Garst v. Harris*, 177 Mass. at 74 (citing *Guerin v. Stacey*, 175 Mass 595 (1900); *Chase v. Allen*, 79 Mass. 42 (1859)). See also *Lynde v. Thompson*, 84 Mass. 456 (1861) for the general rule. Therefore, the plaintiff kept his twenty-one dollar award. Justice Holmes did not choose between a prospective and retrospective view of damages attributable to the breach; both views were implicitly recognized, neither was precluded.

§ 4.2.4   *Morrison v. Richardson*, 194 Mass. 370 (1907)

Although *Morrison v. Richardson*, 194 Mass. 370 (1907) was decided after Justice Holmes was appointed to the Supreme Court of the United States, the opinion (written by Justice Morton) cites both *Guerin* and *Garst* and reflects Justice Holmes's approach in its analysis of the liquidated damages clause in a contract for the supply of construction materials.

Practice Note

The supply contract would no doubt today be governed by Article 2 of the Uniform Commercial Code. See U.C.C. §§ 2-102 and 2-105(1), the main scope sections. The supply contract was entered into because Morrison owned an unfinished building which he intended to make into commercial rental space. His contractor had failed to finish the job, so Morrison undertook to finish it himself and to that end made a supply contract with Richardson for doors, sashes, windows, and blinds. If the contract were governed by Article 2 of the U.C.C., the rule for evaluating the liquidated damages clause would be found in U.C.C. § 2-718(1), which by its express terms allows a "second look" at a stipulated damages clause in light of actual damages attributable to a breach.

The contract contained a delivery schedule and a provision allowing Morrison ten dollars per day as damages if Richardson failed to meet the schedule. When Richardson failed to deliver on time, Morrison sued. A jury found for Morrison, but the trial judge refused Morrison's proposed instruction that the ten dollars per day be treated as a valid liquidation of damages, a ruling to which Morrison took exception. On appeal, the Supreme Judicial Court took up the issue whether the per diem clause was a penalty or liquidated damages. With careful reasoning and citations to many authorities, the court reversed. While taking account of the words used by the parties in their contract, the court also advised that "the circumstances under which the contract was entered into, the subject matter and the situation of the parties, may and should be taken into account in determining the sense in which the parties used them and what their intention was." *Morrison v. Richardson*, 194 Mass. at 376. Thus, a close factual analysis, with due regard for the difficulty of fixing an exact amount for delay damages, resulted in a reversal. The clause was valid and enforceable.

Practice Note

According to the court, "[f]rom the nature of the case the damages would not be easy to determine and the parties may well have chosen to agree upon them beforehand. Neither do we think that the fact that Morrison rented a part of the premises and used a part of the doors affects his right to recover the stipulated damages. He was in possession of the premises when the contract was entered into, and it was contemplated that the things should be used as furnished and that there might be partial breach to which the liquidated damages would apply as well as to an entire breach. *Morrison v. Richardson*, 194 Mass. at 376–77.

§ 4.2.5　　Summation

It is fair to inquire whether Justice Holmes and case law following in his wake altered the path of liquidated damages law. On close reading of the cases, an increased stress on freedom of contract is discernible, but this did not fundamentally alter the trajectory of the law. Several points support this conclusion. First, Justice Holmes's opinions show that he sought the intent of the contracting parties, as precedent required. Second, ascertaining intent often required an inference from the nature of the contract as to the damages that would probably flow from a breach. Third, the difficulty in estimating damages counted in favor of finding a valid liquidation. Finally, there was a discernible movement away from earlier opinions where there was a tendency, perhaps a preference, to find a penalty rather than an enforceable liquidated damages clause. But, any change of course was slight. There was no sharp break with precedent. Justice Holmes's opinions were well anchored in Massachusetts precedents, including *Lynde v. Thompson*. He did sometimes highlight the evidence of intent manifested in the contractual language agreed upon, but the nature of the contract breached, and a contemplation of damages attributable to a breach, anticipated or actual, as the record allowed, were invariably parts of Justice Holmes's analytical approach; an approach which continued even after his departure from the court.

CHAPTER 5

Claims to Deposits: Deposits Fixing the Limits of Damages and the Parallel Law of Forfeiture

Gary L. Monserud, Esq.
New England Law | Boston

§ 5.1   Introduction 5–1

§ 5.2   Retention of Deposits Pursuant to Contract: Cases
         Where a Liquidated Damages Analysis Was Applied
         to Deposits.. 5–2

         § 5.2.1   Garcin v. Pennsylvania Furnace Co., 186 Mass.
                    405 (1904) 5–2

         § 5.2.2   Kaplan v. Gray, 215 Mass. 269 (1913) 5–3

         § 5.2.3   Dubinsky v. Wells Bros. Co. of N.Y., 218 Mass.
                    232 (1914) 5–4

         § 5.2.4   Summation 5–4

§ 5.3   Excursus: The Parallel Doctrine of Forfeiture Where
         Retention of Deposits Was Allowed Apart from the Law
         of Liquidated Damages 5–5

         § 5.3.1   Donaghue v. Parkman, 161 Mass. 412 (1894) 5–6

         § 5.3.2   Keefe v. Fairfield, 184 Mass. 334 (1903)............... 5–7

         § 5.3.3   Smith v. McMahon, 197 Mass. 16 (1907)............. 5–8

         § 5.3.4   King v. Milliken, 248 Mass. 460 (1924) 5–8

§ 5.4   Conclusions 5–9

         § 5.4.1   Burden of Proof.. 5–9

§ 5.4.2   Prospective Versus Retrospective Analysis 5–10

§ 5.4.3   Forfeiture...5–10

§ 5.4.4   Forfeiture and Judicial Scrutiny 5–10

§ 5.4.5   Evaluating Stipulated Damages Clauses..............5–10

CHAPTER 5

Claims to Deposits: Deposits Fixing the Limits of Damages and the Parallel Law of Forfeiture

Gary L. Monserud, Esq.
New England Law | Boston

Scope Note

This chapter addresses the development of the law of liquidated damages in relation to deposits prior to the promulgation of the first *Restatement of the Law of Contracts* in 1932. It then briefly summarizes the law of forfeiture, a parallel doctrinal development, as it pertained to part performance or deposits.

§ 5.1   INTRODUCTION

To this point in my survey of Massachusetts case law, none of the cases have arisen from a claim to a deposit made and agreed upon as liquidated damages. The probable explanation is that deposits made by buyers in real estate contracts were often retained by the seller in the wake of a buyer's breach under the law of *forfeiture. See generally* Milton R. Friedman & James Charles Smith, 2 *Friedman on Contracts and Conveyances of Real Property* § 7:1.5 (Practicing Law Institute, 2011). Nonetheless, in the latter years of the nineteenth century and the early years of the twentieth century, the Supreme Judicial Court issued a few opinions, some involving interests in real estate, wherein a party's right to retain a deposit was analyzed under the law of liquidated damages, even if the contract stipulated that on default a *forfeiture* would occur. The following three cases, of varied fact patterns, illustrate the development of the law of liquidated damages in relation to deposits prior to the promulgation of the first *Restatement of the Law of Contracts* in 1932. I will then briefly summarize the law of forfeiture, a parallel doctrinal development, as it pertained to part performance or deposits.

§ 5.2   RETENTION OF DEPOSITS PURSUANT TO CONTRACT: CASES WHERE A LIQUIDATED DAMAGES ANALYSIS WAS APPLIED TO DEPOSITS

§ 5.2.1   *Garcin v. Pennsylvania Furnace Co.*, 186 Mass. 405 (1904)

Garcin entered into a contract to purchase substantially all of the assets of Pennsylvania Furnace Co., a going concern. The contract did not use the term "liquidated damages," but it explicitly provided for a forfeiture of Garcin's deposits to Pennsylvania Furnace if Garcin breached. *Garcin v. Penn. Furnace Co.*, 186 Mass. 405, 411 (1904). Garcin made his deposits as consideration for an extension of the closing date. The "deposits" were delivery of $25,000 cash and 2,000 shares of stock with a par value of $100 per share to a third party. Garcin failed, without legal excuse, to close as agreed, although Pennsylvania Furnace was ready, willing, and able. He thereafter filed a bill in equity seeking return of his deposits; the bill was denied. When the case came before the Supreme Judicial Court on the procedural question of whether a demurrer to the bill in equity should be sustained, the court phrased the relevant inquiry as: "what was the intention and meaning of the parties?" On close examination of the contract, the justices concluded that "[w]e think it plain that the parties intended them (cash and stock) to be retained as liquidated damages." *Garcin v. Penn. Furnace Co.*, 186 Mass at 415 (citing *Guerin v. Stacey*, 175 Mass 595 (1900); *Garst v. Harris*, 177 Mass. 74 (1900); *Keefe v. Fairfield*, 184 Mass. 334, 68 N.E. 342 (1903)). Hence, the provision for a *forfeiture* was deemed to be a valid liquidated damages clause, though the opinion reveals nothing about damages the parties might have envisioned at the time of contracting or about damages actually incurred. Discernment of *intent*—without regard to the reasonableness of the deposits in relation to anticipated or actual damages—was sufficient to sustain the seller's claim. At first glance the analysis seems superficial; however, given the nature of the transaction, it is reasonable to assume that actual damages, either prospectively or retrospectively, would have been difficult to estimate in the absence of another buyer with a firm offer on the table. The seller retained the deposit.

Practice Note
On the facts, it is admittedly not possible to make any judgment about the *reasonableness* of the forfeiture. Nonetheless, since the contract was for the sale of a going concern, and the number of prospective buyers was probably limited, the damages may well have been substantial and difficult to ascertain. Assessing a market value for assets such as those described would be a tricky undertaking.

§ 5.2.2 *Kaplan v. Gray*, 215 Mass. 269 (1913)

Wridgway, the owner of letters patent for lamp shades on road vehicles, granted Gray a license to manufacture shades within his patent. Gray in turn promised to manufacture a minimum of 1,000 lamp shades and to pay royalties of one dollar per shade. Additionally, Gray deposited $500 with Wridgway ostensibly for two purposes: first, this deposit would serve as security for royalties; and second, if Gray breached the license agreement, the $500 was to be *forfeited* as liquidated damages. Wridgway assigned his interest in the letters patent to Kaplan (hence the caption on the case). Gray breached by making only twenty-five shades on which he paid twenty-five dollars as royalties, leaving Kaplan short by $975 of his expected minimum royalties. Kaplan retained the $500, and sued to collect an additional $475. In order to clear the way to actual damages, he sought a declaration that the $500 agreement was void.

The precise question that eventually came before the Supreme Judicial Court was whether a demurrer to the bill should be sustained. Answering this question required a decision about the deposit: was the $500 deposit a sum that validly liquidated damages and barred any further claim, or could Kaplan have it set aside in order to claim higher, actual damages? While admitting the intention of the parties was not free from doubt, the court determined that the parties had intended the deposit to serve as liquidated damages, and therefore, the $500 was the limit of Kaplan's claim. The case is unusual because instead of a breaching buyer (herein licensee) trying to recover a deposit by proving that its retention would be punitive, the licensor tried to invalidate the clause so that he could make a higher damage claim. The court was content to allow the forfeiture clause as a firm ceiling on damages, based upon the parties' intent, inferred from the record.

Practice Note

The court noted that the stipulated damages were short of actual damages and consequently could not be deemed punitive. In the 1990s one of the fears expressed by court critics was that persons in the position of Kaplan might succeed in invalidating liquidated damages clauses clearing a path for higher actual damages, if courts took a retrospective look at stipulated damages clauses. This approach would leave buyers exposed for more than their deposits. Any proposal for exceptions to the "single look" rule should take account of this concern.

§ 5.2.3   *Dubinsky v. Wells Bros. Co. of N.Y.*, 218 Mass. 232 (1914)

Wells Bros., a general contractor, obtained the contract to construct the Filene Building in Boston. The work included demolition of old buildings and removal of the materials. For the demolition work, Wells Bros. entered into a subcontract with Dubinsky by the terms of which Dubinsky agreed to do the demolition work and to remove the materials in return for title to those materials. Wells Bros. had discretion to remove Dubinsky from the site and to terminate his contract if his work proved unsatisfactory. As per the contract, Dubinsky deposited $1,500 with Well Bros. "to be forfeited in case the other conditions of the contract [were] not satisfactorily carried out." *Dubinsky v. Wells Bros. Co. of N.Y.*, 218 Mass. 232, 237 (1914). Dubinsky's crew was the object of multiple complaints. *Dubinsky v. Wells Bros. Co. of N.Y.*, 218 Mass. at 235–36. Exercising powers allowed by the contract, Wells Bros. gave notice to clean things up within forty-eight hours. Being dissatisfied with Dubinsky's response, Well Bros. gave notice of termination, took over the site, and claimed the materials from the building that was being demolished.

Contending that his termination was wrongful, Dubinsky sued. The case was given over to a master who found that Dubinsky's termination was made in good faith within the powers allowed Wells Bros. by contract, but determined, among other things, that if Wells Bros. had acted prudently, it could have finished the wrecking and removal of materials without incurring any additional expense. Consequently, according to the master's report, Wells Bros. was entitled to only nominal damages. Therefore, the trial judge ordered that the $1,500 deposit, less five dollars for nominal damages, be refunded.

With respect to the deposit of $1,500, the Supreme Judicial Court ruled that "it was intended by the parties to secure performance and was not intended to be retained by the defendant as liquidated damages." The order that $1,495 be returned to Dubinsky was sustained. Whether intent was inferred from the absence of actual damages, the text of contract, or the context is not clear, but intent as discerned from the record governed the outcome. It seems probable that the absence of actual damages made the invalidation of the clause more palatable than if there had been substantial damages attributed to a breach by Dubinsky.

§ 5.2.4   Summation

In two of the selected cases, the deposits were held to constitute a liquidation of damages; in the third case the deposit was deemed a penalty. In the early twentieth century, there were other Massachusetts cases involving deposits claimed as liquidated damages, *see e.g., Perry v. Wilson Bros., Inc.*, 260 Mass. 519(1927) (sustaining a lessor's retention of a deposit equal to one month's rent when lessor reentered on lessee's breach and incurred expenses in reletting and for a time relet at a price below that in the breached lease); *Courogenis v. Kerr*, 255 Mass. 536 (1926) (sustaining lessor's retention of a $1,100 deposit on lessee's breach of a lease); *Lieberman v. Lavene*, 253 Mass. 579 (1925) (sustaining a lessor's retention of a $200 deposit made by a lessee as security when the lessee was granted permission to assign the lease to a third party); *Davis-Hill Co., Inc. v. Wells*, 254 Mass. 118 (1925) (sustaining a claim against a surety on a secondary promise to refund a $1,000 deposit made by plaintiffs on entering into an agreement to serve as distributors of goods); *Wheaton Bldg. & Lumber Co. v. City of Boston*, 204 Mass. 218 (1910) (allowing an owner to retain a bid deposit on a contractor's wrongful failure to enter into a contract after his bid was accepted); *Hall v. Middleby*, 197 Mass. 485 (1908) (holding that a lessee's trustee in bankruptcy was entitled to lessee's deposit on lessor's wrongful actions), but the three cases selected are representative of the judicial approach employed. The cases exhibit a common quest. In determining whether there should be a refund to a buyer or lessee or other contracting party in breach, the inquiry was always fundamentally the same: what did the parties intend? Sometimes the intent to liquidate damages was inferred or assumed, with little or no comment. At other times, an estimate of actual damages, or the absence thereof, was part of the context. There was no stress upon either a prospective or retrospective point of view, and labels did not control. In these cases, an agreement for a *forfeiture* was treated as if the parties had agreed to liquidate damages.

§ 5.3 EXCURSUS: THE PARALLEL DOCTRINE OF FORFEITURE WHERE RETENTION OF DEPOSITS WAS ALLOWED APART FROM THE LAW OF LIQUIDATED DAMAGES

During the era when deposits were first analyzed under the law of liquidated damages, there arose a parallel line of authorities allowing aggrieved sellers in real estate cases to retain deposits without any consideration of whether or not the parties intended to liquidate damages. This was the law of forfeiture which had two branches: there was consensual forfeiture based upon agreement of the contracting parties, and nonconsensual forfeiture allowed by law with no inquiry into the parties' intentions. Cases involving the law of forfeiture are part of the legal context in which the current law of liquidated damages should be evaluated.

§ 5.3.1   *Donaghue v. Parkman*, 161 Mass. 412 (1894)

Donaghue's bid of $13,000 for a parcel of real estate was accepted by an auctioneer. Pursuant to a written contract he thereafter signed, Donaghue made a $500 deposit and expressly agreed "to forfeit said sum to the use of seller should I fail to comply with the residue of said terms." *Donaghue v. Parkman*, 161 Mass. 412, 413 (1894). Without legal excuse, Donaghue failed to complete the transaction, but nonetheless sued for return of the $500. The trial judge, without a jury, decided that the seller could rightfully retain the deposit. On appeal, the Supreme Judicial Court gave Donaghue short shrift:

> The first and principal question is whether a purchaser at a sale by auction, who has made a deposit of money under an agreement that it shall be forfeited to the use of the seller if he fails to comply with the terms of the sale, can recover back the deposit. It is well settled that he cannot. . . . Where the agreement contains a clause of forfeiture, all the authorities agree the deposit cannot be recovered back. In *Kelly v. Thompson* it is said by Mr. Justice Ames: "[w]hen purchaser expressly stipulates that a payment on account . . . actually made by him, is to be forfeited if by his own fault the purchase shall not go into effect, he may reasonably be understood to mean that it shall not be reclaimed in whole or in part. The distinction between a penalty and liquidated damages does not apply to a case of that description.

Donaghue v. Parkman, 161 Mass. at 413–14 (quoting *Kelly v. Thompson*, 101 Mass. 291 (1869)).

Thus, in 1894 an agreement to forfeit a deposit was different from an agreement to liquidate damages, at least in the minds of the justices that decided *Donaghue v. Parkman*. In a dictum the *Donaghue* court alluded to another doctrine, recognized in England and elsewhere: "[i]t is held in other cases that, *even if there is no clause of forfeiture in the agreement, a purchaser who violates his contract cannot recover his deposit." Donaghue v. Parkman*, 161 Mass. at 413 (citing *Ex Parte Barell*, 10 Ch. App. 512; *Depree v. Bedborough*, 4 Giff. 479; *Howe v. Smith*, 27 Ch. Div. 89) (emphasis added). Therefore, in *Donaghue*, we can discern two lines of cases bearing upon forfeitures of deposits: forfeitures by agreement without the scrutiny given to stipulated damages clauses, and forfeiture by law, apart from any agreement, due to an uncured breach by the buyer. The frequency of cases allowing a consensual forfeiture diminished in Massachusetts, possibly because such clauses were increasingly subjected to analysis as liquidated damages clauses, *e.g., Garcin v .Penn. Furnace, Co.*, 186 Mass. 405 (1904), or because clauses were drafted by legal counsel with eyes on cases involving liquidated damages clauses, thereby triggering an analysis under that line of authorities.

§ 5.3.2   *Keefe v. Fairfield*, 184 Mass. 334 (1903)

Keefe entered into a written agreement to buy a building from Fairfield, promising to pay the purchase price in ten-dollar-per-month installments. The contract provided further that if Keefe failed to make a monthly payment and did not cure within thirty days, the seller (Fairfield) would be released from all obligations, and that seller "shall have the right to retain for his own use as liquidated damages for such failure all moneys previously paid on account for such principal sum." *Keefe v. Fairfield*, 184 Mass. 334, 334 (1903). Keefe defaulted after making $210 in payments, and thereafter, when Fairfield refused to accept further payments, sought to reclaim that which he had paid. The trial judge denied his claim. On appeal, the Supreme Judicial Court sustained the result, allowing the seller to retain the deposit, and justified the result based on two distinct jurisprudential grounds: the law of forfeiture, and the law of liquidated damages. According to the court, resort to the law of liquidated damages was unnecessary because forfeiture was justified as a matter of law when Keefe breached and failed to cure within the time stipulated.

Practice Note

The Supreme Judicial Court recognized a dual rationale for seller's retention of the payments. First, the court recognized the doctrine of forfeiture without citation or explanation in the following language: "[t]he case stated in the bill of exceptions seems to be merely an attempt of one who has voluntarily made payments under a contract, and who has broken the contract by failing to make other payments as they became due, to recover back what he paid to the other party to the contract, who has not broken it, and who stands ready to perform it. Manifestly, there can be no recovery in such a case, and none of the rulings requested could be given in such a case. This alone is enough to dispose of the exceptions." *Keefe v. Fairfield*, 184 Mass. at 336. The court went further, saying "most of the requests for rulings seem to have been made upon an assumption that the defendant . . . has treated the contract as void, and has retained the money as liquidated damages. If the facts were in accordance with this assumption, the rulings requested upon the apparent ground that the money cannot be retained as liquidated damages, and that the provision must be treated as declaring a forfeiture, upon which actual damages should be assessed, were rightly refused." *Keefe v. Fairfield*, 184 Mass. at 336 (citing *Guerin v. Stacey*, 56 N.E. 892 (1900); *Garst v. Harris*, 177 Mass. 72 (1900); *Wallace v. Smith*, 21 Ch. Div. 243; and *Atkins v. Kinnier*, 4 Exch. 776–83).

§ 5.3.3   *Smith v. McMahon*, 197 Mass. 16 (1907)[*]

McMahon, having agreed to buy certain real estate from Smith, signed a memorandum binding himself, and at the time of signing deposited $500 with the broker (Green). Subsequently, fearing an abutter's likely objection to the transfer of a liquor license in connection with the sale, McMahon decided not to go forward. Smith sued the broker for the $500 deposit whereupon McMahon was admitted as a defendant since he sought return of the deposit. The trial judge entered judgment for Smith (the seller), to which McMahon took exception. The Supreme Judicial Court affirmed, allowing Smith (the seller) to retain the deposit. The court was clear on the rule: "the case stands as it would have stood, if the money had been paid to the plaintiff [seller] himself, in which case it is clear that, upon defendant's refusal to take a deed and complete the purchase, the plaintiff would have been entitled to retain the money." *Smith v. McMahon*, 197 Mass. 16, 18–19 (1907). Inasmuch as the court deemed it unnecessary to cite any authority for seller's right to retain the deposit, the right must have been deemed self-evident. *Smith* has often been cited as authority for the seller's right to retain a deposit, apart from any liquidated damages clause. *See, e.g., Macurdy v. Carver*, 328 Mass. 434 (1952); *Devore v. Good*, 321 Mass. 84 (1947); and *King v. Milliken*, 248 Mass. 460 (1924).

§ 5.3.4   *King v. Milliken*, 248 Mass. 460 (1924)

King and Milliken signed an agreement wherein King agreed to buy a parcel of real estate, along with specified personal property, for $8,000. King made a $500 deposit. The closing was set for November 10, 1921. After multiple extensions, due to proceedings in the Land Court, Milliken was ready, willing, and able to convey title in accord with the agreement. King did not appear, but sued for return of his deposit, apparently in the belief that he was excused due to delay in the Land Court. The trial judge entered judgment for Milliken, allowing him to retain the $500 deposit.

---

[*] This case is sometimes cited as *Smith v. Green. See, e.g., Beck v. Doore*, 319 Mass. 707 (1946).

The Supreme Judicial Court sustained the trial judge. In justification, the court stated simply, "it was the plaintiff who made default in performance of his contract; and the defendant was ready and willing to fulfill his obligations. In such circumstances the defaulting purchaser ordinarily is not entitled to recover a deposit which he has made in part payment." *King v. Milliken*, 248 Mass. at 463. Instead of setting forth seller's right to the deposit as self-evident, as in *Smith*, the court anchored its holding in nine cases, seven from foreign jurisdictions. One such citation was to *Lawrence v. Miller*, 86 N.Y. 131 (1881), generally deemed the seminal case justifying forfeiture of a deposit on buyer's default, in the absence of any agreement allowing forfeiture. The court linked the law of Massachusetts to a strong majority nationwide: buyers forfeit deposits on breach whether or not a liquidated damages clause has been agreed upon.

King v. Milliken has never been overruled and has been cited by the Supreme Judicial Court in a line of cases ending in 1981. *See, e.g., Sechrest v. Safiol*, 383 Mass. 568 (1981) (buyer's failure to use reasonable efforts to satisfy conditions precedent to his obligations under a purchase and sale agreement justified seller's retention of a $3,800 deposit); *La Valle v. Cataldo*, 343 Mass. 332 (1961) (buyer who refused to go through with the transaction on bank's approval of his mortgage application could not get his deposit back); *Berger v. Victory Realty Trust*, 329 Mass. 74 (1952) (seller was not obliged to have tenant dispossessed as buyers contended, hence, buyers in breach could not recover their deposit); *Macurdy v. Carver*, 328 Mass. 434 (1952) (buyer on breach forfeited his deposit and could recover no part of it). In reflecting upon the future of the law of liquidated damages, especially as that law pertains to real estate transactions, it is prudent to remember that there is a parallel doctrine that has allowed seller's retention of a deposit on buyer's breach of a contract for the conveyance of real estate, even in the absence of a stipulated damages clause. *See* Milton R. Friedman & James Charles Smith, 2 *Friedman on Contracts and Conveyances of Real Property* § 7:1.5 (7th ed. 2011).

§ 5.4   CONCLUSIONS

Through selected cases, I have sought to trace the law of liquidated damages in Massachusetts from the law's deep roots in England to the eve of the first Restatement of the Law of Contracts. I made a few observations and conclusions along the way and will add a few more here.

§ 5.4.1   Burden of Proof

The Supreme Judicial Court did not assign a burden of proof. Neither the challenger nor the party trying to uphold a clause was explicitly assigned the burden of either invalidating or validating a clause. In the era of Justice Holmes, it is arguable that the court moved toward a *presumption* of enforceability in cases where parties used the appropriate language and toward the opposite presumption when the parties designated a sum as a penalty, but there was no expressly articulated burden of proof.

§ 5.4.2   Prospective Versus Retrospective Analysis

The Supreme Judicial Court did not in any discernible sense choose a prospective or a retrospective method of analysis; a so-called second look was neither approved nor precluded. When proof of actual damages, or lack thereof, was evident in the record, such facts were recognized as pertinent in ascertaining the probable intent behind a clause.

§ 5.4.3   Forfeiture

In cases involving deposits, particularly in cases arising from failed real estate transactions, the Supreme Judicial Court recognized and developed an independent law of forfeiture whereby an aggrieved seller was allowed to retain deposits, usually made as part payment, even in the absence of any stipulated damages clause.

§ 5.4.4   Forfeiture and Judicial Scrutiny

When a clause explicitly stipulated that a buyer on default would forfeit payments made in the event of breach, such a clause was usually enforced as written without the judicial scrutiny normally given a liquidated damages clause. On the other hand, in some cases, forfeiture clauses were subjected to the same scrutiny as liquidated damages clauses. Hence, the doctrines surrounding forfeiture and liquidated damages tend to overlap.

§ 5.4.5   Evaluating Stipulated Damages Clauses

The Supreme Judicial Court never explicitly adopted a test, either two-prong or three-prong, for evaluating stipulated damages clauses. Ostensibly, the inquiry was always about the intent of the contracting parties, yet the opinions reveal that there were common factors of importance routinely given close attention, including the probable actual damages on breach. Results were generally fact-driven as courts searched for the probable intent of the parties.

Practice Note

On close examination of the case law, it is arguable that the Supreme Judicial Court was cautiously moving toward a tiered method of analysis before the first *Restatement of the Law of Contracts* was promulgated. A case illustrating this point is *Putnam Machine Co. v. Mustakangas*, 236 Mass. 376 (1920), in which a father agreed to an apprenticeship contract for his minor son to learn the machinist trade. In the contract, he promised that if his son breached, he (the father) would pay the machinist $100 as "ascertained and liquidated damages." When the son breached, the master sued. The trial judge found the liquidated damages clause unenforceable. The Supreme Judicial Court reversed with the following explanation: "[f]rom the nature of the undertaking and the subject matter of the contract, it might be difficult to determine the exact amount of damages. The parties might well agree upon them when the contract was made; it does not appear that they are excessive. It is expressly stated that the defendant was to pay $100 as ascertained and liquidated damages if the agreement was not fulfilled by his son. There is no suggestion of a penalty, the language indicates the intention of the parties to be that the sum agreed upon should be treated as liquidated damages and not as a penalty." *Putnam Mach. Co. v. Mustakangas*, 236 Mass. at 378. The analytical method set forth was compatible—more or less—with the two-prong test included in the first *Restatement of the Law of Contracts* (1932), which treated liquidated damages in § 339 and deposits in § 340.

CHAPTER 6

The *Restatement of Contracts* (1932): A Two-Prong Test Replaces the Quest for the Intent of the Contracting Parties

Gary L. Monserud, Esq.
New England Law | Boston

§ 6.1   **Introduction** **6–1**

§ 6.2   **The Origins of Section 339** **6–3**

§ 6.3   **Prospective Versus Retrospective Analysis** **6–6**

§ 6.4   **Did the Massachusetts Supreme Judicial Court Adopt Section 339 of the Restatement?** **6–8**

CHAPTER 6

The *Restatement of Contracts* (1932): A Two-Prong Test Replaces the Quest for the Intent of the Contracting Parties

Gary L. Monserud, Esq.
New England Law | Boston

Scope Note

This chapter discusses the two-prong test embodied in Section 339 of the *Restatement of Contracts* entitled, "Liquidated Damages and Penalties," as well as Section 340 entitled "Money Deposits as Liquidated Damages." This Chapter concludes with a discussion of case law showing the adoption of a two-prong test into Massachusetts law.

§ 6.1   INTRODUCTION

The law in Massachusetts was greatly impacted by the promulgation of the first *Restatement of the Law of Contracts* in 1932, for which Professor Samuel Williston was the Reporter. Section 339, entitled "Liquidated Damages and Penalties," states as follows:

> (1) An agreement, made in advance of breach, fixing the damages therefor, is not enforceable as a contract and does not affect the damages recoverable for the breach, unless
>
> – the amount so fixed is a reasonable forecast of just compensation for the harm that is caused by the breach; and
>
> – the harm that is caused by the breach is one that is incapable or very difficult of accurate estimation.

> (2) An undertaking in a penal bond to pay a sum of money as a penalty for non-performance of the condition of the bond is enforceable only to the extent of the harm proved to have been suffered by reason of such non-performance, and in no case for more than the amount named as a penalty, with interest.

Section 340 entitled "Money Deposits as Liquidated Damages" states as follows:

> A sum of money or other property deposited by a promisor as security for performance by him and against loss to the other party, to be forfeited in case of breach, may be either a penalty or liquidated damages in accordance with the rule stated in Section 339(1).

It is apparent in Section 340 that deposits of money to be forfeited on breach should be evaluated according to the regular rules for evaluating liquidated damages clauses, as was usually the case in Massachusetts before the *Restatement*. It is equally apparent that subsection (2) of Section 339 limits enforcement of penal bonds to actual damages proved ex post, thus reiterating and clarifying the compensatory principle established in case law. The focus here will be on subsection (1) of Section 339 with respect to which I aim to answer three questions:

- What was the origin of this two-prong test?

- Was it intended exclusively as an ex ante (prospective) test or was it designed to allow ex post (retrospective) inquiries into actual damages?

- To what extent was Section 339 adopted or relied upon by the Supreme Judicial Court in Massachusetts?

Practice Note

Neither the text of Section 340, nor its comment, nor the single illustration following say anything about the law of forfeiture apart from explicit agreements. I presume, therefore, that Professor Williston and his collaborators did not intend to extinguish nonconsensual forfeitures wherever case law allowed such forfeitures to be enforced.

Practice Note

Illustration 8 under Section 339 demonstrates the compensatory principle as follows: "A executes a bond binding himself to pay B the sum of $10,000, on condition to be void, however, if C, who is B's cashier, shall properly account for all moneys entrusted to him. C defaults to the extent of $500. B can recover on the bond no more than the amount of the loss, not $10,000."

§ 6.2   THE ORIGINS OF SECTION 339

Even though the first *Restatement* did not list Professor Williston's sources, because he authored a multivolume treatise on contracts, a revision of which appeared in 1936, see Samuel Williston, *A Treatise on the Law of Contracts* (rev. ed. by Samuel Williston and George Thompson 1936), it is reasonable to search for legal history behind the *Restatement* in his revised treatise, especially where it contains citations to the pertinent *Restatement* sections. Liquidated damages is a topic given substantial treatment in the 1936 revised treatise. *See* Samuel Williston, 3 *A Treatise on the Law of Contracts,* Chapter XXVIII, §§ 776–79 (rev. ed. 1936).

One of the first points of consequence is Professor Williston's side-lining of the inquiry concerning the parties' intentions in adopting a clause stipulating damages. While he acknowledged a long line of cases wherein courts had enunciated the importance of discerning contracting parties' intentions, he concluded that "the first step towards a clear understanding of the matter is to recognize that the determination of whether or not a particular provision is penal or merely provides for liquidated damages only does not depend on the natural meaning of the language used by the parties," Samuel Williston, 3 *A Treatise on the Law of Contracts,* § 777 at 2185 (rev. ed. 1936). That view ran contrary to Justice Holmes's viewpoint and collided with roughly 120 years of case law in Massachusetts. Professor Williston assumed that in many cases a scrivener chose the contract language, and that the contracting parties were often unaware of the legal implications of word choices, saying

> In every case, either of penalty or of liquidated damages, the parties have manifested a clear intention that the sum stated in the contract shall be paid in the contingency which has occurred. If their intention is to be given effect, every penalty will be enforced. If, however, by intention of the parties is meant their intention that the particular provision in question shall be liquidated damages or shall be a penalty, it should be observed that most people who make contracts know nothing about these terms or what they connote. If they do know that there is a distinction made by the law, the surest way of indicating that they mean one or the other is to call it by its appropriate name; and when contracts

> are drawn by lawyers the sum stipulated for is usually
> called liquidated damages, but courts rightly pay little
> attention to the name given to a sum payable in terms
> on breach of a contract.

Samuel Williston, 3 *A Treatise on the Law of Contracts* § 777 at 2185 (rev. ed. 1936).

Hence, instead of focusing upon intent, Professor Williston focused upon the reasonableness of the estimate at the time of formation, and on that point he cited to *Restatement* § 339(1) and selected cases. Samuel Williston, 3 *A Treatise on the Law of Contracts* § 777 at 2185 (rev. ed. 1936). Thus, § 339(1) was prescriptive as much as descriptive.

While case law from several jurisdictions through deliberation and debate may have flowed into the drafting of Section 339(1), it does appear from Professor Williston's citations that decisions made by the Supreme Court of Connecticut were the main underpinnings for the test adopted in Section 339(1), 3 Samuel Williston, *A Treatise on the Law of Contracts,* § 778 n.11 (rev. ed. 1936) (citing *Schoolnick v. Gold*, 89 Conn. 110 (1915); and *Banta v. Stamford Motor Co.*, 89 Conn. 551 (1914)). Writing many decades later, Professor E. Allan Farnsworth opined that it was the Supreme Court of Connecticut which first enunciated a test for judicial use in evaluating stipulated damages clauses. E. Allen Farnsworth, *Contracts* § 778 n.11 (4th ed.). Of the Connecticut cases preceding the *Restatement*, the preeminent case setting forth a test was *Banta v. Stamford Motor Co.*, 89 Conn. 51 (1914).

The case arose from a contract for the construction of a yacht for the price of $5,500. Delivery was due on or before September 1, 1911. The contract contained an incentive clause allowing Stamford Motor five dollars per day for early delivery and a liquidated damages clause allowing Banta fifteen dollars per day for delay. When Stamford Motor failed to deliver until November 25, Banta claimed $1,275 in delay damages, more than the balance owing on the contract. Banta sued for the liquidated damages, won at the trial court, and Stamford Motor appealed.

Practice Note

Currently, this case would be governed by Article 2 of the U.C.C. because the yacht would be considered "specially manufactured goods" recognized in Section 2-105(1). Therefore, U.C.C. § 2-718(1) would provide the applicable rule for evaluating the liquidated damages clause. This subsection states: "Damages for breach by either party may be liquidated in the agreement but only at an amount which is reasonable in light of the anticipated or actual harm caused by the breach, the difficulties of proof of loss, and the inconvenience or nonfeasibility of otherwise obtaining an appropriate remedy. A term fixing unreasonably large liquidated damages is void as a penalty." By the reference to *actual damages*, the rule herein contained authorizes a "second look" to ascertain reasonableness. As of June 2013, no reported decision in Massachusetts has applied this section.

Stamford Motor's lawyer based his argument mainly upon the fact that the yacht was a pleasure boat, not intended for any commercial use; accordingly, Banta had not suffered any measurable, compensable loss. Upholding the liquidated damages clause, the Supreme Court of Connecticut set forth a three-prong analytical test:

- The damages to be anticipated as resulting from the breach must be uncertain in amount or difficult to prove;

- there must have been an intent on the part of the parties to liquidate them in advance; and

- the amount stipulated must be a reasonable one—that is to say, not grossly disproportionate to the presumable loss or injury.

Banta v. Stamford Motor Co., 89 Conn. at 667 (citing *Associated Hat Mfrs. v. Baird United Co.*, 88 Conn. 333 (1914); and *Dean v. Conn. Tobacco Corp.*, 88 Conn. 619 (1914)).

Due to Professor Williston's suspicions about attempts to discern intent, he and his cohorts dropped the middle prong and with slight rephrasing and adjustments, Section 339 was fashioned. The introductory words in Section 339 suggest a presumption against enforceability because "an agreement, made in advance of breach, fixing the damages therefor, is not enforceable, unless . . ." the two-prong test is met.

We need not guess about the manner in which Section 339 was contemporaneously viewed by the legal community in Massachusetts. In 1935 scholars and distinguished members of the Massachusetts bar collaborated for the publication of two volumes of *Massachusetts Annotations to the Restatement of the Law of Contracts*. Massachusetts Bar Association of the City of Boston (American Law Institute Publishers 1935). Section 339 was introduced with this succinct comment: "[t]he results of the Massachusetts decisions are in substantial harmony with this section, *although the form in which the results are stated differs materially therefrom.*" Massachusetts Bar Association of the City of Boston, *Massachusetts Annotations to the Restatement of the Law of Contracts* § 339 at 199 (American Law Institute Publishers 1935) (emphasis added). This was a candid recognition of that which my study of earlier case law has demonstrated, namely, that for more than a century prior to the promulgation of the *Restatement*, the

Massachusetts courts (like many others) primarily searched for evidence of the probable intent of the parties behind clauses for stipulated damages. Surveying prior case law, the authors of the 1935 study determined that the Massachusetts courts would likely have decided the cases as they did if the *Restatement* test had been applied, but the opinions ("the form in which the results are stated") would have rested upon the criteria included in Section 339 rather than the presumed intent of the parties.

§ 6.3   PROSPECTIVE VERSUS RETROSPECTIVE ANALYSIS

One of the major issues in recent times has been the division between courts which examine liquidated damages clauses only from the vantage point of formation (ex ante) and those which take a second look (ex post) and invalidate a clause if it stipulates damages grossly disproportionate to damages actually incurred, even if the clause was reasonable at the time of formation. Which view did Section 339 embody? A careful examination of the text of Section 339, its legislative history, and its official comments yields a reasonably certain answer.

First, consider the text of Section 339(1) which provides that a clause is not enforceable unless "(a) the amount so fixed is a reasonable forecast of just compensation for the harm that is caused by the breach, and (b) the harm that is caused by the breach is one that is incapable or very difficult of accurate estimation." A forecast, as referred to in subsection (a), *is necessarily prospective*. Subsection (b) does not state whether the estimation of harm (which must be very difficult or incapable of being made) refers to the time of breach or formation, but there is solid evidence that an ex ante test was intended by the drafters. One piece of evidence is Tentative Draft No. 8 of Section 330 (an antecedent to Section 339) submitted to the members of the American Law Institute for discussion in May, 1930. Section 330 of Tentative Draft 8 stated as follows:

> (1) An agreement, made in advance of breach, fixing the damages therefor, is not enforceable as a contract and does not affect the damages recoverable for the breach, unless
>
> — the amount so fixed is a reasonable forecast of just compensation for an injury that is incapable or very difficult of accurate estimation; and
>
> — it appears after the injury has occurred that the agreed amount is not *grossly disproportionate thereto* (italics added).

Contemplating the language of subsection (b), it seems indisputable that Tentative Draft No. 8 recommended a retrospective analysis of the stipulated sum in relation to actual harm caused by the breach. The deletion of this language in favor of the language adopted in Section 339(1)(b) strongly suggests a movement away from a retrospective analysis in assessing the reasonableness of the sum agreed upon. Moreover, the 1935 revised edition of Professor Williston's treatise, citing Section 339 stated that "the matter would be much simplified if it were clearly recognized and stated that *the reasonableness of the agreed sum looked at as of the time when the contract was made is the only important thing.*" Samuel Williston, 3 *A Treatise on the Law of Contracts*, § 778 at 2190 (rev. ed. 1936) (emphasis added). It seems reasonably clear that a purpose behind Section 339 was to instruct the courts to analyze the reasonableness of stipulated damages clauses prospectively.

But, there is more to the story. Comment (e) to subsection (1) of Section 339 authorizes a no-damages defense when a party sues to enforce a stipulated damages clause. In relevant part it states that "[i]f the parties honestly but mistakenly suppose that a breach will cause harm that will be incapable or very difficult of accurate estimation, when in fact the breach causes no harm at all or none that is incapable of accurate estimation without difficulty, their advance agreement . . . is unenforceable." *Restatement of the Law of Contracts* § 339 cmt e. The comment goes on to advise that evidence of a mistake made at the time of contracting is admissible. Just as any agreement might be rendered unenforceable by proof of a mutual mistake, a liquidated damages clause could be rendered unenforceable by proof that the estimate proved later to have been a mistake. Differently viewed, if it could be proved ex post that a breach caused no harm, the drafters believed that the parties had made a mistake in liquidating damages because there was nothing to liquidate. Again, the revised edition of Professor Williston's treatise tends to substantiate this viewpoint where it states "there cannot well be any other liquidated damages for a breach which causes an injury, the extent of which is mathematically certain, than the very sum mathematically determined." Samuel Williston, 3 *A Treatise on the Law of Contracts* § 783 at 2201–02 (rev. ed. 1936). Zero is mathematically certain. Furthermore, even if damages are not mathematically certain, but "as a matter of obvious fact fall within narrow limits, not only is a sum much beyond those limits unreasonable, but the parties must be regarded as chargeable with notice of that fact." Samuel Williston, 3 *A Treatise on the Law of Contracts* § 783 at 2201–02 (rev. ed. 1936). Hence, great disparity between actual harm and the liquidated sum provides a basis upon which to infer either that the original estimate was not reasonable or that the parties made a mistake which can render the liquidated damages clause voidable. Consequently, while there is good evidence that Section 339 was intended to promote a two-prong ex ante analysis, the official comments and Professor Williston's treatise make it clear that postbreach evidence of either actual damages or the absence thereof were intended to serve in some cases to negate a clause on alternative grounds: mutual mistake or an inference undercutting the reasonableness of the original estimate. Thus, the first *Restatement* did not preclude all post-breach analyses of liquidated damages clauses. The *Restatement's* allowance of a retrospective analysis did not go wholly unnoticed in case law. Quite the contrary; in 1989 the First Circuit Court of Appeals quoted extensively from Comment (e) in a case where the court invalidated a $200,000 lump sum liquidated damages clause on a record that showed no net loss attributable to breach. *See Colonial at Lynnfield v. Sloan*, 870 F.2d 761, 765 n.6 (1st Cir. 1989).

§ 6.4   DID THE MASSACHUSETTS SUPREME JUDICIAL COURT ADOPT SECTION 339 OF THE RESTATEMENT?

The Supreme Judicial Court appears, without any announcement, to have adopted the test embodied in Section 339(1) of the first *Restatement of the Law of Contracts* without casting aside Massachusetts pre-*Restatement* precedents which have been cited frequently into the twenty-first century. Since the 1940s, the court has commingled case law which precedes the *Restatement*, where the focus was on the intent of the parties, with the *Restatement* test drawn from non-Massachusetts sources, which eschews any inquiry into intent. Perhaps it was the conceptual and linguistic differences between the deep reservoir of case law in Massachusetts and the two-prong test in Section 339 that caused the courts to be sparing in their application of Section 339 in decades after 1932. Perhaps this commingling of earlier case law and the *Restatement* test is one reason for abiding interpretive challenges in reading later Massachusetts cases. The mingling of cases that turned on intent with a tiered test that eschewed intent has made the case law interesting, and not always easy to understand.

The first citation to Section 339 by the Supreme Judicial Court was in *Commissioner of Insurance v. Massachusetts Accident Co.*, 310 Mass. 769 (1942), a case involving rent acceleration. The court justified its decision by citation to six Massachusetts cases, and double as many cases from other jurisdictions, before sandwiching a citation to Section 339 between citations to two other secondary authorities, one of which was Professor Williston's treatise. The court's next citation to Section 339 was in *Security Safety Corp. v. Kuznicki*, 350 Mass. 157 (1966). The citation to Section 339 followed the statement that "[t]his case is governed in all respects by *A-Z Servicenter, Inc. v. Segall*. . . . For aught that appears, the damages in the event of breach were not going to be difficult of ascertainment" (*citing A-Z Servicenter Inc. v. Segall*, 334 Mass. 672 (1956)). This suggests that *A-Z Servicenter* was decided in whole or in part on the application of the *Restatement* test, or at least was consistent with Section 339, but nowhere in the *A-Z Servicenter* opinion is there any mention of Section 339.

Practice Note

In *A-Z Servicenter v. Segall,* the court used a test akin to Section 339(1), but the court cited *Putnam Machine Co. v. Mustakangas*, 236 Mass. 376 (1920); *Makletzova v. Diaghileff*, 227 Mass. 100 (1917); *Garst v. Harris*, 177 Mass. 72 (1900); *Fisk v. Gray*, 93 Mass. 132 (1865); and *Shute v. Taylor*, 46 Mass. 61 (1842)—all of which preceded the *Restatement* and turned (ostensibly) on the intent of the parties.

Whence came the formulation used in *A-Z Servicenter* which appears so similar to the test embodied in Section 339(1)? My hunch—only a hunch—is that the court took the formulation either directly from Section 339(1), without citing it, or from Professor Williston's treatise, revised edition, Section 776, both of which were cited in the plaintiff's appellate brief on the appeal in the *A-Z Servicenter* case. Suffice it to say that a slight reformulation of the two-prong *Restatement* test from Section 339(1), or a test consistent with Section 339(1), was imported quietly into Massachusetts case law by 1956, but thereafter, the Supreme Judicial Court and the lower courts continued to support their decisions by citations to case law from before the *Restatement*. The two-prong test became a fixed part of our jurisprudence, central to arguments for decades, though Section 339 has seldom been cited in appellate opinions.

CHAPTER 7

The Rise of the "Second Look Rule" in Real Estate Sales

Gary L. Monserud, Esq.
New England Law | Boston

§ 7.1   The Path to *Shapiro v. Grinspoon* and its "Second Look" Rule.. **7–1**

§ 7.1.1   *A-Z Servicenter, Inc. v. Segall*, 334 Mass. 672 (1956) 7–1

§ 7.1.2   *Security Safety Corporation v. Kuznicki*, 350 Mass. 157 (1966) 7–4

§ 7.1.3   *Warner v. Wilkey*, 2 Mass. App. Ct. 798 (1974)..... 7–5

§ 7.1.4   *Lynch v. Andrew*, 20 Mass. App. Ct. 623 (1985) ... 7–6

§ 7.1.5   *Colonial at Lynnfield, Inc. v. Sloan*, 870 F.2d 761 (1st Cir. 1989)... 7–7

§ 7.1.6   *Schrenko v. Regnante*, 27 Mass. App. Ct. 282 (1989) 7–8

§ 7.1.7   *Shapiro v. Grinspoon*, 27 Mass. App. Ct. 596 (1989) 7–9

§ 7.2   The Bar's Reaction to *Shapiro v. Grinspoon* and the Second Look Rule **7–14**

CHAPTER 7

The Rise of the "Second Look Rule" in Real Estate Sales

Gary L. Monserud, Esq.
New England Law | Boston

Scope Note

This chapter extends the story of the development of the law of liquidated damages in Massachusetts through the latter half of the twentieth century and into the twenty-first century, with an intense focus on real estate sales. This chapter aims to explain the development of the "second look rule" as it pertains to deposits made pursuant to purchase and sale agreements for real estate. More precisely, this chapter is about the *development, articulation, and bar criticism* of the second look rule in real estate cases when breaching buyers sought return of their deposits in times of rapid inflation in the real estate market.

§ 7.1 THE PATH TO *SHAPIRO V. GRINSPOON* AND ITS "SECOND LOOK" RULE

§ 7.1.1 *A-Z Servicenter, Inc. v. Segall*, 334 Mass. 672 (1956)

This case arose from a contract for the purchase and sale of a gas station. The buyer agreed to a purchase price of $20,000, signed a promissory note payable over fifteen years with interest at the rate of 11.2 percent on the outstanding balance, and granted seller a purchase money mortgage on the property. Segall (seller) insisted that the mortgage and promissory note be in the amount of $41,400 (principal plus interest computed for fifteen years), and the buyer acquiesced. *A-Z Servicenter, Inc. v. Segall*, 334 Mass. 672, 673 (1956). Regarding damages, the note stipulated that "whenever any default in the performance of the conditions of the mortgage securing this note shall continue for a period of thirty days, then at the option of the holder of this note, the entire amount of $41,400 as set forth above less any payments made hereon shall be immediately due and payable as liquidated damages and not as a penalty." Thus, the stipulated damages consisted of the total amount of the note, less payments made.

The buyer defaulted, having paid a total of $2,970, less than $500 of which was allocated against the principal. Segall initiated a foreclosure action, claiming the entire balance of the note as liquidated damages, and was granted a decree allowing the foreclosure. When the foreclosure was advertised, the buyer filed suit, seeking a declaration of the amount due, and discharge of the debt on payment of the amount judicially determined. A trial judge decreed that the amount rightly owing was $24,821, a sum which included outstanding principal and accrued interest, but not the entire unpaid balance as stipulated. Hence, the judge refused to enforce the clause which purportedly liquidated the damages.

The seller appealed, arguing that the liquidated damages clause (allowing the unpaid balance due on the note), should have been enforced. The Supreme Judicial Court sustained the trial judge's decision, holding that the clause was a penalty. While the court acknowledged that an acceleration clause triggered by breach and designated as a computation of liquidated damages was lawful, the court ruled that to survive scrutiny, such a clause could rightly include interest only "if the acceleration extended no further than to include interest actually due at the time of breach." *See A-Z Servicenter, Inc. v. Segall*, 334 Mass. at 675. The unearned interest at the point of breach was not a realistic estimate of actual damages.

In support of its decision, the court first set forth the uncontroversial proposition that the enforceability of a stipulated damages clause depends on the circumstances of each case. *See De Cordova v. Weeks*, 246 Mass. 100 (1923); *Int'l Paper Co. v. Priscilla Co.*, 281 Mass. 22 (1932). As to the test for enforceability, the court used the following formulation:

> Where actual damages are difficult to ascertain and where the sum agreed upon by the parties at the time of the execution of the contract represents a reasonable estimate of actual damages, such a contract will be enforced.

A-Z Servicenter, Inc. v. Segall, 334 Mass. at 675 (citing *Garst v. Harris*, 177 Mass. 72 (1900); *Putnam Mach. Co. v. Mustakangas*, 236 Mass. 376 (1920)).

Although the first clause could conceivably refer to either the time of formation or the time of breach, read as a whole, this formulation appears to be consistent with the *prospective* approach to evaluating a stipulated damages clause embodied in § 339 of the *Restatement*. But, after the citations, the court flipped the test upside down and stated:

> But where the actual damages are easily ascertainable
> and the stipulated sum is unreasonably and grossly
> disproportionate to the real damages from a breach,
> or is unconscionably excessive, the court will award
> the aggrieved party no more than his actual damages.

A-Z Servicenter, Inc. v. Segall, 334 Mass. at 675 (citing *Shute v. Taylor*, 5 Metc.
61, 46 Mass. Rep. 61 (1842); *Makletzova v. Diaghileff*, 227 Mass. 100(1917);
Fisk v. Gray, 11 Allen 132, 93 Mass. 132 (1865)).

If one reads this language detached from the "time of the breach" language preceding the quotation, it appears to approve a *retrospective* test because it speaks
of "real damages" and "actual damages," and of possible proportionality and
unconscionability of stipulated damages in comparison to actual damages. It is
doubtful that Justice Ronan, who wrote the *A-Z Servicenter* opinion, intended
any break with precedent or had the objective of cutting a new path in the law.
Nonetheless, his language was susceptible to being support for a second look
(retrospective) analysis, and later courts viewed *A-Z* as the genesis of the second
look rule. To round out the analysis, the court warned against using the term
"liquidated damages" as a cloak to hide "a sum of money out of proportion to
and differing greatly from the actual damages ordinarily arising from a breach."
A-Z Servicenter, Inc. v. Segall, 334 Mass. at 675 (citing *Shute v. Taylor*, 5 Metc.
61, 46 Mass. Rep. 61 (1842); *Comm'r of Ins. v. Mass. Accident Co.*, 310 Mass.
769 (1942); and *Kothe v. R.C. Taylor Trust*, 280 U.S. 224 (1930) (reference to
"actual damages ordinarily arising from a breach" points toward an analysis
based upon the nature of the contract)).

Practice Note

As indicated at the end of Chapter 6, the source of the rule applied
in *A-Z Servicenter, Inc.* is perplexing since the rule employed seems
to be a slight rephrasing of Section 339 of the first *Restatement of
the Law of Contracts*; yet the *Restatement* is not cited. Moreover,
the only post-*Restatement* case that had cited Section 339, *Commissioner of Insurance v. Massachusetts Accident Co.*, 310 Mass.
769 (1942), was cited only for the general principle that a penalty
cannot be hidden beneath the term "liquidated damages." I suspect
the court took the test from Professor Williston's treatise.

Apart from what the court said, did the decision turn on a comparison of actual
and stipulated damages? In a limited way, it did. There was a second look only
in the sense that the court noted the time of breach, the principal owed, and the
interest accrued to the date upon which the trial court's decree was entered—all
with reference to the schedule of payments in the note. The trial court did simple
arithmetic to compute actual damages (earned interest), and the Supreme Judicial

Court approved. It would be inaccurate to contend that the court blinded itself to the material facts at the time of the breach, or postbreach facts for that matter, but the court never suggested that it would have been appropriate to consider Segall's postbreach losses, if any, apart from calculable interest. The court simply made a practical judgment considering the express terms of the note.

Practice Note

In *A-Z Servicenter, Inc. v. Segall*, an alternative approach could have involved an inquiry into Segall's consequential damages, meaning lost interest payments. Segall was not merely the seller, but was also the lender. For example, it would have been possible to compare postbreach interest rates to the 11.2 percent interest rate to which Segall was entitled under the note. If postbreach interest rates were less, and Segall could have earned, for example, only 3.2 percent, the breach arguably would have caused Segall damages, i.e., loss of interest not recoverable by reinvestment. The court did not take this approach nor did Segall's lawyer argue for any damages of such a nature.

§ 7.1.2　　*Security Safety Corporation v. Kuznicki*, 350 Mass. 157 (1966)

In this case, the Supreme Judicial Court, in an opinion by Chief Justice Wilkins, relied on *A-Z Servicenter, Inc.* to sustain a trial judge's refusal to enforce a liquidated damages clause in a contract for the installation of a fire protection system, when the homeowners unjustifiably cancelled the morning after the signing of the contract. The liquidated damages clause would have awarded the aggrieved contractor one-third of the contract price on the homeowner's breach. In support of the decision, Chief Justice Wilkins used language that subsequently enhanced the legitimacy of a second look:

> The case is governed in all respects by *A-Z Servicenter, Inc. v. Segall* [citation omitted]. For aught that appears, the damages in the event of breach were not going to be difficult of ascertainment.... *Time was lacking for an opportunity for the plaintiff to incur much expense of performance. The stipulated sum is unreasonably and grossly disproportionate to the real damages from the breach.* In these circumstances, the aggrieved party will be awarded no more than his actual damage.

Security Safety Corp. v. Kuznicki, 350 Mass. at 158 (emphasis added).

The words "[t]ime was lacking for an opportunity . . . to incur much expense of performance" point toward a retrospective approach (second look), as do the words "the real damages from the breach." Moreover, the italicized language presumes that the contractor's rightful claim would be for reliance damages, meaning sums actually expended in reliance on the contract. *See, e.g., Restatement (Second) of the Law of Contracts* § 344(b). If the court had considered that the contractor might have been entitled to his lost expectation interest, meaning his benefit of the bargain, *see, e.g., Restatement (Second) of the Law of Contracts* § 344(a), one-third of the contract price might have been reasonable in the circumstances and within the contemplation of the parties at the time of contracting. However, nothing suggests that there was a serious effort at the trial court level to demonstrate actual losses corresponding reasonably to the stipulated percentage, nor did the Supreme Judicial Court lament the lack of evidence about probable expectation losses. The court made a reasonable judgment that the contractor's actual losses were minimal and affirmed without saying explicitly whether an ex post analysis should be employed or not. The same can be said about *Manganaro Drywall, Inc. v. Penn-Simon Construction Co.*, 367 Mass. 563 (1970).

§ 7.1.3 *Warner v. Wilkey*, 2 Mass. App. Ct. 798 (1974)

This appears to be the first case in which *A-Z Servicenter, Inc.* was deemed authoritative for a decision arising from an aborted contract for the sale of real estate. After the buyers failed to close, the seller commenced an action for specific performance. The disappointed seller (Warner) was able to arrange a sale to a second buyer, however, so the trial judge awarded the sum agreed upon as liquidated damages, though only a part of that sum had been prepaid as a deposit. The buyers appealed, and the Massachusetts Appeals Court upheld the award of liquidated damages to the seller. The opinion from the Massachusetts Appeals Court contained the following statement, justifying the result:

> The judge was right in invoking the clause in the contract entitling the plaintiff to retain the defendants' pre-closing deposit as "liquidated damages" [citations omitted]. He was also right in assessing as damages the unpaid balance of the amount agreed upon as a deposit. The amount was not so disproportionate to plaintiff's losses and expenses caused by defendants' breach as to make the liquidated damages clause unenforceable as a penalty. See *A-Z Servicenter, Inc. v. Segall,* 334 Mass. 672, 675, 138 N.E.2d 266 (1956), and the cases cited. In determining the amount of those losses and expenses, the judge properly considered the plaintiff's liability for the broker's commission on the

> abortive sale *as well as the difference between the agreed purchase price and the lesser price for which is was actually sold.*

Warner v. Wilkey, 2 Mass. App. Ct. 798, 798 (1974) (emphasis added).

The rescript opinion is exceedingly brief. Nowhere does the court speak explicitly of a "retrospective" or "ex post" analysis, but giving the language its plain meaning, that evidence of a postbreach resale price was a matter rightly considered by the trial judge, the opinion could (and did) become one more link in a chain of cases leading to an explicit adoption of the second look rule. This decision did not cause alarm—at least so far as is discernible from bar journals—probably because the liquidated damages clause was enforced, and there was nothing that overtly signaled a doctrinal shift.

§ 7.1.4   *Lynch v. Andrew*, 20 Mass. App. Ct. 623 (1985)

In this case, seller and buyers executed a purchase and sale agreement with a clause stipulating that the buyers' deposit of $24,500 would be retained by the seller in the event of the buyers' breach. The buyers then defaulted. When they sued for a refund of their deposit, the trial judge allowed a partial refund on the grounds that retention of the whole of the deposit amounted to a penalty in the circumstances. In lieu thereof, the trial judge awarded $8,400 actual damages. *Lynch v. Andrew*, 20 Mass. App. Ct. 623, 624 (1985). The Appeals Court upheld the trial judge's finding of breach by the buyers, but reversed as to the liquidated damages clause. In a scholarly review of the pertinent law, Justice Kass gave a respectful nod to Justice Holmes ("so far as precedent permits the proper course is . . . not to undertake to be wiser than the parties"), *Lynch v. Andrew*, 20 Mass. App. Ct. at 627 (citing *Guerin v. Stacey*, 175 Mass. 595 (1900)), and then quoted from the opinion in *Warner v. Wilkey* to set forth the rule that "contract provisions that clearly and reasonably establish liquidated damages should be enforced if 'not so disproportionate to the losses and expenses caused by defendant's breach' as to constitute a penalty." *Lynch v. Andrew*, 20 Mass. App. Ct. at 627 (citing *Warner v. Wilkey*, 2 Mass. App. Ct. at 799). Looking at the terms of the contract before the court, it was clear that in the wake of the buyers' default one-half of the deposit was allocated to the broker, so the seller would actually be left with $12,700, not $25,400, if the liquidated damages clause were enforced. Additionally, the seller had enumerated many elements of actual damages, several of which would rightly be classified as consequential and difficult to estimate with exactitude. Noting these claims, Justice Kass concluded:

> This is not a case in which the house sold within days of the first buyer's default, at about the same price,

> and without complicating factors which make the ac-
> tual damages difficult to calculate with precision. It is
> not a case in which the liquidated damages provision is
> grossly disproportionate to a reasonable estimate of ac-
> tual damages. . . . When losses are difficult to quantify,
> considerable deference is due the parties' reasonable
> agreement as to liquidated damages.

Lynch v. Andrew, 20 Mass. App. Ct. at 628.

Justice Kass was willing, and thought it proper, to take account of economic realities both at the time of and following breach, as shown by the record. Yet there was no announcement of any rule change. The propriety of considering postbreach consequences to the seller was a given in light of precedent. The opinion implied that if a house sold for about the same price as agreed upon in the aborted contract (or presumably for more than the contract price) *within days* and *without complicating factors*, the result might have been different.

§ 7.1.5   *Colonial at Lynnfield, Inc. v. Sloan*, 870 F.2d 761 (1st Cir. 1989)

For those who study liquidated damages clauses, 1989 was a banner year in Massachusetts. The first case of consequence was *Colonial at Lynnfield, Inc. v. Sloan*, 870 F.2d 761 (1989), in which the judges of the First Circuit Court of Appeals *assumed* that Massachusetts courts had adopted a second look rule. *Colonial at Lynnfield, Inc. v. Sloan*, 870 F.2d at 765. The facts pertaining to the transaction are complex. Suffice it to say that a corporate seller entered into an agreement with buyers for the sale of a 49 percent interest in a hotel. The buyers breached, and the seller tried to claim a $200,000 lump sum that had been agreed upon as a liquidated damages amount. A federal district judge upheld the clause. On appeal, the judges of the First Circuit agreed that if the clause were evaluated only *prospectively*, when the parties agreed to it, "it was a reasonable estimate of difficult-to-ascertain damages." *Colonial at Lynnfield, Inc. v. Sloan*, 870 F.2d at 765. However, writing for the First Circuit, Judge Coffin asserted that "Massachusetts law clearly envisions a retrospective appraisal of a liquidated damages provision in certain circumstances." *Colonial at Lynnfield, Inc. v. Sloan*, 870 F.2d at 765. For authority, he cited *A-Z Servicenter, Inc. v. Segall*, *Lynch v. Andrew*, *Warner v. Wilkey*, and S*ecurity Safety Corporation v. Kuznicki*. Applying this retrospective approach, the court invalidated the liquidated damages clause and reversed, because the record established that the seller had gained $251,000 by a second sale which was only possible after the plaintiffs breached. In light of this second sale, the liquidated damages clause was a penalty, and the trial judge had erred by enforcing it. On the basis of the authorities cited, the First Circuit judges made the only reasonable judgment they could about the law of liquidated damages in Massachusetts as that law had developed by early 1989.

Practice Note

The First Circuit judges also relied in part on *Restatement (First) of Contracts* § 339(e). *See Colonial at Lynnfield, Inc. v. Sloan*, 870 F.2d at 765 n.6 (1st Cir. 1989). Comment (e) plainly authorized a no-actual-damages defense to a claim for liquidated damages.

§ 7.1.6   *Schrenko v. Regnante*, 27 Mass. App. Ct. 282 (1989)

Schrenko v. Regnante, 27 Mass. App. Ct. 282 (1989), was decided a few weeks following *Colonial at Lynnfield*. The case arose from the buyers' breach of a purchase and sale agreement on a house for $360,000. The buyers made a $16,000 deposit designated as liquidated damages; however, the sellers reserved the power to elect actual as opposed to liquidated damages. *Schrenko v. Regnante*, 27 Mass. App. Ct. at 283. After the buyers' default, the sellers' lawyer advised by letter that "it is sellers' present intention to retain your deposit in the amount of $16,000 as liquidated damages and to hold you liable for any additional damages that may be or are incurred by my clients as a result of your failure to consummate the purchase of the premises." *Schrenko v. Regnante*, 27 Mass. App. Ct. at 284. It is apparent that the sellers were angling to collect both liquidated *and* actual damages. The buyers sued for return of their deposit. The trial judge, applying a strictly prospective rule, granted summary judgment for the sellers allowing them to retain the $16,000.

The Appeals Court analyzed the buyers' appeal in light of *Lynch v. Andrew*, wherein Justice Kass had indicated the resale price might make a difference in evaluating a liquidated damages clause. The record established that the closing on the failed transaction had been scheduled for November 12, 1985, and that on December 19, 1985, a little more than one month later, the sellers had resold the property for $25,000 more than the breaching buyers had agreed to pay. Even though the sellers incurred substantial expenses attributable to the breach, amounting to more than $18,000, it appeared that sellers made an economic gain on account of the buyers' default. *See Schrenko v. Regnante*, 27 Mass. App. Ct. at 284. On this record, the Appeals Court reversed and ordered the deposit, with interest, returned to the buyers. Yet, the court stopped short of explicitly endorsing a second look rule. Because the sellers had elected to claim their actual damages (as the clause allowed), the stipulated sum in the circumstances was deemed a penalty provision. Thus, the Appeals Court sidestepped the issue whether or not the trial judge had erred by refusing to consider the resale price.

Practice Note

According to the court, "the clause, in effect, gives the sellers the right to consider the damages unliquidated and to seek additional damages beyond the amount of the forfeited deposit. The sellers by letter sought to exercise that right. By doing so, the $16,000 deposit, instead of being a settlement agreed upon in advance, became, at the seller's option, only the minimum amount they would receive as compensation for their losses. According to the terms of the agreement, that minimum amount had to be accepted in settlement only in the event of a loss in the amount of the deposit or less. The clause, therefore, at least when the sellers chose to exercise their rights within thirty days to seek additional damages, provided for a penalty, not liquidated damages. In these unusual circumstances, in our view, it would not be equitable for the sellers, having benefited financially as a result of the buyers' breach, to retain the deposit." *Schrenko v. Regnante*, 27 Mass. App. Ct. at 286–87.

In *Schrenko,* the Appeals Court expressly acknowledged for the first time the split among jurisdictions: a majority in 1989 enforced liquidated damages clauses even when sellers resold the subject property for the same or a higher price; in a minority of jurisdictions, the courts regarded liquidated damages clauses in such circumstances as windfalls or penalties that ought not be enforced. *Schrenko v. Regnante*, 27 Mass. App. Ct. at 286, n.4. The court also took note of *Colonial at Lynnfield, Inc. v. Sloan*, wherein the First Circuit had invalidated a clause, applying Massachusetts law, but the Appeals Court neither approved nor disapproved of the First Circuit's use of the data about the resale in its retrospective analysis. *Schrenko v. Regnante*, 27 Mass. App. Ct. at 286, n.4. Therefore, whether the ex post (retrospective) review would be endorsed remained an open question.

§ 7.1.7 *Shapiro v. Grinspoon*, 27 Mass. App. Ct. 596 (1989)

It was not until *Shapiro v. Grinspoon*, 27 Mass. App. Ct. 596 (1989), that the Massachusetts Appeals Court clearly embraced the second look rule, *requiring* a retrospective analysis in a real estate case. *Shapiro* arose from a failed contract for the purchase and sale of an apartment complex. The seller was Regency Park, a limited partnership (in which Grinspoon was a general partner). Shapiro and Regan (buyers) entered into negotiations for the purchase of the complex. A troublesome point in the negotiations was the fact that Metropolitan Life Insurance Company (Metropolitan) held a mortgage for $6.5 million on the property which, by its terms, required a hefty fee for prepayment. Nonetheless, the parties signed a letter of intent with all essential terms in October 1985, at which time buyers made a $50,000 deposit. In December 1985, the parties signed a purchase and sale agreement setting the purchase price at $16,500,000, and the buyers made an additional $450,000 deposit bringing their total deposit to $500,000.

In early 1986, the buyers advised they were exercising a power to terminate the agreement on account of the prepayment penalty demanded by Metropolitan, claiming that the prepayment amount insisted upon by Metropolitan triggered their right of termination. *See Shapiro v. Grinspoon*, 27 Mass. App. Ct. at 598 (quoting ¶ 9 of the purchase and sale agreement). The buyers failed to show up at the scheduled closing. It is true that a literal reading of the contract might plausibly have allowed buyers' termination, and accordingly, the buyers demanded return of their $500,000 deposit. *Shapiro v. Grinspoon*, 27 Mass. App. Ct. at 600. The seller declined, so the buyers sued for a refund.

Eschewing a literal reading of the prepayment clause, the trial judge found the buyers in breach, and steadfastly applying the single look rule, held that $500,000 was a reasonable forecast of damages likely to flow from a breach by the buyers, at the time the purchase and sale agreement was executed. Therefore, the seller was allowed to retain the deposit.

Justice Warner, writing for the appeals court, sustained the trial judge's finding that the buyers were in breach. On the subject of liquidated damages, he began by stating that both prospective *and* retrospective views were required under the Massachusetts case law. With respect to the *prospective view* applied to the undisputed facts, Justice Warner stated that "[t]he judge was correct . . . in concluding that the amount of liquidated damages was a reasonable forecast, as of the time of execution of the contract, of damages that would result from plaintiffs' breach." *Shapiro v. Grinspoon*, 27 Mass. App. Ct. at 603. That did not end the inquiry. Justice Warner noted that in *Schrenko v. Regnante*, decided two months earlier, the court had "discussed whether a later profitable sale should be considered in determining the reasonableness of a liquidated damages provision at the time of the required retrospective examination," and had "reserved the question." *Shapiro v. Grinspoon*, 27 Mass. App. Ct. at 603–04. He then justified a reversal, explaining the court's reasons in the following language:

> We now hold that enforceability is not affected by a later profitable sale standing alone. The relevance, if any, of a later profitable sale is only to the value of the property at the time of breach. We think the disproportionateness and excessiveness of which our cases speak should be measured, as of the time of the breach, against the actual losses caused by the breach, that is, those uncompensated damages, as, for example, mortgage service costs, taxes, and legal and accounting expenses,

> which flow directly from a defaulting party's actions in connection with the transaction. The plaintiffs may show that, *at the time of breach*, the property could have been sold for a price higher than what the plaintiffs agreed to pay so as to sufficiently compensate the defendants for damages attributable to the breach.

Shapiro v. Grinspoon, 27 Mass. App. Ct. at 603–04 (emphasis in the original).

This ruling about the admissibility of evidence of value at the time of breach was extremely important on the facts established in the record. The record showed that a little more than four months after the failed closing, the seller had resold the property for $17,000,000, resulting in a net gain of approximately $300,000 over what the seller would have received if Shapiro and Regan had gone through with the deal. Under the holding, this resale was relevant to the market price on the date of breach, and a trial judge was supposed to consider the market price at the date of breach (to estimate actual damages) and compare those damages to the stipulated sum.

The holding was narrow. The court did not approve of an approach under which a resale at the contract price or higher would ipso facto invalidate a liquidated damages clause. Rather, the court held that the resale price could be used as proof to negate actual damages. There was nothing radical in this holding. While referred to thereafter as a "second look rule," it could more exactly be described as a no-actual-damages defense, precisely what was allowed by Official Comment (e) to Section 339 of the first *Restatement. See Law of Liquidated Damages in Massachusetts* § 6.2 (MCLE, Inc., 2013). The opinion was well anchored in Massachusetts case law as well. Moreover, Justice Warner cited two cases as persuasive authorities: *Vines v. Orchard Hills*, 181 Conn. 501, 435 A.2d 1022 (1980), wherein the Connecticut Supreme Court approved evidence of a resale price as one factor to be considered in ascertaining whether or not any damages were incurred, and *Colonial at Lynnfield, Inc. v. Sloan*. Finally, Justice Warner found support in the *Restatement (Second) of Contracts* § 356, making particular references to Official Comment (b) and Illustration 4, which in combination advise that a liquidated damages clause should not be enforceable in a case where the record makes clear that *no damage was caused by the breach*.

Practice Note

Official Comment (b) to the *Restatement (Second) of the Law of Contracts* states as follows: "Under the test stated in Subsection (1), two factors combine in determining whether an amount of money fixed as damages is so unreasonably large as to be a penalty. The first factor is the anticipated or actual loss caused by the breach. The amount fixed is reasonable to the extent that it approximates the actual loss that has resulted from the particular breach, even though it may not approximate the loss that might have been anticipated under other possible breaches. See Illustration 2. Furthermore, the amount fixed is reasonable to the extent that it approximates the loss anticipated at the time of the making of the contract, even though it may not approximate the actual loss. See Illustration 3. The second factor is the difficulty of proof of loss. . . . A determination whether the amount fixed is a penalty turns on a combination of these two factors. If the difficulty of proof of loss is great, considerable latitude is allowed in the approximation of anticipated or actual harm. If, on the other hand, the difficulty of proof of loss is slight, less latitude is allowed in that approximation. If, to take an extreme case, it is clear that no loss at all has occurred, a provision fixing a substantial sum as damages is unenforceable." Thus, the threshold question is whether or not damages are easily ascertainable.

Practice Note

Illustration 4 to the *Restatement (Second) of the Law of Contracts* § 356 sets out a case built upon the facts of Illustration 3 wherein a contractor is by agreement subject to a $1,000 per diem assessment for each day of delay in finishing a racetrack. The contractor finished ten days late. However, the fact is that the owner of the racetrack was not licensed to operate the track during the period of the delay; hence, the delay caused no damages. Since the damages to the racetrack owner (zero damages) are not difficult to ascertain, the clause "provides for a penalty and is unenforceable on grounds of public policy."

With the opinion in *Shapiro*, the Appeals Court linked Massachusetts to the minority viewpoint that allows a second postbreach look to consider whether or not actual damages were incurred. If the opinion had gone this far, and no farther, it might have unsettled a few minds, but it probably would not have caused a firestorm. It was in setting out instructions for the trial judge on remand, that an unwelcome opaqueness crept in, and an unnecessary dictum garbled the opinion. Consider the instructions pertaining to remand, which the opinion broke down into three steps, the language of which is taken literally from *Shapiro v. Grinspoon*, 27 Mass. App. Ct. at 605:

> Step 1:   In sum, the judge should first determine whether the actual damages to the defendants are difficult to ascertain. If they are, in view of the the reasonableness of the forecast of those damages, the liquidated damages provision should be enforced.

Shapiro v. Grinspoon, 27 Mass. App. Ct. at 605.

Was the difficulty of ascertaining damages to be judged first from the vantage point of formation? Or was the question about the difficulty of ascertaining damages always to be considered only at the time of breach? Although what Justice Warner envisioned as a first step is not totally clear, I surmise that a trial judge was supposed to begin with a retrospective analysis asking: Are damages difficult to ascertain? If the answer was affirmative, then the judge was supposed to consider whether the forecast was reasonable. If so, enforce the clause. If this analysis is correct, the court was requiring first a retrospective, and secondarily, a prospective inquiry. This seems to be at variance with a two-point prospective analysis as a starting point, endorsed by *A-Z Servicenter* and subsequent cases.

> Step 2: If not, he should consider whether the sum of $500,000 is so "unreasonably and grossly disproportionate" to or is "unconscionably excessive" of, the actual damages caused by the breach so as to make the liquidated damages a penalty. See *A-Z Servicenter v. Segall*, 334 Mass. 672 (1956).

Shapiro v. Grinspoon, 27 Mass. App. Ct. at 605.

What is the antecedent to which "if not" refers? I assume that it refers to the first question posed under Step 1, namely: are actual damages difficult to ascertain? If that assumption is correct, and a trial judge finds that the actual damages are not difficult to ascertain (whether the damages are zero or otherwise), then the judge should inquire about proportionality and ask whether in light of actual damages the stipulated sum is unconscionably excessive. If so, the clause must not be enforced. This seems to be truly a second look, a retrospective analysis.

> Step 3: Finally, if the judge determines that the liquidated damages provision is unenforceable, and that the defendants' [sellers'] losses exceed the difference between the contract price and the saleable value of the property at the time of breach, he should award to the defendants the amount of actual damages."

Shapiro v. Grinspoon, 27 Mass. App. Ct. at 605.

This language at first may seem benign and sensible, but as the meaning sinks in, Step 3 is very unsettling. Surely, this step was a dictum, entirely unnecessary for the decision, because on the record nobody suggested that the seller in *Shapiro* suffered damages beyond the $500,000 on deposit, if any damages whatever were suffered. On the contrary, the defendants appear to have profited by the resale. The language of Step 3 directed, however, that a trial judge should tear up a liquidated damages clause if damages were underliquidated; an approach at variance with virtually all authorities. As stated in Comment (a) to Section 356 of the *Restatement (Second) of Contracts*, "[a] term that fixes an unreasonably small amount as damages may be unenforceable as unconscionable. *See Section* 208." The language in Step 3 was unfortunate, unnecessary, and it was alarming to some seasoned real estate lawyers. *Shapiro* very soon became a lightning rod for criticism from the bar.

Practice Note

The doctrine upon which underliquidating clauses are invalidated is the doctrine of unconscionability rather than the test derived from the common law cases and the *Restatements*. See E. Allan Farnsworth, *Contracts* § 12.18 at 811 (4th ed.): "[s]ince it is the in terrorem effect that is objectionable, the proscription applies only if the stipulated sum is on the high, rather than the low, side of conventional damages although a provision stipulating an unreasonably small amount . . . might be stricken under the section on unconscionable contracts or clauses" (quoting U.C.C. § 2-718, cmt. 1). Both the *Restatement (Second)* § 208 and U.C.C. § 2-302 (the sections pertaining to unconscionability) are generally construed as requiring proof of both substantive and procedural unconscionability. Thus, invalidating a clause because the stipulated damages are too small has usually been greatly more difficult than the dictum in Step 3 of the *Shapiro* instructions implies.

§ 7.2 THE BAR'S REACTION TO *SHAPIRO V. GRINSPOON* AND THE SECOND LOOK RULE

Shapiro v. Grinspoon was the law for about a decade in Massachusetts, but the holding and the dictum were the objects of intense criticism. While a few months elapsed before comments appeared in print, reactions from members of the practicing bar to *Shapiro v. Grinspoon* and *Colonial at Lynnfield, Inc. v. Sloan* were critical, sometimes stinging. The first critical assessment, written by Jeffrey Sacks and Robert Daniszewski, appeared in the Boston Bar Journal in the spring of 1990. Their article was a scholarly and thorough analysis of *Shapiro* and *Colonial*, criticizing each court's use of Massachusetts precedent as well as the application of *Restatement (Second) of Contracts* § 356. More importantly, the authors highlighted what they discerned as negative policy implications. The authors were especially perturbed about the lack of predictability in Massachusetts in the wake of *Shapiro*, expressing the fear that contracting parties could never rest easy about the enforceability of a liquidated damages clause, no matter how reasonable at the time of formation, if a disgruntled party was always at liberty to sue and get a retrospective analysis. *See* 34 *Bos. Bar J.* at 14. Unpredictability, they contended, would lead to increased litigation, thereby destroying the risk allocation and peace of mind intended by negotiating damages ex ante. *See* 34 *Bos. Bar J.* at 15. Increased litigation would destroy the efficiency provided by a remedy duly negotiated at the time of contracting. *See* 34 *Bos. Bar J.* at 15. The *Shapiro* court displayed a sense of fair play, the authors wryly noted, by making both buyers and sellers *equally insecure*: sellers might be required to return deposits to defaulting buyers, but defaulting buyers might be liable beyond their deposits for actual damages, if the liquidated damages provisions failed an analysis allowed by *Shapiro*. *See* 34 *Bos. Bar J.* at 14–15. Fundamentally, the authors objected to what they perceived as a judicial infringement on freedom of contract. *See* 34 *Bos. Bar J.* 14.

As to the court's use of precedent, the authors took particular issue with the court's reading of *A-Z Servicenter, Inc.*, arguing, that on a careful reading of that case, the court had determined only that the damages (including interest earned) were determinable on the basis of the note itself, not by taking a second look. They argued that the phrase "the time of the execution of the contract" in the *A-Z Servicenter* opinion reasonably referred to both judicial inquiries: Were damages difficult to assess? Was the estimate made by the parties reasonable? *See* 34 *Bos. Bar J.* at 14. Hence, they argued, the *Shapiro* court made a questionable, probably erroneous, reading of *A-Z Servicenter*, wrongly making it into a "second look" case. The authors also thought that the First Circuit in *Colonial* had misapplied *Lynch v. Andrew*, elevating dicta to a new rule.

Practice Note

I think there is legitimacy to this criticism. In *Lynch v. Andrew*, 20 Mass. App. Ct. 623 (1985), Justice Kass declined to invalidate the liquidated damages clause stating that this was not a case wherein a resale without complications occurred within a short time after the first buyer 's default. The second look question remained open.

As to the use of Section 356 of the *Restatement (Second)*, Sacks and Daniszewski particularly argued against the use of Illustration 4, which sets forth a hypothetical case wherein the owner of a racetrack entered into a contract for the construction of a grandstand for $1,000,000 by a fixed date, and the contract stipulated that for each day of delay, the contractor would be liable for $1,000 in liquidated damages. The contractor finished ten days late. However, the owner of the racetrack delayed thirty days beyond the contractor's deadline in obtaining governmental permission to operate the racetrack, and consequently, suffered no damages attributable to the contractor's delay. The *Restatement* advises that since the owner's loss (zero) is not difficult to prove, the liquidated damages clause is "unenforceable on the grounds of public policy." *Restatement (Second) of Contracts* § 356, cmt. b, Illustration 4.

A construction contract, according to Sacks and Daniszewski, bears no resemblance to a contract for the sale of real estate because risk allocations are fundamentally different. While in the racetrack hypothetical, the owner bore the risk of not having a permit, in a typical real estate case certain risks associated with ownership of the property pass to the buyer only on consummation of a sale. *See* 34 *Bos. Bar J.* at 14.

Therefore, the analogy simply does not hold up since there will be *some loss or increase in risk* to a seller when a buyer defaults.

Whether Sacks and Daniszewski spoke for a great number of practicing lawyers, I cannot say, but their views were echoed and amplified by an article published in the *Massachusetts Lawyer's Weekly*, June 28, 1993, authored by Attorney William V. Hovey. After a speedy recapitulation of case law running from *A-Z Servicenter* through *Shapiro*, he asked rhetorically:

> But why can't normal, consenting adult buyers and sellers agree to breach damages in advance? If I can agree to pay $1 million for a widget, why can't I agree to pay the manufacturer $50,000 if I breach my contract to buy the widget whether the manufacturer's cost is $20,000 or $80,000. What is wrong with a penalty under a contract fairly and knowledgeably entered into? Isn't the law interested in resolving disputes, rather than creating conflicts? Why does the Appeals Court hate real estate attorneys? Are real estate attorneys becoming judicially paranoid?

William V. Hovey, "Avuncular Advisor: Breaching Buyers Exposed," *Massachusetts Lawyers Weekly*, June 28, 1993 at 2.

Maybe the justices on the *Shapiro* court and the First Circuit judges who decided *Colonial at Lynnfield* harbored a hatred for real estate lawyers, and plotted to make their lives miserable, but I sincerely doubt it. Furthermore, I doubt that many real estate lawyers developed a generalized paranoia about the courts on account of a disturbance of common assumptions pertaining to liquidated damage clauses. In fact, there is an answer to one of the rhetorical questions posed by Mr. Hovey: parties can agree to damages in advance so long as the agreement does not run afoul of the case law that has divided liquidated damage from penalties for two centuries in Massachusetts, and much longer in England. While Mr. Hovey's frustration was understandable, his challenging rhetoric arguably obscured the fundamental issue: how can a proper balance be maintained between freedom of contract and the compensatory principle in the context of real estate sales?

Reading further in Attorney Hovey's article, it becomes apparent that his main concern derived from that unfortunate third step for trial judges near the end of the *Shapiro* opinion which advised that a trial judge should invalidate a liquidated damages clause if it stipulated damages that were too low in light of seller's actual damages. Mr. Hovey advised that "we owe a duty to our buying clients to make it crystal clear that the common provision limiting damages for a buyer's breach to the deposit may not be enforceable and that as a consequence a breaching buyer may have to pony actual damages suffered by the seller." *See* William V. Hovey, "Avuncular Advisor: Breaching Buyers Exposed," *Massachusetts Lawyers Weekly*, June 28, 1993 at 3. The frustration evident at this point is understandable, and I wholeheartedly subscribe to the concern raised. Setting a limit to a party's liability in the event of default has been an important function of stipulated damages clauses for a long time. *See, e.g., Kaplan v. Gray*, 215 Mass. 269 (1913) (nonbreaching party tried to invalidate a $500 liquidated damages clause in order to claim actual damages nearer $1,000. The Supreme Judicial Court held that the $500 liquidated damages clause set the limit; the party aggrieved could not have it set aside to claim greater damages).

Given the concern for setting a limit on damages for a defaulting buyer, and the ambiguities in the remand instructions in *Shapiro*, there was some justification for negative reactions. I take issue, however, with the notion that *Shapiro* and *Colonial at Lynnfield* were either radical departures from the historic path of the law bearing upon liquidated damages or perverse interpretations of *A-Z Servicenter.* Judicial consideration of the actual consequences of a breach had long been evident in reported cases as established in earlier chapters of this book. Intent at formation was often inferred from the observable consequences of breach. Moreover, the *Shapiro* style of analysis involving some consideration of probable actual damages in testing out the enforceability of a liquidated damages clause was evident in cases between *A-Z Servicenter* and *Shapiro*—well before 1989. Consequently, the result in *Shapiro* need not have taken the bar completely by surprise. In any event, given the dissatisfaction, a decade after *Shapiro*, the time was ripe for a reexamination of the rules for evaluating liquidated damages clauses in real estate contracts.

CHAPTER 8

The Demise of the Second Look Rule

Gary L. Monserud, Esq.
New England Law | Boston

§ 8.1   *Kelly v. Marx*, **428 Mass. 877 (1999)** **8–1**

§ 8.2   **Bar Reaction to** *Kelly v. Marx* **8–5**

§ 8.3   **Refinements in the Single Look Rule: Assigning
a Burden of Proof and Negating Liquidated Damages
by Specific Performance** **8–7**

CHAPTER 8

The Demise of the Second Look Rule

Gary L. Monserud, Esq.
New England Law | Boston

Scope Note

This chapter focuses upon the demise of the second look rule when the Supreme Judicial Court decided *Kelly v. Marx*, which overruled *Shapiro v. Grinspoon*, discussed in Chapter 7, and established a single look rule. This chapter also reviews the bar's reaction to *Kelly v. Marx* as well as case law that extended and refined the implementation of the single look rule.

§ 8.1   *KELLY V. MARX*, 428 MASS. 877 (1999)

Kelly v. Marx, 428 Mass. 877 (1999) presented the perfect fact pattern for a reexamination of *Shapiro v. Grinspoon*. John and Pamela Kelly (buyers) and Steven and Merrill Marx (sellers) entered into a purchase and sale agreement for residential property. The buyers made a 5 percent deposit amounting to $17,750 which was agreed upon as liquidated damages if the buyers defaulted. *Kelly v. Marx*, 44 Mass. App. Ct. 825, 826. The buyers defaulted, apparently because they were not able to sell their old house and were dependent upon the expected proceeds to consummate the transaction with sellers. The sellers retained the deposit even though they were able to resell their house for $360,000, $5,000 more than buyers had agreed to pay. The second sale was consummated within about three weeks of the closing date set for the contract that was breached.

The buyers sued for a refund of their deposit. On cross motions for summary judgment, the Superior Court judge allowed the sellers to retain the deposit, concluding that the liquidated damages clause allowing the 5 percent deposit was customary and neither unreasonable nor excessive, even though the sellers produced no proof of actual damages attributable to the breach. The Massachusetts Appeals Court reversed the decision upon the buyers' appeal. The court recognized that taking a prospective look only, the trial judge had made a correct analysis. *Kelly v. Marx*, 44 Mass. App. Ct. at 829. Relying mainly on *Shapiro*, the justices took a *second look* and disagreed with the trial judge's disposition, because the record showed no actual damages incurred by the sellers. *Kelly v. Marx*, 44 Mass. App. Ct. at 830–31. As summarized by Justice Jacobs, who authored the opinion, "there are no damages to liquidate." *Kelly v. Marx*, 44 Mass. App. Ct. at 831.

> **Practice Note**
>
> The trial judge recognized the approach required by *Shapiro* and sought to apply it as is apparent in the following: "[o]n the record before the court, there is, concededly, no evidence that the Marxs incurred any actual damages, such as mortgage service costs, taxes, and legal or accounting expenses, as a direct result of the Kellys' breach. See *Shapiro*, 27 Mass. App. Ct. at 604. In the circumstances at bar, however, where the damages are <u>not</u> difficult to ascertain, the court is to consider whether the sum of money awarded under the liquidated damages clause is 'so unreasonably and grossly disproportionate' to, or is 'unconscionably excessive' of, the actual damages so as to make [the Clause] a penalty." Trial Court decision at 5.

This case was, in the court's view, an extreme case involving no loss, as described in Comment (b) to *Restatement (Second)* § 356; hence, the majority rested the decision on the compensatory principle. Realizing that some members of the bar were unhappy with *Shapiro v. Grinspoon*, Justice Jacobs acknowledged that the second look approach was "not lacking for critics," and even suggested that the criticisms raised against *Shapiro* "may well call for legislative remediation or for a departure from *Shapiro v. Grinspoon*, as advocated by the dissent." *Kelly v. Marx*, 44 Mass. App. Ct. at 829. In two impressive appendices, the court set out by jurisdiction a list of twenty-two courts which favored the single look approach and twenty courts which seemed to apply a second look approach. *Kelly v. Marx*, 44 Mass. App. Ct. at 832–33

Justice Spina dissented, stressing the objectives of liquidated damages clauses, apart from the compensatory principle, and he opined that the majority's decision undermined the certainty of result and peace of mind expected by parties who had agreed in advance to a clause "eminently suitable for the circumstances." *Kelly v. Marx*, 44 Mass. App. Ct. at 834. He also questioned whether the "second look" approach was rightly derived from *A-Z Servicenter*, stating that "it is unclear whether that case anticipated any progeny." *Kelly v. Marx*, 44 Mass. App. Ct. at 833. Thus, he opposed the reversal on policy grounds and questioned whether the doctrine enunciated in *Shapiro* was rightly grounded in precedent. The Supreme Judicial Court granted the sellers' application for further appellate review, and in an opinion by Justice Ireland (now Chief Justice), the court agreed with Justice Spina. The court clearly rejected the retrospective analysis (second look rule) in favor of a prospective analysis, a *single look* at the time of contract formation, *Kelly v. Marx*, 428 Mass. at 880, hence, the trial judge was correct in finding five percent reasonable. Justice Ireland summarized the court's application of law to the facts as follows:

> Viewing the facts at the time of contract formation, the liquidated damages were a reasonable estimate of the damage to the defendants. The deposit, five per cent of the purchase price, was a reasonable forecast of defendants' losses that would result if the buyers were to breach the agreement. These costs could arise from a host of issues relating to finding another buyer and waiting for an uncertain period of time before selling their property, and in light of the risk of an undeterminable loss that is dependent on many factors (primarily the shape of the real estate market at the time of the breach). The sum is not grossly disproportionate to the expected damages arising from a breach of the sale agreement nor is it 'unconscionably excessive' so as to be defeated as a matter of public policy.

Kelly v. Marx, 428 Mass. at 882.

The methodology for trial judges after this decision was clear: scrutinize the liquidated damages clause from the vantage point of formation and ask only two questions:

- Were actual damages in the event of breach difficult to estimate?

- Was the estimate fixed by the parties a reasonable forecast of damages?

The answer to the first question is nearly always affirmative because real estate markets can rise or fall unexpectedly. If the answer to both questions is affirmative, the inquiry is concluded. The clause should be enforced. Resale prices as evidence of market prices at the time of breach are, therefore, irrelevant.

Practice Note

After the recent crash in the real estate markets (2008–2009), it is generally difficult to quarrel with an affirmative answer to the first question if it asks whether an advance computation of the *amount of damages that will be incurred on buyer's breach* can be made at the time of formation. But, there is an ambiguity inherent in the question:

"were damages in the event of breach difficult to estimate?" It could mean that the court must ask whether ex ante the damages would be difficult or impossible to compute *at the time of breach.* If this is the meaning of the question, an affirmative answer is less probable in many cases. The ambiguity inherent in the first prong was explored in detail by Professor Melvin Eisenberg in an article entitled "The Limits of Cognition and the Limits of Contract," 47 *Stan. L. Rev.* 211, 230–31 (Jan. 1995).

By deciding in favor of a single look rule, the court necessarily negated or limited the holdings of some Massachusetts precedents. While Justice Ireland's opinion did not delve deeply into case law, he took note of the "many decisions" allowing a second look in the wake of *A-Z Servicenter, Inc.,* though the second look rule was articulated most notably in *Shapiro. See Kelly v. Marx,* 428 Mass. at 879 ("Many decisions, following *A-Z Servicenter, Inc. v. Segall,* have concluded that liquidated damages should be measured, first, by assessing the reasonableness of the liquidated damages in light of the parties' ability to anticipate damages at contract formation, and second, against the actual damages resulting from the breach. This was evident, most notably, in the *Shapiro* case, on which the Appeals Court relied and which contained a three-step analysis based on the *Shapiro* court's interpretation of the *A-Z Servicenter* opinion."). Any cases authorizing a second look were hereafter of limited (if any) value as precedent. Likewise, the opinion rejected the application of *Restatement (Second)* § 356 to the facts of the *Kelly* case, at least Illustration 4 thereof, upon which the *Shapiro* court had relied. *See Kelly v. Marx,* 428 Mass. at 880 n.4 ("We disagree with the *Restatement's* Illustration. It contradicts the express language of § 356(1) which permits liquidated damages where the agreement is 'reasonable in light of the anticipated *or* actual loss' (emphasis added). In the Illustration, the liquidated damages were reasonable in light of the owner's anticipated or potential loss, and therefore should have been enforced."). Instead, Justice Ireland turned to case law, chiefly *Watson v. Ingram,* 124 Wash. 2d 845, 881 P.2d 247, wherein the Supreme Court of Washington had adopted a single look rule for pragmatic reasons. It was this opinion from the Supreme Court of Washington, and a supporting law review article, James A. Weisfield, Note, "'Keep the Change!'; A Critique of the No Actual Injury Defense to Liquidated Damages—*Lind Building v. Pacific Bellevue Developments,* 55 Wash. App. 70, 776 P. 2d 977 (Div. 1) *review denied,* 113 Wash. 2d 1021, 781 P.2d 1322 (1989)," 65 *Wash. L. Rev.* 977 (1990), upon which Justice Ireland chiefly relied in explicating the policies that undergirded the holding. He wrote:

> In addition to meeting the parties' expectations, the "single look" approach helps resolve disputes efficiently by making it unnecessary to wait until actual

> damages from a breach are proved. By reducing chal-
> lenges to a liquidated damages clause, the "single
> look" approach eliminates uncertainty and tends to
> prevent costly future litigation. The "second look" by
> contrast, undermines the "peace of mind and certain-
> ty of result" . . . the parties sought when they con-
> tracted for liquidated damages. . . . In other words,
> the parties must fully litigate (at great expense and
> delay) that which they sought not to litigate.

Kelly v. Marx, 428 Mass. at 881 (citing *Watson v. Ingram*, 124 Wash. 825, 881 P.2d 247 (1994)).

In a single stroke, the Supreme Judicial Court swept away the legacy of *Shapiro* and the case law that led to it. The great strengths of Justice Ireland's opinion are its clarity and the absence of useless quibbling about the meaning of precedents such as *A-Z Servicenter, Inc.* Justice Ireland saw one issue, *see Kelly v. Marx*, 428 Mass. at 879 ("The question before us is whether enforceability of a liqui-dated damages clause is to be tested by analyzing the circumstances at time of formation, the prospective or 'single look' approach, or when the breach occurs, the retrospective or 'second look' approach"), went for the jugular, and in a straightforward opinion, set the bench and bar on a fresh course. Yet, there is one sentence in a note at the end of Justice Ireland's opinion that should not be for-gotten: "We reiterate our view that '[a] term fixing unreasonably large liquidated damages is unenforceable on grounds of public policy as a penalty.'" *Kelly v. Marx*, 428 Mass. at 882 n.6 (citing *Restatement (Second) of Contracts* § 356(1)). The full implications of this sentence have yet to be developed.

§ 8.2 BAR REACTION TO *KELLY V. MARX*

There was no eruption of criticism following the Supreme Judicial Court's deci-sion in *Kelly v. Marx*. It appears that the Supreme Judicial Court's decision was favorably received. A very favorable analysis is found in an article published by Attorney Mark Robbins in the March/April 2000 issue of the Boston Bar Jour-nal. Mark D. Robbins, "Another Look at the 'Second Look' Doctrine: Enforcing Liquidated Damages Clauses Without Hindsight," 44 *Boston Bar J.* 8 (2000). Mr. Robbins began with a review of the *Kelly* case, and strongly supported the Supreme Judicial Court's decision on policy grounds. He went so far as to sug-gest that "[g]iven the nearly even split among other states on this issue, the SJC's decision will provide a powerful incentive to use a choice of law provision se-lecting Massachusetts law in instances where a liquidated damages clause is to be an important feature of a contract." 44 *Boston Bar J.* at 22. He also pointed out something in the court records that may serve as a slight corrective in reading *Kelly*, namely, that the sellers (Marx) *claimed* damages attributable to the breach, though they failed to quantify or set forth any proof of actual damages in support of their motion for summary judgment. The absence of proof does not establish that sellers suffered no damages. Common sense suggests otherwise, given the hassles of a second sale and the necessity of maintaining and insuring property longer than would have been necessary had the first sale gone through as planned.

Practice Note

Mr. Robbins's summary on this point is as follows: "In discovery responses and in summary judgment submissions, the defendants did not attach any monetary figure to, or in any way quantify, any actual damages they claimed to have incurred. These actual damages were described as twenty days of property maintenance and related expenses, as well as legal fees and loss of rental income from a rental apartment on the property." Mark D. Robbins, "Another Look at the 'Second Look' Doctrine: Enforcing Liquidated Damages Clauses Without Hindsight," 44 *Boston Bar J.* at 8 (citing *Kelly v. Marx*, 44 Mass. App. Ct. 825, 820 & nn.8–9 (1998)).

The bulk of Mr. Robbins's article consists of a careful analysis of the opinion in *A-Z Servicenter, Inc.* and the opinions in earlier cases; some of which were cited in *A-Z*, in support of his argument that the second look rule never had sound doctrinal underpinnings in Massachusetts case law. In effect, he sought to demonstrate what Chief Justice Ireland in *Kelly* avoided: courts citing *A-Z* and its predecessors for the second look rule had gone off the rails, badly misunderstanding the cases. Mr. Robbins found a foundation for the single look rule in *Chase v. Allen*, 79 Mass. (13 Gray) 42 (1859), and a full articulation of the rule in *Lynde v. Thompson*, 84 Mass. (2 Allen) 456 (1861) (cited at Mark D. Robbins, "Another Look at the 'Second Look' Doctrine: Enforcing Liquidated Damages Clauses Without Hindsight," 44 *Boston Bar J.* 9 (2000)). While I fully acknowledge the scholarship upon which Mr. Robbins based his views, I take issue with him on one point. I disagree with his reading of *Lynde v Thompson*. Indeed, *Lynde v. Thompson* does have language consistent with a prospective mode of analysis and that nothing therein stated explicitly justifies the so-called second look, but it is equally plain that the court in 1861 was not deciding between a single look and second look approach. *Lynde v. Thompson* was decided more than seventy years before the prospective test in the first *Restatement* was promulgated, and more than eighty years before the Supreme Judicial Court cited the test. In 1861 the courts in Massachusetts were scrutinizing the record for multiple factors, as grounds upon which *to infer the intent of the parties* at the time of contracting. During the long history of liquidated damages law in

Massachusetts, prior to *Kelly v. Marx,* courts generally *did not preclude* a judicial look at the actual consequences of breaches. Because there are circumstances in which a second look may be appropriate, and in fact, even in the post-*Kelly* era, a second look has not always been avoided, rereading the case law can be important for charting a course for the future.

§ 8.3 REFINEMENTS IN THE SINGLE LOOK RULE: ASSIGNING A BURDEN OF PROOF AND NEGATING LIQUIDATED DAMAGES BY SPECIFIC PERFORMANCE

There is unanimity on the rule that the enforceability or unenforceability of a liquidated damages clause is a matter exclusively for the court, E. Allan Farnsworth, *Contracts* § 12.18 at 813 (4th ed.), but jurisdictions have long been divided on the burden of proof when enforceability is put in issue. *See, e.g.,* 2 Milton R. Friedman & James C. Smith, *Friedman on Contracts and Conveyances of Real Property* § 7:1.5 (citing *Chaffin v. Ramsey,* 555 P.2d 459 (Or. 1976)). Until 2006 no appellate court in Massachusetts had decided which party had the burden of proof, and the risk of nonpersuasion, when a stipulated damages clause was challenged. The implications of *Kelly v. Marx* and its practical application are less than complete without an understanding of where the burden now lies after the decision in *TAL Financial Corp. v. CSC Consulting, Inc.,* 446 Mass. 442 (2006).

Onward Technologies, Inc. (which subsequently merged with CSC Consulting Service, Inc.) leased office equipment from TAL. *See TAL Fin. Corp. v. CSC Consulting, Inc.,* 446 Mass. at 424. Alleging breach, TAL sued for damages, including liquidated damages, under the terms of the lease agreement. The trial judge held that lessee was in breach, see *TAL Fin. Corp. v. CSC Consulting, Inc.,* 446 Mass. at 427–28, and allowed actual damages but refused to enforce the liquidated damage clause, finding it grossly disproportionate to a reasonable estimate of actual damages at the time of formation. *See TAL Fin. Corp. v. CSC Consulting, Inc.,* 446 Mass. at 425. TAL appealed, arguing inter alia that the liquidated damages clause should have been enforced. The Supreme Judicial Court took the case on direct appellate review to address one issue, namely, "the proper allocation of the burden of proof when a party in contractual default seeks to void a provision in a contract providing for the payment of liquidated damages." *TAL Fin. Corp. v. CSC Consulting, Inc.,* 446 Mass. at 423 (the court took the case on its own motion).

The court may have taken this case because the First Circuit, applying Massachusetts law, had opined in 2001 that if the Supreme Judicial Court were to decide the issue, "it would assign the burden of proving unenforceability of a liquidated damages clause to the party raising that defense." *Honey Dew Assocs., Inc. v. M & K Food Corp.*, 241 F.3d 23, 27 (1st Cir. 2001). As it turned out, the First Circuit judges had guessed correctly. Writing for an undivided Court, Justice Greaney stated: "[w]e hold that the burden of proof rests with the party challenging the provision's enforcement." *TAL Fin. Corp. v. CSC Consulting, Inc.*, 446 Mass. at 423. Applying that rule, the court sustained the trial judge's ruling that the liquidated damages clause in the lease was not enforceable under the test required by *Kelly v. Marx*.

Practice Note

The court noted that if the parties had raised the issue, U.C.C. § 2A could rightly have been applied because the contract in question was a lease of goods. If § 2A had been applied, § 2A-504 would have provided the governing rule. However, neither party brought this to the attention of the trial judge. The case had been decided applying the rule of *Kelly v. Marx* which became the law of the case. *TAL Fin. Corp. v. CSC Consulting, Inc.*, 446 Mass. at 431. The justices discerned no reason why the burden of proof would be different under § 2A-504: "[w]hile we do not decide the question, we are aware of no reason why the allocation of the burden of proof, as settled above, would not be the same under the UCC." *TAL Fin. Corp. v. CSC Consulting, Inc.*, 446 Mass. at 431.

The court followed the modern trend, placing the burden on the party challenging enforcement of the clause: "Any reasonable doubt as to whether a provision constitutes a penalty or a legitimate liquidated damages clause should be resolved in favor of the aggrieved party. We thus join the majority of courts in other States that have considered the question. *See, e.g., Chisholm v. Reitler*, 143 Colo. 288, 252 P.2d 794 (1960); *Clampit v. A.M.R. Corp.*, 109 Idaho 145, 149, 706 P.2d 34 (1985); *Pav-Saver Corp v. Vasso Corp.*, 143 Ill. App. 3d 1013, 1019, 97 Ill. Dec. 760, 493 N.E.2nd 423 (1986); *Rodriguez v. Learjet, Inc.*, 24 Kan. App. 2d 461, 464–65, 946 P.2d 1010 (1997); *Shallow Brook Assocs. v. Dube*, 135 N.H. 40, 50, 599 A2d 132 (1991); *MetLife Capital Fin. Corp. v. Wash. Ave. Assocs. L.P.*, 159 N.J. 484, 496, 732 A.2d 493 (1999); *P.J. Carlin Constr. Co. v. City of N.Y.*, 59 A.D. 2d, 847, 848, 399 N.Y.S.2d 13 (N.Y., 1977); *Illingsworth v. Bushong*, 297 Or. 675, 690, 688 P.2d 379 (1984); *Chamberlain Livestock Auction, Inc. v. Penner*, 462 N.W.2d 479, 484 (S.D. 1990); *Wassenaar v. Panos*, 111 Wis. 2nd 518, 526, 331 N.W.2d 357 (1983)."

Practice Note

The Supreme Judicial Court also rested its burden of proof decision on two Massachusetts cases wherein the burden of proof had been assigned, albeit in cases not involving liquidated damages. The first case was *Town Planning & Engineer Association., Inc. v. Amesbury Specialty Co.*, 369 Mass. 737 (1976), in which the court placed the burden of proving the alleged illegality of a service contract on the party asserting this defense (the proof failed). The second case was *Hastings Associates., Inc. v. Local 369 Building Fund, Inc.*, 42 Mass. App. Ct. 162 (1997), in which the court placed the burden of proving the illegality of the transfer of a liquor license on the party asserting illegality (the proof sufficed).

Practice Note

According to *Black's Law Dictionary* (9th ed.): "Presumption. . . . Most presumptions are rules of evidence calling for a certain result in a given case unless the adversely affected party overcomes it with other evidence. A presumption shifts the burden of production or persuasion to the opposing party, who can then rebut or overcome the presumption." Since a clause will be upheld if the challenger does not muster sufficient proof of nonenforceability, there is a presumption in favor of enforcement.

Subsequent case law shows the difficulty of meeting this burden. It has proven nearly impossible to convince appellate judges that any estimate at the time of contracting was unreasonable, given the vagaries of the marketplace. *See, e.g., NPS, LLC v. Minihane*, 451 Mass. 417(2008).

A further refinement of the *Kelly v. Marx* rule was soon to come. Recall that Justice Ireland advised in a dictum in *Kelly v. Marx* that some clauses might be stricken as excessive and therefore contrary to public policy. *Kelly v. Marx*, 428 Mass. at 882 n.6. This caveat proved prophetic, as illustrated by *Perroncello v. Donahue*, 448 Mass. 199 (2007). In April 1998, Donahue (seller) entered into a purchase and sale agreement with Perroncello (buyer) for a property on Beacon Street for the negotiated price of $2,250,000. Perroncello made a deposit of $150,000 designated as liquidated damages in the event of buyer's default. *See Perroncello v. Donahue*, 448 Mass. at 200. The agreement provided that closing would occur on or before May 6, 1998. Perroncello negotiated an extension, putting the closing over into June, but the closing did not occur in June either. The facts are a little murky; however, Perroncello eventually filed suit claiming damages for breach of contract, and asked for an accounting with respect to his $150,000 deposit. *See Perroncello v. Donahue*, 448 Mass. at 201.

Donahue counterclaimed, and after fruitless discussions, filed an offer of judgment for specific performance, intending to force Perroncello's hand on his professed desire to consummate the transaction. The motion judge granted Donahue's motion ordering a conveyance upon tender of the price, but preserved each party's claims against the other for damages. A closing took place on September 23, 1998 at which time the $150,000 deposit was counted as part of the payment of the agreed-upon purchase price. Nonetheless, Donahue pressed his claim for $150,000 as liquidated damages. The judge allowed only actual damages, designated as carrying costs, for a part of the time that elapsed after the first closing date was extended. *See Perroncello v. Donahue*, 448 Mass. at 202–03.

Donahue appealed, claiming inter alia that the motion judge had erred by disallowing liquidated damages in light of *Kelly v. Marx*. The Massachusetts Appeals Court agreed with Donahue, demonstrating a literal and complete faithfulness to the holding in *Kelly v. Marx*. In the language of Justice Doerfer, who wrote for the court:

> The judge ruled that Donahue could not recover the liquidated damage established in the contract even if there were a breach, since that would exceed his expectation interest from the contract. This was error. In *Kelly*, a seller was allowed to recover a deposit as liquidated damages even when the seller eventually sold the property for *more* than the original contract price . . . .
>
> Perroncello [buyer] argues that this case can be distinguished from *Kelly* because here the *original* buyer eventually purchased the property at the original contract price. This, however, is not a distinction supported by the text of *Kelly*. The parties here negotiated a liquidated damages amount that was fair to each side based on their unique concerns and circumstances surrounding the agreement, and their individual estimate of damages in the event of breach. While the particular aftermath of this breach was an unusual one, that aftermath is irrelevant to an assessment of the clause's conscionability.

Perroncello v. Donahue 64 Mass. App. Ct. at 569–70.

This illustrates the application of the single look rule with the utmost scrupulousness. But, there was a further review, and a reversal, on the ground that liquidated damages are an alternative to specific performance. Writing for the Supreme Judicial Court, Justice Cordy opined that while specific performance and liquidated damages are not inconsistent in the sense that both are predicated upon the validity of a contract, the seller necessarily *must elect* either the liquidated damages and retention of title, or passage of title for the price. *See Perroncello v. Donahue*, 448 Mass. at 204 (citing *McMahon v. McMahon*, 122 S.C. 336, 115 S.E. 293 (1922); *Slaughter v. La Compagnie Francaises Des Cables Telegraphiques*, 119 F. 588 (2nd Cir. 1902), *cert. denied*, 191 U.S. 574 (1903); *Connihan v. Thompson*, 111 Mass. 270 (1873); *Lynch v. Andrew*, 20 Mass. App. Ct. 623 (1985)). Of course, actual damages, e.g., carrying costs during part of the delay in closing, were allowable, as the trial judge had correctly assumed. But, the Appeals Court had erred in allowing seller the price and the $150,000 deposit, because "[t]he law of contracts is intended to give an injured party the benefit of the bargain, not the benefit of the bargain and a windfall." *Perroncello v. Donahue*, 448 Mass. at 206 (citing *Situation Mgt. Sys., Inc. v. Malouf, Inc.*, 430 Mass. 875 (2000)). Hence, the opinion ends with a ringing endorsement of the compensatory principle; the party aggrieved is entitled to his or her lost expectancy, no more. The result was reached by considering postbreach facts (specific performance) which a literal application of *Kelly* would proscribe. It seems clear that in *Perroncello* the Supreme Judicial Court refined the *Kelly v. Marx* rule by allowing, if not a "second look," then at least a "postbreach peek" when the transaction was consummated between the original parties. If there were absolutely no exceptions to the single look rule, surely Justice Doerfer's opinion would have been correct, but a windfall would have been allowed.

The result in *Perroncello* was well-anchored, and seems fair. Yet, this leaves us in an odd situation. For example, if the judges in *Colonial at Lynnfield* had been obliged to follow *Kelly*, and the single look rule had been scrupulously applied in that case, the sellers would have gained more than $250,000 on a second sale (albeit with some extra costs incurred) *and $200,000 extra in liquidated damages*. On the other hand, if specific performance had been decreed, and the judges followed *Perroncello*, then in exchange for the original price on closing, the seller would have been precluded from collecting the liquidated damages. The result is that if an aggrieved seller gains a decree for specific performance, he or she is always limited to the actual contract price plus any provable actual damages, but if an aggrieved seller resells to a third party at any price (possibly gaining significantly on a resale), liquidated damages will nonetheless be allowed. The differing treatment is hard to justify.

Kelly v. Marx created a good rule, but it needs a limit (with possible exceptions) because its application to some facts will otherwise submerge the compensatory principle. The long-term benefit of recognizing a limit with exceptions (is not *Perroncello v. Donahue* already one exception?) would be a rebalancing of the law with respect to liquidated damages, so that the compensatory principle retains a vital role and is not overwhelmed by a rigid adherence to *Kelly v. Marx* and liberty of contract or the appearance thereof.

CHAPTER 9

An Evaluation of *Kelly v. Marx*: Strengths, Weaknesses, and the Need for Exceptions to the Single Look Rule

Gary L. Monserud, Esq.
New England Law | Boston

§ 9.1   **Justifications for the Single Look Rule** 9–1

      § 9.1.1   Predictability 9–1

      § 9.1.2   Fixing Direct Damages upon Buyer's Breach 9–2

      § 9.1.3   Capturing Consequential Damages Upon
                      Buyer's Breach 9–3

      § 9.1.4   Efficiency 9–4

      § 9.1.5   Compensation for the Buyer's "Option"
                      under a Purchase and Sale Agreement 9–5

      § 9.1.6   Punishment versus Windfall 9–6

      § 9.1.7   Seller as Risk-Bearer 9–7

      § 9.1.8   Liquidated Damages and Forfeiture 9–8

      § 9.1.9   Facilitating Efficient Breaches 9–9

      § 9.1.10   Summary 9–9

§ 9.2   **An Argument for a Principled Limitation
on the Application of the Single Look Rule** 9–9

§ 9.3   **The Application of the Second Look Rule When
Stipulated Damages Exceed the Norm: Revisiting
Colonial at Lynnfield** 9–14

      § 9.3.1   Knowledge of the Agreement 9–16

§ 9.3.2   Actual Economic Loss 9–16

§ 9.3.3   Proportionality of Stipulated Damages.................9–17

CHAPTER 9

An Evaluation of *Kelly v. Marx*: Strengths, Weaknesses, and the Need for Exceptions to the Single Look Rule

Gary L. Monserud, Esq.
New England Law | Boston

Scope Note

As noted by the Massachusetts Appeals Court and the Supreme Judicial Court in their respective opinions in *Kelly v. Marx,* the single look rule is applied in a slight majority of jurisdictions. Nearly as many jurisdictions have adopted the second look rule. Arguments can be made for both. Based on precedent, the Supreme Judicial Court could reasonably have left the *Shapiro* holding (allowing a second look) as the law of the Commonwealth. Considerations of the policies advanced or thwarted by the choice of rules chiefly undergirded Justice Ireland's opinion in *Kelly v. Marx.* This chapter will explore further why the single look rule was arguably a workable and wise choice, and will also set forth an argument for exceptions to the single look rule.

§ 9.1 JUSTIFICATIONS FOR THE SINGLE LOOK RULE

§ 9.1.1 Predictability

Predictability is one of the justifications for the single look rule because it does usually make the consequences of breach more predictable than a second look rule. If seller and buyer, and their counsel, understand at the time of signing a purchase and sale agreement that the seller will be able to retain the deposit in the event of buyer's default, and that the deposit *will be the limit of buyer's liability* for default, the consequences of a buyer's default are fairly well fixed. The *Shapiro* rule did, to some extent, leave a seller uncertain about his or her rights to the deposit on a buyer's default. Moreover, on account of the dictum near the opinion's end, a buyer might reasonably have felt uncertain about his or her maximum liability for default before *Kelly*. The argument that a single look rule serves predictability, gives the parties a sense of security, and preserves peace of mind has the ring of truth in it.

§ 9.1.2   Fixing Direct Damages upon Buyer's Breach

A second justification for the *Kelly v. Marx* rule is that it allows the contracting parties to fix a sum that includes direct damages that might not be easily provable after a buyer's breach. On buyer's breach, in the absence of an enforceable stipulated damages clause, the seller has a claim to direct damages measured by the difference between the contract price and market price on the date of breach, assuming, of course, that the market price is less than the contract price. *See, e.g., Abrams v. Reynolds Metal Co.*, 340 Mass. 704 (1960). Fixing market price is necessarily an inexact art. The challenge of proving direct damages was well articulated in an amicus brief filed in the *Kelly v. Marx* appeal wherein it was argued that the traditional market versus contract price measure "may be a perfectly adequate measure of damages in the case of peanut oil, or coffee, or shares of listed securities . . . . That is not the case with real estate which is not fungible and is indeed unique." *See* Brief of Amici Curiae, The Abstract Club and the Massachusetts Conveyancers Association, Inc., filed with the Supreme Judicial Court for the *Appeal in Kelly v. Marx* at 15–16 (citing 14 *Powell on Real Property* ch. 81 ¶ 882 [2][b] (1993 ed.); *Greenfield Country Estates Tenants Ass'n, Inc. v. Deep*, 423 Mass. 81, 88 (1996)). Because market price is a more or less sophisticated guess as to what a willing buyer would pay on any given day, a second look finding a resale above contract price does not necessarily prove the absence of direct damages.

Although courts commonly allow evidence of a resale price as evidence of market price on the date of breach, the resale price is not deemed definitive as to market price. *See* Prof. James M. Fischer, *Understanding Remedies* § 167 at 823 (LexisNexis, 2nd ed.). The resale might have been a stroke of good fortune, not a certain indicator of market price on the date of breach. As a practical matter, resale price can only help a factfinder make *an inference* about market price at the time of breach. In a hot market, a prospective estimate by the parties may not be inferior to a retrospective inference by experts using a resale price. It is presumptuous to assume that a second look necessarily results in a more exacting analysis than a prospective estimate, especially if a resale occurs weeks or months following breach.

Practice Note

Recall that in *Shapiro v. Grinspoon*, the Appeals Court was careful to state that the purpose of allowing evidence of the resale price was only as an indicator of market price on the date of breach. Indeed, the law might have been different. More than thirty years ago, the Commissioners on Uniform State Laws promulgated the Uniform Land Transactions Act. If it had been adopted, the relevant section, which was Section 504(a), would have fixed the difference between a resale price and the contract price as the appropriate measure of damages when a buyer defaulted. However, neither Massachusetts nor any other state adopted the proposed rule which would have made the seller's damage computations in real estate cases analogous to a seller's damages under U.C.C. § 2-706. *See* Marion W. Benfield, Jr., "Wasted Days and Wasted Nights: Why the Land Acts Failed," 20 *Nova L. Rev.* 1037 (Spring, 1996).

§ 9.1.3   Capturing Consequential Damages Upon Buyer's Breach

On a buyer's default, a seller will often (perhaps nearly always) suffer consequential damages, even if the common law rule (contract price minus market price) yields zero. The seller may have intended to use the expected consideration for purchase of a different property, or for paying a debt, or for any number of purposes particular to the seller's needs and interests. Any delay in sale will normally cause the seller to incur more-than-expected costs for insurance, maintenance, and utilities. With respect to residential real estate, any homeowner who has engaged in a purchase or sale of a house realizes that considerable time must be invested to make it happen. Days missed at work, trips to lawyers and lenders, and time invested in phone calls, e-mails, and faxes all amount to investments in a transaction, the value of which is lost when the transaction is aborted due to a buyer's default. An aborted commercial transaction can consume untold hours and outlays in advertisements, preparations for another sale, negotiations, and preservation of the property until a later disposition, if any can be arranged. Beyond these transactional costs, there are the anxiety and frustration commonly arising from a default and the disappointment that goes with it and necessitates a second round of transactional investments. Even if the common law rule (contract minus market price) yields no damage, this does not truly mean that no damage was suffered by the party aggrieved, even though such damage might be difficult or impossible to quantify and prove in court.

Practice Note
There is an academic debate in progress about what can count as actual damages for those courts that allow a second look to test actual damages against liquidated damages. *See, e.g.*, Gregory Scott Crispi, "Measuring 'Actual Harm' for the Purpose of Determining the Enforceabililty of Liquidated Damages Clauses," 41 *Houston L. Rev.* 1579 (2004–2005). Professor Crispi has argued that reasonably certain and unavoidable damages can rightly be liquidated; he would not require that damages be foreseeable. The argument assumes that some damages not necessarily allowable in court may rightly be captured by a liquidated damages clause.

A liquidated damages clause can capture consequential damages, proof of which would be precluded by traditional limitations in court. This was recognized by the Supreme Court of Wisconsin in 1983, in an opinion upholding a liquidated damages clause in an employment contract. According to this court, "actual harm suffered and damages that would be awarded in a legal action for breach of contract may not be the same. Nevertheless, in providing for stipulated damages, the parties to the contract could anticipate types of damages not usually awarded by law." *Wassenaar v. Panos*, 331 N.W.2d 357, 355–56 (Wis. 1983) (decision by Justice Abrahamson). *See also Wassenaar v. Panos*, 331 N.W.2d at 366 ("The usual arguments against allowing recovery for consequential damages—that they are not foreseeable and that no dollar value can be set by a court—fail when the parties foresee the possibility of such harm and agree on an estimated amount."). This view makes good, practical sense. Parties ex ante might reasonably anticipate some damages not usually provable or allowed, given legal limitations. Indeed, raw damages actually suffered, but not translatable into provable damages, can leave an aggrieved seller far short of his or her lost expectation interest. A well thought out liquidated damages clause may fine-tune justice, allowing a measure of damages nearer lost expectancy than a judicial award subject to the limitations imposed by law.

§ 9.1.4   Efficiency

A fourth justification for *Kelly v. Marx* is efficiency. Writing in favor of the single look approach in *Kelly v. Marx*, Justice Ireland opined that the single look rule "tends to prevent costly future litigation," while "[t]he 'second look,' by contrast, undermines the 'peace of mind and security of result . . . the parties sought when they contracted for liquidated damages.' It increases the potential for litigation by inviting the aggrieved party to attempt to show evidence of damage when the contract is breached, or more accurately, evidence of damage flowing from the breach, but occurring sometime afterwards. In other words, 'the parties must fully litigate (at great expense and delay) that which they sought not to litigate.'" *Kelly v. Marx*, 428 Mass. 877, 881 (1999) (citing *Watson v. Ingram*, 124 Wash. 2d 845, 851–52, 881 P.2d 247 (1994)). As to private expenditures, if the parties fully expect that a clause will be enforced, neither has an incentive to spend money on litigation. With respect to residential properties, where the deposits subject to liquidated damages clauses commonly run from $5,000 to $25,000 (as indicated in the reported cases), legal fees and costs will often exceed the deposit, especially if a disposition cannot be made on motions or if an appeal is taken. Sparing the parties legal costs and fees is a great gain. On the public side, judges, juries, and court personnel may be called upon at public expense to carry out the process of settling upon actual damages if a stipulated damages clause is rendered unenforceable on a second look. It is self-evident in reading the opinions in *Shapiro* and *Colonial at Lynnfield* that the allowance of a second look resulted in considerable monetary outlays by the parties and brought judges and others into the drama at substantial public expense.

§ 9.1.5   Compensation for the Buyer's "Option" under a Purchase and Sale Agreement

A fifth justification for the single look rule lies in recognition of the fact that when any buyer enters into a purchase and sale agreement, that buyer receives a *benefit*, even if the buyer subsequently walks away from the contract. The benefit lies in the *option* within the agreement. I am not using the term *option* in a technical sense, meaning only an irrevocable offer. *See Black's Law Dictionary* (9th ed.) (an option is "a contractual obligation to keep an offer open for a specific period, so that the offeror cannot revoke the offer during that period"). *See also Restatement (Second) of the Law of Contracts* § 25 ("[a]n option contract is a promise which meets the requirements for the formation of a contract and limits the promisor's power to revoke an offer."). I mean to stress rather that by binding the seller, the buyer has obtained a right to a property for a fixed price on set terms, a right which in virtually any context has *some value*. Allowing a seller to retain a reasonable deposit if a buyer fails to consummate a deal is, in part, a reasonable compensation for the benefit obtained. This point was powerfully made in an Amicus Curiae brief filed in the *Kelly v. Marx* appeal.

Practice Note

In the Brief of Amici Curiae, The Abstract Club and the Massachusetts Conveyancers Association, Inc. at 26–27, it was argued that "[t]he landowner may think he has made a better deal for himself in insisting on a purchase and sale agreement, rather than an option, but in reality he is mistaken. If we come to understand that the Kellys truly held an option to buy the Marx's property and could decide, as they did, not to proceed to purchase it, we can see more clearly why they should not now be heard to reclaim their deposit. How one-sided it would be to allow them to do so! Had they decided to buy, the Marxes would have been bound to sell at the agreed price even though (as we now know but no one could have known when the agreement was made) another buyer was waiting in the wings ready to pay a higher price."

When any buyer defaults on a purchase and sale agreement, whatever the buyer's reasons, the buyer has had the benefit of binding the seller to the point of buyer's default. During this period, the buyer was able to assess the situation and speculate about the advantages and disadvantages of going forward. The buyer's legal right to hold the seller to the agreement prior to default, therefore, is a benefit which renders it plausible that a seller might be justly compensated by retention of the deposit, although the benefit may be difficult to measure.

§ 9.1.6   Punishment versus Windfall

A sixth justification for the single look rule is that a seller's gain upon buyer's default is not necessarily a punishment in any sense but rather a windfall, to which a lucky seller is arguably entitled. Assume that a seller and buyer enter into a purchase and sale agreement for a horse farm in Hamilton, Massachusetts, for the price of $5 million, and the buyer defaults; the seller may, a few months later through good contacts, find a buyer with a passion for polo and fox hunting who is ready and willing to pay $7 million. In a sense, it is true that the first buyer's breach gained the seller $2 million, and if there was a 5 percent deposit on the breached contract ($250,000), the seller's retention of the deposit pursuant to a liquidated damages clause might feel irksome. However, being irked is different from being punished. Neither law nor equity guards against any and all windfalls. Arguably, the windfall belongs to the seller who benefitted from good connections and serendipity. Narrowing the time between the breach of the first contract and the resale may strengthen an argument against seller's enrichment, but should the time of resale really matter? A breaching buyer's claim to a deposit lies in restitution since the buyer no longer has enforceable rights under the contract. In *Perroncello v. Donahue*, Justice Cordy's opinion prudently disallowed both specific performance and liquidated damages to avoid a windfall in violation of the compensatory principle. But, the law of restitution has evolved to prevent not enrichment, but unjust enrichment to a nonbreaching party.

Practice Note

The extent to which Massachusetts courts will recognize a breaching party's claim for restitution is beyond the scope of this book; however, v. 1 of the recently promulgated *Restatement (Third) of the Law of Contracts, Restitution and Unjust Enrichment*, begins in Section 1

with the following general principle: "[a] person who is unjustly en-
riched at the expense of another is subject to liability in restitution."
Not every unbargained-for gain is unjust. *See also* Dan B. Dobbs, 1
Dobbs Law of Remedies, § 4.1(1) at 551–52 (2nd ed.) where he
states: "[r]estitution is a simple word but a difficult subject, partly because restitutionary ideas appear in many guises. In spite of their di-
versity restitution claims are bound by a major unifying thread. Their
purpose is to prevent the defendant's *unjust enrichment* by capturing
the gains the defendant secured in a transaction" (emphasis added).

§ 9.1.7   Seller as Risk-Bearer

The seller is normally a risk-bearer for an extended period of time when a buyer
breaches. While the law pertaining to risks (fire, floods, and the like) can be allocated by contract, the default rule seems to leave the risk on the owner during
the executory period as is reflected in following statement from *Massachusetts
Practice*:

> Where a purchase and sale agreement is silent as the
> situation wherein premises are destroyed or damaged
> by accidental fire, the risk of loss follows ownership.
> It therefore follows that in such case, the agreed gran-
> tor cannot recover or retain any part of the purchase
> price if such destruction occurs before conveyance to
> the agreed grantee. If the agreed grantee has paid mon-
> ey to the agreed grantor as a deposit or as a part pay-
> ment of the purchase price, such sum may be recov-
> ered back on the grounds of a failure of consideration.

Talty, Talty, and Braunstein, 5 *Massachusetts Practice*, § 3:38 at 99 (citing *Wells
v. Calman*, 107 Mass. 514 (1871); and *Thompson v. Gould*, 37 (20 Pick)).

The seller may negotiate a clause requiring the buyer to purchase insurance, or
to assume the risk allocated by law to the seller, but if the buyer fails to purchase
adequate insurance and simply walks away from the deal, the defaulting buyer
will be a poor candidate from whom to seek compensation peaceably if the
property suffers serious loss or destruction. If the seller bears any risk for a time
longer than initially bargained for, that detriment (or potential detriment) can
rightly be viewed as a justification for retention of some benefit by the seller.

§ 9.1.8   Liquidated Damages and Forfeiture

Liquidated damages clauses can be viewed as a substitute for a seller's common law right to retain payments on buyer's default under the doctrine of forfeiture. *See Law of Liquidated Damages in Massachusetts* ch. 5 (MCLE, Inc. 2013). As noted earlier, there is an abundance of case law in Massachusetts and elsewhere pursuant to which a seller has been entitled to retain a defaulting buyer's payment made as part performance on a real estate sales contract without any explicit agreement allowing retention. *See, e.g., Smith v. McMahon*, 197 Mass. 16 (1907); *King v. Milliken*, 248 Mass. 460 (1924); *Beck v. Doore*, 319 Mass. 707 (1946). Forfeiture in failed real estate contracts has long been an accepted remedy for the aggrieved seller, quite apart from whether or not the forfeiture would withstand scrutiny under the law pertaining to liquidated damages.

Practice Note

The modern law on this subject is summarized in Dan B. Dobbs, 3 *Dobbs Law of Remedies*, § 12.9(4) at 264–65: "Forfeitures of initial deposits may . . . be upheld on the ground that the earnest money deposit operates like a fee for an option to purchase and is not a forfeiture at all, or on the similar ground that it represents performance due under the contract rather than damage for breach . . . . When the forfeiture claimed is not an earnest money deposit, but installments paid by a purchaser who is in default, the case is different. Although courts once felt compelled to refuse restitution to the defaulting buyer, courts today are more inclined to respect the buyer's 'equity' by allowing him to recover installments paid minus the seller's actual damages. But, even so, the courts in this situation do not return fully to the harsh rule against 'penalties.'"

Of course, the doctrine can lead to inequities. Warring with some success against the unrestricted law of forfeiture under real estate contracts was an accomplishment of Professor Arthur Corbin. *See* Arthur L. Corbin, "The Right of a Defaulting Vendee to the Restitution of Instalments Paid," XL *Yale L. J.* (May 1931). Although the law of liquidated damages has largely displaced the law of forfeiture in modern real estate contracts, courts might rightfully note that historically the community's sense of justice has not been offended by the seller retaining something of value when a buyer defaults, even if damages are not proved. Naturally, any doctrine that restricts a breaching buyer's claim to deposits or part payments made before breach can serve as an inducement to perform. A buyer able to perform, but contemplating breach, even an efficient breach, may weigh the costs and elect to perform when the negative economic consequences are certain or nearly certain. Placing some costs on breach and thereby enhancing the probabilities of performance should not be viewed as bad policy. An inducement does not necessarily constitute punishment. Rather, a seller's right to retain a reasonable sum under the single look rule can be seen as an equitable right, a recognition that the seller has been inconvenienced by the buyer's breach, and should be allowed something of value on account of the inconvenience, even if no actual damages are provable.

§ 9.1.9 Facilitating Efficient Breaches

The single look rule may facilitate efficient breaches. Parties, especially buyers, can better assess their risks if alternative opportunities in the marketplace arise. If the consequences of breach will be less than the benefits, a party may elect breach on economic grounds. Suppose a buyer enters into a contract to purchase a parcel of land for $1,000,000 intending to build a hotel, and makes a 5 percent ($50,000) deposit designated as liquidated damages. Before closing, the buyer happens upon a parcel better located for the price of $850,000. If buyer's damages for breach will be limited to the deposit of $50,000, and the buyer can with reasonable certainty obtain the second parcel, an election that gains the buyer $100,000 makes economic sense. Since the *Kelly v. Marx* rule allows the deposit to serve as a limit on the seller's damages for the buyer's breach, the rule tends to facilitate efficient breach. *See, e.g.,* John Edward Murray, Jr., *Murray on Contracts* § 118[C] at 752 (LexisNexis, 5th ed.).

§ 9.1.10 Summary

In choosing the single look rule, the Supreme Judicial Court made a decision with multiple policy implications. I have elaborated upon nine arguments that go some distance toward justifying the *Kelly v. Marx* single look rule. There is no sound reason to mount a campaign against *Kelly v. Marx,* which would almost certainly be a losing campaign in any event. The single look rule should be retained for its many advantages, but its application should be limited in a principled way to avoid injustices.

§ 9.2 AN ARGUMENT FOR A PRINCIPLED LIMITATION ON THE APPLICATION OF THE SINGLE LOOK RULE

The best general rules humankind can devise may not do justice in unusual circumstances. Powerful parties may by strategic calculation cloak an abusive term beneath an accepted rule that normally advances both private and public interests, or fair-minded bargainers may unwittingly manifest agreement upon a contract term that later proves oppressive. Some situations will inevitably put a strain on the single look rule. Justice Ireland acknowledged as much near the end of the *Kelly v. Marx* opinion, stating that "[a] term fixing unreasonably large liquidated damages is unenforceable on grounds of public policy as a penalty." *Kelly v. Marx*, 428 Mass. 877, 882 n.6 (citing *Restatement (Second) of Contracts* § 356(1)). The single look rule adopted in *Kelly v. Marx* should not be the final word on stipulated damages in Massachusetts.

Leaving aside installment land contracts where a default after many payments can create a particular stress on the rules, *see, e.g.*, Arthur L. Corbin, "The Right of a Defaulting Vendee to the Restitution of Instalments Paid," XL *Yale L. J.* (May, 1931), consider only cases involving deposits pursuant to purchase and sale agreements and those agreements where a percentage of the price has been agreed upon as damages for buyer's default. The strain that can arise by an unlimited application of the single look rule is illustrated easily by varying the facts of *Kelly v. Marx*. Suppose instead of 5 percent ($17,750), John and Pamela Kelly had deposited 15 percent ($53,250) or 20 percent ($71,000); and suppose further that on signing the purchase and sale agreement, John and Pamela tendered their life savings, planning on a promised loan, which did not come through. Should the Marxes (sellers) be allowed to retain $53,250 or $71,000 if they were lucky enough to resell within a reasonable time to a third party (as reported) for $360,000? One can argue that "a deal is a deal," and only fools would make such a deal without a financing contingency clause. That is surely a hard-nosed approach that some persons might accept. But, if one's sense of fairness is aroused by the foregoing variation, it seems apparent that the justifications for the *Kelly v. Marx* rule, and its general acceptance by the bar, are contingent upon deposits, or any part payments designated as liquidated damages, being *reasonable*.

What counts as reasonable may not always be self-evident. *Kelly v. Marx, Shapiro v. Grinspoon*, and other cases discussed in Chapter 7 illustrate that in both residential and commercial sales agreements, 5 percent, or something slightly less, is customary and deemed reasonable as a deposit. In a recent New York decision, 10 percent was deemed reasonable in a contract for a sale of a residence. *See Hegner v. Reed*, 770 N.Y.S.2d 87 (App. Div. 2d Dep't) (2003). In *Kelly v. Marx*, Justice Ireland favorably cited *Watson v. Ingram*, in which the Supreme Court of Washington adopted the single look rule where the buyer, Watson, made a $15,000 deposit on a purchase and sale agreement for $355,000. *Watson v. Ingram*, 124 Wash. 2d 845, 881 P2d 247 (1994). Hence, the deposit was under 5 percent of the purchase price. The Supreme Court of Washington affirmed lower court rulings allowing seller's retention of the deposit, even though the seller was able to resell for the contract price. Not only the facts of *Kelly v. Marx*, but the facts underlying the single foreign case relied upon as persuasive authority, demonstrate that the single look rule as enunciated in Massachusetts rests upon reasonableness. *Kelly v. Marx* was not an invitation for courts to honor any and all stipulated damages clauses agreed upon.

In some jurisdictions, a reasonableness limitation has been imposed by statute, coupled with a legislative abrogation of the no-actual-damages defense, so long as the parties stipulate for damages within the limits allowed by statute. Such is the case in the state of Washington where the legislature has imposed a 5 percent limit as a safe harbor rule. *See* RCWA 64.04.005. The statute did not apply to *Watson* because the contract had been entered into prior to the effective date of the statute, but the court took note of this legislative directive. *Watson v. Ingram*, 881 P.2d 250 n.2. California has adopted similar legislation setting a 3 percent limit on stipulated damages clauses in contracts for residential real estate. *See* Cal. Civ. Code § 1675. Jurisdictions differ as to what happens when parties stipulate for damages beyond the legislatively approved minimum. In Washington, if a stipulation goes over 5 percent, a common law analysis is triggered. *See* RCWA 64.04.005 (2). California has dealt with clauses in excess of the statutory maximum differently, by shifting the burden; the party trying to enforce the clause, if it exceeds three percent in a contract for a residential sale, must prove that it is reasonable in the circumstances. *See* Cal. Civ. Code § 1675 (d).

It would be helpful if the Massachusetts legislature followed Washington or California and regulated deposits under purchase and sale agreements. Justice Jacobs, writing for the majority in the Appeals Court opinion in *Kelly v. Marx,* and commenting on the no-actual-damages defense allowed in *Shapiro* remarked: "[i]t is arguable that such considerations may well call for legislative remediation or for departure from *Shapiro v. Grinspoon*, as advocated by the dissent." *Kelly v. Marx*, 44 Mass. App. Ct. at 829. Legislative action to guide the courts in evaluating liquidated damages clause has not been forthcoming in the wake of *Kelly v. Marx*. Legislation would be appropriate and could be helpful by guiding conveyancers, as well as courts, as to what is reasonable, and by setting out the consequences of making unreasonable stipulations. Assuming that there will be no legislative limits on stipulated damages clauses in Massachusetts in the foreseeable future, however, the question arises as to what courts should do in a case where a seller claims a sum substantially in excess of accepted norms, perhaps 15 or 20 percent of the purchase price, or if the parties agree to a lump sum having no apparent relationship to a purchase price.

I contend that *Kelly v. Marx* should be limited in its application to claims for 5 percent deposits or such other percentage as is established as reasonable and customary among honorable players in the marketplace at the time. Deposits of 5 percent on real estate contracts may be lower than in prior times, partly because of market conditions. 5 percent may not be the norm in decades to come, but the enforcement of a liquidated damages clause, applying the single look rule, should be contingent upon the deposit being *reasonable in relation to the contract price, at this time, 5 percent, more or less.* Otherwise, the single look rule is susceptible to becoming an instrument of oppression.

The question then arises: if the stipulated damages in a purchase and sale agreement consist of a percentage chosen that materially overshoots the accepted norm, or a lump sum arbitrarily chosen, what should the trial judge do? The choices are:

- never mind the sum chosen, and enforce the clause as written, since it is nearly impossible in volatile markets for any challenger to prove that from the vantage point of formation any sum chosen was necessarily unreasonable under all contingencies;

- declare the clause unenforceable, and allow actual damages, if any can be proved, whether more or less than the sum agreed upon; or

- develop a principled fall-back approach whereby a trial judge can evaluate a clause that outruns the norm or otherwise raises serious questions of fairness in the context.

I am arguing for the third course.

I propose that in any case wherein a party challenges the enforceability of a stipulated damages clause in a purchase and sale agreement (whether for residential or commercial property), *see, e.g., Colonial at Lynnfield, Inc. v. Sloan,* 870 F.2d 761 (1st Cir. 1989), the trial judge should determine first whether the clause falls within the norm (now 5 percent) or is materially beyond the norm, or is simply a lump sum not necessarily related to the purchase price. If the clause is within the norm, the clause should be enforced, barring duress or some other common law basis for avoiding the contract. Any "no-actual-damage" defense should be rejected. Summary judgment will in the ordinary course be appropriate in accordance with *Kelly v. Marx.*

Practice Note

In addition to duress, grounds for avoidance include undue influence, misrepresentation, mutual and unilateral mistake, and unconscionability. Barring extraordinary circumstances, only unconscionability provides a basis for a judge to invalidate a stipulated damages clause, leaving the remainder of the contract intact. *See Restatement (Second) of the Law of Contracts* § 208, and U.C.C. § 2-302 and its Official Comment. The other grounds for avoidance will nearly always pertain to the whole of a contract, not the stipulated damages clause alone.

However, if the challenger establishes that the stipulated sum is materially higher than the norm, or is a lump sum having no obvious relationship to the contract price, then the trial judge should shift the burden of proof to the party trying to enforce the clause, requiring that party to prove its enforceability in context.

Practice Note

In Massachusetts, the burden had not been placed on the challenger until the Supreme Judicial Court's decision in *TAL Financial Corp. v. CSC Consulting, Inc.*, 446 Mass. 442, (2006). A respectable minority of jurisdictions, including Maine, Arkansas, and Tennessee have gone the opposite direction. *See Pacheco v. Scoblionko*, 532 A.2d 1036 (Me., 1987); *Mcilvenny v. Horton*, 227 Ark. 826 (1957); and *Patterson v. Anderson Motor Co.*, 45 Tenn. App. 35, 319 S.W.2d 492 (1958). Additionally, some jurisdictions (at least on some contracts) have statutory presumptions that stipulated sums are penalties, and therefore the parties trying to sustain the clauses must assume a burden. *See, e.g., Coldwell Banker v. Meide & Son, Inc.*, 422 N.W.2d 375 (N.D. 1998); *Fisher v. Schmeling*, 520 N.W.2d 820 (N.D., 1994); *see* N.D. Code § 9-08-4; *Waggoner v. Johnston*, 408 P.2d 761 (1965) (citing 15 O.S. 1961, §§ 214, 215); and *Util. Consumers' Action Network, Inc. v. AT&T Broadband of S. California*, 135 Cal. App. 4th 1023 (2006) (citing Cal. Civ. Code § 1671 which in consumer contracts places the burden on the party trying to enforce the clause, and in other contracts places the burden on the challenger).

The party now bearing the burden of proof should be required to prove

- that the clause was *knowingly agreed upon* by the party seeking to avoid the clause;

- that the nonbreaching party suffered a net economic loss attributable to the breach; and

- that the sum stipulated is not grossly disproportionate to raw actual damages caused by the breach.

See generally Wassenaar v. Panos, 331 N.W.2d 257 (Wis. 1983).

If the party seeking enforcement fails to meet that burden, then the aggrieved party should be limited to actual damages, though the stipulated sum should in all events serve as the limit of the breaching party's liability in the case.

Practice Note

One of the primary reasons for the bar's frustration with the single look rule from *Shapiro v. Grinspoon*, 27 Mass. App. Ct. 596 (1989), was that it allowed for unlimited damages against a breaching buyer if the stipulated damages clause was invalidated on a second look. *See* William V. Hovey, "Avuncular Advisor: Breaching Buyers Exposed," *Massachusetts Lawyers Weekly* (June 28, 1993). It is, therefore, important that if a second look is allowed in unusual cases, where the sum stipulated is alleged to be too high, the stipulated sum should nonetheless stand as a limitation on buyer's damages. In principle, this was accomplished with respect to penal bonds in § 339(2) of the first *Restatement of Contracts* which provided: "An undertaking in a penal bond to pay a sum of money as a penalty for non-performance of the condition of the bond is enforceable only to the extent of the harm proved to have been suffered by reason of such non-performance, *and in no case for more than the amount named as a penalty, with interest*" (emphasis added). Following the same principle, a stipulated damages clause should serve as an upper limit, unless the seller proves that damages were underliquidated, and therefore unconscionable. *See Restatement (Second) of the Law of Contracts* § 208.

§ 9.3   THE APPLICATION OF THE SECOND LOOK RULE WHEN STIPULATED DAMAGES EXCEED THE NORM: REVISITING COLONIAL AT LYNNFIELD

To bolster and better explain my argument for a principled second look in cases where the stipulated damages clause runs afoul of the norm, I will revisit *Colonial at Lynnfield, Inc. v. Sloan*, 870 F.2d 761 (1st Cir. 1989), in which the First Circuit judges, prior to *Kelly v. Marx*, declined to enforce a liquidated damages clause, assuming that Massachusetts case law required a retrospective look. Recall that in 1980, the Colonial Inn at Lynnfield, Inc. (Colonial), suffering from financial stress, entered into an agreement to sell a 49 percent interest for $3,375,000 and that the purchase and sale agreement contained a liquidated damages clause fixing the sum of $200,000 as damages for buyer's failure to close. The reason for selecting the sum of $200,000 is not clear from the record. The deal collapsed. The parties quarreled about fault. Colonial sold a 50 percent interest in the hotel to another party for $3.7 million and thereafter filed suit to enforce the $200,000 liquidated damages clause.

The buyers raised multiple defenses, one of which was that the liquidated damages clause amounted to a penalty, "being disproportionate to any reasonable estimate of damage that plaintiff might suffer." *Colonial at Lynnfield, Inc. v. Sloan*, 870 F.2d at 763. The trial judge awarded liquidated damages, applying the single look rule. The First Circuit judges agreed that *prospectively*, damages in the event of buyer's default were difficult to estimate, and that ex ante the $200,000 estimate was reasonable. Yet, the judges extended the analysis, believing on the basis of precedent that Massachusetts law required a "retrospective appraisal of a liquidated damages provision in certain circumstances." *Colonial at Lynnfield, Inc. v. Sloan*, 870 F.2d (citing *A-Z Servicenter, Inc.*, 334 Mass. 672 (1956); *Lynch v. Andrew*, 20 Mass. App. Ct. 683 (1985); *Security Safety Corp. v. Kuznicki*, 350 Mass. 157 (1966); *Warner v. Wilkey*, 2 Mass. App. Ct. 798 (1974); *Restatement of Contracts* § 339; *Restatement (Second) of Contracts* § 356, cmt. a). Therefore, the trial judge had erred by not considering whether the clause constituted a penalty when viewed retrospectively. The court deemed the record sufficient to show, Colonial's arguments notwithstanding, that Colonial suffered no damages on account of the breach, but rather the record established "that Colonial made a profit of $251,000 . . . as a result of defendants' breach." *Colonial at Lynnfield, Inc. v. Sloan*, 870 F.2d at 766. Citing *Restatement (Second) of the Law of Contracts* § 356, Comment (b), the court classified this case as an "extreme case" in which no loss incurred, hence, a case where the clause was necessarily invalid. *Colonial at Lynnfield, Inc. v. Sloan*, 870 F.2d at 767.

If the case had arisen after *Kelly v. Marx*, there would presumably have been no second look, and the trial judge's ruling would have been affirmed. Yet neither the reasoning nor the result in *Colonial at Lynnfield* should be lightly cast aside. Rather, the case can be seen as illustrative of the need for the limit on the single look rule that I am espousing. If the same fact pattern, or one similar, were to appear, a trial judge could in good conscience shift the burden of proof. To be sure, this requires creating an exception to *TAL Financial Corp. v. CSC Consulting, Inc.*, 446 Mass. 442 (2006), in which the Supreme Judicial Court followed a modern trend. But, for equitable reasons, the presumption of enforceability should not hold in a case where the damages stipulated do not accord with the norm that underlies the rule. Shifting the burden is a practical first step because, if the court assumes in retrospect a worst case scenario (markets plummet), it is virtually impossible for a buyer to prove by a preponderance that *any* estimate at the time of contracting was not proportionate to damages that might someday, somehow have to have been incurred by the seller on buyer's breach. In a worst case scenario, a property reasonably valued at $500,000 at the time of formation could be worth 50 percent of the contract price, or less, at the time of breach, if there were a severe and sudden crash in the market. Hence, the *TAL* rule is workable and enhances efficiency in the garden variety cases, but it places too heavy a burden on the party least able to muster the relevant evidence when the situation justifies closer judicial scrutiny.

If the judge shifts the burden of proof, then the judge should require the party trying to enforce the clause to come forward with proof on the following three-point analytical pathway.

§ 9.3.1   Knowledge of the Agreement

The party seeking to enforce the a clause should be required to establish that the clause was *knowingly agreed upon*, either by a signature on the clause, or proof of negotiations about the clause, or by admission of the party seeking to avoid it. Signature requirements of some sort on clauses that are peculiarly sensitive are common, sometimes statutorily required. *See, e.g.,* U.C.C. § 2-205. The simple fact that the seller or a third party furnished a standard form contract should not render a clause unenforceable. Even proof that the buyer signed an adhesion contract should not ipso facto void the clause. But, if the clause was in fine print, or buried in a lengthy contract, and there is no credible evidence that the buyer knowingly agreed to it, the seller should not be able to have the benefits of the clause when the sum stipulated goes beyond the norm or is otherwise suspect. Given the sophistication of the parties in *Colonial at Lynnfield,* and the record showing extended negotiations, there is little doubt that the clause was knowingly agreed upon.

Practice Note

Black's defines the term "adhesion contract" as "[a] standard-form contract prepared by one party, to be signed by another party in a weaker position, usu. a consumer, who adheres to the contract with little choice about its terms." *Black's Law Dictionary* (9th ed., West).

§ 9.3.2   Actual Economic Loss

If proof is forthcoming that a clause was knowingly agreed upon, the trial judge should require that the party trying to enforce the clause (seller) come forward with some credible evidence of actual economic loss caused by the breach, actual loss not negated by benefits from continued use, or gains made on disposition of the subject property. If the seller refuses or fails, the analysis should stop at this point. That was the end point in *Colonial at Lynnfield* where (according to the First Circuit) the seller was unable to establish any net loss. *See Colonial at Lynnfield, Inc. v. Sloan,* 870 F.2d at 766. Instead of a no-actual-damages defense, what I am proposing is a *some-actual-damages requirement* for enforcement.

§ 9.3.3   Proportionality of Stipulated Damages

If there were *credible evidence* of any net loss, the judge should ask: Are the damages stipulated grossly disproportionate to what appear to be actual damages attributable to the breach? This question takes account of the caveat in *Kelly v. Marx*, 428 Mass. at 886 n.6, and makes sense of language strewn throughout the case law, usually appended to test questions bearing upon validity, i.e., that stipulated damages must not be "excessive" or "grossly disproportionate to actual losses." *See, e.g., Shapiro v. Grinspoon*, 27 Mass. App. Ct. 596 (1989); and *A-Z Servicenter v. Segall*, 334 Mass. 627 (1956). The trial judge should not be required to make an unconscionability analysis under *Restatement (Second) of Contracts* § 208, or U.C.C. § 2-302, both of which usually require both procedural and substantive unconscionability. Rather, the court should make an assessment as to whether the party seeking to enforce the clause has in good faith come forth with credible evidence of actual damages bearing a reasonable relationship to the stipulated sum. A high degree of certitude as to actual damages should not be required, only a good-faith showing that, given the nature of the case, the proportionality criterion is met. *See, e.g., Wassenaar v. Panos*, 331 N.W.2d 357 (Wis. 1983)

Applying this approach, *Colonial at Lynnfield* might in good conscience be decided as the First Circuit judges decided it. This second-look-in-limited-circumstances approach is more consistent with *Restatement (Second) of Contracts* § 356 than is the unlimited application of the single look rule. Judicial adoption of this fall-back second look rule for cases beyond the norm would have four positive effects. First, this approach would encourage buyers and sellers, and their legal counsel, to agree upon stipulated damages within accepted norms. Lawyers and bargaining parties would tend to give the stipulated damages clause more careful thought if they wanted to avoid the scrutiny of a second look. Second, if parties in good faith agreed upon a stipulated sum in excess of the prevailing norm, there would be a principled analytical pathway whereby the clause could be salvaged if there were a solid justification for it. Stipulated sums that would be excessive in the ordinary run of cases might very well be justified, for example, if a seller had to invest heavily to clear up title, or to clean up a toxic site, or if the seller agreed to substantial improvements to make the property fit for a buyer's special use. In such cases a court should be at liberty to enforce a clause well beyond the norm under the pathway suggested herein. Third, if a party trying to enforce a clause in excess of prevailing practices were to fail, a speedy settlement would be probable, for a rare claimant would set out to prove actual damages by a preponderance if he or she failed in the lesser challenge of making a good-faith showing of some proportionality between raw actual damages and the stipulated sum.

Fourth, and importantly, recognizing that a failure to liquidate rightly *is not a failure to limit* damages, this second look proposal provides security for a buyer. *See* U.C.C. § 2-718(1), § 2-719 (distinguishing between liquidation of damages and limitations on damages). Whatever is agreed upon should be the maximum limit of a buyer's exposure on default. The clause sets the limit of what a buyer could reasonably foresee. Any other rule destroys a buyer's reasonable expectation and makes life uneasy for buyer's legal counsel. Taking away the agreed sum as a limit opens a door to multiple objections and would render any second look exception problematic.

Aside from practical advantages, the second look as a fall-back rule would bring the case law of the future into line with the case law of the nineteenth and early twentieth centuries in Massachusetts. The courts would continue to play a defined and reasonably expected role in closely scrutinizing the unusual cases to make sure that excessive sums are not taken to the detriment of the compensatory principle. With a principled second look applied in unusual cases, liquidated damages clauses in purchase and sale agreements should be manageable and workable with little judicial intervention for decades to come.

The much thornier problems derive from liquidated damages based upon acceleration clauses in lease and license agreements, the subject next to be explored. The long history of liquidated damages in Massachusetts is especially relevant in examining clauses in these kinds of agreements. The cases pertaining to purchase and sale agreements establish the necessary background.

The author wishes to acknowledge Robert Guman, his former Contracts student at New England Law | Boston, for his assistance in researching this chapter.

CHAPTER 10

The Extension of the Single Look Rule to Leases and Licenses: The Question of Mitigation

Gary L. Monserud, Esq.
New England Law | Boston

§ 10.1   **Acceleration Clauses as Stipulated Damages:
The Time Honored Rule** **10–1**

§ 10.2   **The Challenge:** *Cummings Properties, LLC v. Empire
Technologies, Inc.* **(2002)** **10–3**

§ 10.3   *Cummings Properties, LLC v. National Communications
Corporation*: **The Modification of a Venerable Rule
Pertaining to Liquidated Damages** **10–4**

§ 10.4   *NPS, LLC v. Minihane*: **The Single Look Rule Is
Extended from Leases to Licenses, and the Mitigation
Question Is Resolved** **10–5**

CHAPTER 10

The Extension of the Single Look Rule to Leases and Licenses: The Question of Mitigation

Gary L. Monserud, Esq.
New England Law | Boston

Scope Note
This chapter discusses how the single look rule is extended to leases and licenses. It addresses the acceleration clause as a form of liquidated damages, and considers key decisions in this area.

§ 10.1 ACCELERATION CLAUSES AS STIPULATED DAMAGES: THE TIME HONORED RULE

A milestone in the law pertaining to real estate leases was *Commissioner of Insurance v. Massachusetts Accident Co.*, 310 Mass. 769 (1942). The opinion became the touchstone for the adjudication of cases with rent acceleration clauses. In April 1930, Boston Insurance Company (lessor) leased certain premises to the Massachusetts Accident Company (lessee) for a term, with a monthly rent of approximately $1,000. The lessee came upon hard times. The Commissioner of Insurance was appointed as receiver. The lessor made a claim against the receiver for rent for the residue of the lease term (approximately nine months). A single justice allowed rent for only the last month of occupancy, although the lease contained a clause allowing an acceleration of all rents remaining unpaid as liquidated damages.

On review, the Supreme Judicial Court posed the first issue as "whether the provision for the acceleration of the rent calls for a penalty or liquidated damages." *Commissioner of Ins. v. Mass. Accident Co.*, 310 Mass. at 770. The record established that the lessee had bound itself to pay the rent and to multiple other obligations of varying significance. An acceleration clause made all rent for the remainder of the term immediately due and payable on lessee's failure to keep any of the promises enumerated or upon appointment of a receiver. The damages for breach of several of the lessee's promises, for example, to pay for electricity, were easily calculable. For minor breaches, the accelerated rent for the remainder of the lease term would have been disproportionate to the actual damages incurred. It is reasonable to assume that in the circumstances, the accelerated rent could have been a reasonable estimate of damages for abandonment of the premises. Hence, the formula chosen in the lease was proportionate to damages for some possible breaches, disproportionate as to others.

Writing for an undivided court, Justice Ronan stated as follows:

> We think that the clause providing for acceleration of rent in this lease, which must be construed as of the time of its execution and not as of the time of breach, comes within the general rule that, where a lease contains many covenants of varying importance, and where a breach of some of them would result in a loss which could be accurately determined and would be inconsiderable in comparison with the amount required by the lease to be paid although the damage resulting from a breach of some other covenants would be substantial and difficult exactly to ascertain, the sum designated to be paid upon a breach of any of these covenants is a penalty and not liquidated damages.

Comm'r of Ins. v. Mass. Accident Co., 310 Mass. at 771.

The rule relied upon had deep roots in Massachusetts case law, *see Higginson v. Weld*, 14 Gray 165, 80 Mass. 165 (1859); *Fisk v. Gray*, 11 Allen 132, 93 Mass. 132 (1865); *Wallis v. Carpenter*, 13 Allen 19, 95 Mass. 19 (1866); *Makletzova v. Diaghileff*, 227 Mass. 100, (1917); *De Cordova v. Weeks*, 246 Mass. 100 (1923), and was consistent with a case decided by the U.S. Supreme Court in 1930. *See Kothe v. R.C. Taylor Trust*, 280 U.S. 224 (1930) (rent acceleration clause was deemed a penalty when under the lease all rent remaining for the term of the lease was due if lessee filed for bankruptcy or any creditor filed a petition for bankruptcy against the lessee). Additionally, the court cited eleven cases arising in foreign states all of which, more or less, tended to sustain the rule that a stipulated damages clause covering a variety of breaches will not be upheld when it would be punitive as to lesser breaches, even if it would be a fair estimate of damages for significant breaches. *See generally Comm'r of Ins. v. Mass. Accident Co.*, 310 Mass. at 771; *Restatement (Second) of the Law of Contracts* § 339; Samuel Williston, *A Treatise on the Law of Contracts* § 776 (rev.

ed. by Samuel Williston and George Thompson 1936). While the court did not trace the rule back this far, the rule relied upon in *Commissioner of Insurance* had already been applied at the beginning of the nineteenth century in *Astley v. Weldon*, 126 E.R. 1318 (Court of Common Pleas, 1801), and *Kemble v. Farren*, 130 E.R. 1234 (Court of Common Pleas, 1829), English cases that were influential in Massachusetts. The decision broke no new ground. Nonetheless, Justice Ronan's opinion was regarded as the authoritative articulation of the settled law in Massachusetts for well more than fifty years. *See, e.g., A-Z Servicenter, Inc. v. Segall*, 334 Mass. 672, (1956); *Renda v. Gouchberg*, 4 Mass. App. Ct. 786 (1976); *Sentry Ins. v. Firnstein*, 14 Mass. App. Ct. 706 (1982); *DiBella v. Fiumara*, 2004 WL 203101. The challenge to the rule came from clashes between Cummings Properties, LLC, and its tenants when Cummings sought to enforce rent acceleration clauses in its form leases.

§ 10.2 THE CHALLENGE: *CUMMINGS PROPERTIES, LLC V. EMPIRE TECHNOLOGIES, INC.* (2002)

The facts are taken from the opinion issued by the Appellate Division of the District Court Department, 2002 WL 971807 (Mass. App. Div.). Cummings (lessor) and Empire (lessee) entered into a lease of commercial property for a two-year term. The lease provided for an automatic renewal for five years unless either party gave written notice of nonrenewal at least six months before the expiration date. When Empire was late in giving notice of nonrenewal, Cummings elected to hold Empire strictly to the lease terms. Empire defaulted, whereupon Cummings sought in a summary process action to recover possession of the premises and the unpaid rent ($135,091) through the end of the lease term. A district judge allowed repossession of the premises by Cummings, but awarded only $20,263, which was rent calculated through October 2001, far short of the end of the renewal term which was January, 2006.

Cummings appealed to the appellate division raising multiple issues which bore upon its claim for liquidated damages. The judges of the appellate division opined that, while the trial judge had not declared the rent acceleration clause to be unenforceable (but had rather limited its applicability), rendering the clause unenforceable might have been warranted on the basis of *Commissioner of Insurance v. Massachusetts Accident Co.*, because the clause by its terms was triggered by failures of differing significance, such as failure to pay the agreed security deposit, any taxes due, or any substantial invoice for goods or services, as well as failure to pay the rent. *See Cummings Props., LLC v. Empire Techs., Inc.*, 2002 WL 971807, n.2. The case was remanded for a recomputation of actual damages in which the rules on mitigation were pertinent. The stage was set for a future challenge to the rule embodied in *Commissioner of Insurance*.

§ 10.3 *CUMMINGS PROPERTIES, LLC V. NATIONAL COMMUNICATIONS CORPORATION:* THE MODIFICATION OF A VENERABLE RULE PERTAINING TO LIQUIDATED DAMAGES

In 1991, Cummings entered into a lease with National Communications Corporation (National) for the lease of commercial property. The lease was thereafter modified and extended. The last extension expired on March 30, 2006. The lease contained a rent acceleration clause designating rent for the remainder of any unexpired term as liquidated damages in the event of the lessee's default on any of several obligations, as in the *Cummings v. Empire* case. *See Cummings Props., LLC v. Nat'l Communications Corp.*, 449 Mass. 490, 492 n.3 (2007). National defaulted on its obligation to pay rent, and failed to pay a real estate tax charge, whereupon Cummings promptly gave written notice of breach. National failed to cure, and consequently, Cummings filed a complaint for summary process in District Court, seeking possession of the premises and accelerated rent in the sum of $525,643 as damages.

The trial judge awarded possession of the premises, the accelerated rent, and a tax owing, plus interest and costs for a total judgment of $536,760. National appealed to the Appellate Division of the District Court Department, arguing chiefly against the enforcement of the accelerated rent (liquidated damages) provision. The Appellate Division sustained the trial judge's decision granting possession to Cummings but reversed the monetary award based upon accelerated rent as liquidated damages, citing the rule from *Commissioner of Insurance*. *See Cummings Props., LLC v. Nat'l Communications Corp.*, 2004 WL 1662088 at 3. Having declared the rent acceleration clause invalid, the Appellate Division remanded for a computation of actual damages. A district court judge took evidence and computed the actual damages sustained by Cummings as $492,007.94 which was about six percent below the sum awarded as accelerated rent. *See Cummings Props., LLC v. Nat'l Communications Corp.*, 449 Mass. at 493 n.8.

Since the award was close to the liquidated sum computed on the basis of the acceleration clause, on economic grounds alone, Cummings might have been satisfied. Aggressively pursuing a change in the law, Cummings appealed the Appellate Division's ruling that had declared the accelerated rent clause unenforceable. The Supreme Judicial Court took the case from the Appeals Court on its own motion to consider one issue: "whether an accelerated rent provision in a commercial lease constitutes an enforceable liquidated damages provision where the tenant's breach, the failure to pay rent, is deemed by the lease (and agreed by the parties) to be 'significant,' but where, on its face, the provision might also apply to breaches of less significance, to which its application would be dispro-portionate." *Cummings Props., LLC v. Nat'l Communications Corp.*, 449 Mass. at 490. In an opinion by Justice Cordy, the court reversed the District Court Ap-pellate Division, and upheld the liquidated damages clause, modifying its hold-ing in *Commissioner of Insurance v. Massachusetts Accident Co.* "to the extent that in a case of a commercial agreement between sophisticated parties contain-ing a liquidated damages provision applicable to breaches of multiple covenants, it may be presumed that the parties intended the provision to apply only to those material breaches for which it may properly be enforced." *Cummings Props., LLC v. Nat'l Communications Corp.*, 449 Mass. at 495–96 (citing *United Air Lines, Inc. v. Austin Travel Corp.*, 867 F.2d 737 (2d Cir. 1989)); *XCO Int'l, Inc. v. Pac. Scientific Co.*, 369 F.3d 998 (7th Cir. 2004); 11 A. Corbin, *Contracts* § 58.14 (rev. ed. 2005). The acceleration clause was enforced because National had failed to carry its burden of proving that from the vantage point of for-mation, the acceleration clause allowed for damages grossly disproportionate to damages likely to be incurred. *See Cummings Props., LLC v. Nat'l Communica-tions Corp.*, 449 Mass. at 494–95. The court remanded for reinstatement of the award of liquidated damages as per the rent acceleration clause. The court de-clined to rule on whether or not Cummings had failed to mitigate damages be-cause the issue had not been preserved for appellate review.

§ 10.4   *NPS, LLC V. MINIHANE*: THE SINGLE LOOK RULE IS EXTENDED FROM LEASES TO LICENSES, AND THE MITIGATION QUESTION IS RESOLVED

In 2002, while Gillette Stadium was under construction, Paul Minihane entered into a ten-year agreement with NPS (developer) by the terms of which he li-censed two luxury seats, promising to pay $3,770 per seat annually. *See NPS, LLC v. Minihane*, 451 Mass. 417 (2008). Minihane and his guests only used the seats during one season. Having paid only $2,000 and a $7,500 security deposit, Minihane defaulted. Pursuant to a clause in the agreement, NPS gave notice of acceleration of all payments due over the ten-year term of the license, and de-manded the total ($65,500) as liquidated damages, which Minihane refused to pay. *See NPS, LLC v. Minihane*, 451 Mass. at 419 n.2 (quoting from Section 15 of the License Agreement). NPS brought suit claiming the accelerated sum, in-terest, and attorney fees. Minihane defended, arguing that the acceleration clause was punitive, and therefore not enforceable as a liquidated damages provision. After a bench trial, a Superior Court judge agreed with Minihane, finding that the amount due on acceleration was "grossly disproportionate to a reasonable estimate of actual damages made at the time of formation." *NPS, LLC v. Minihane*, 451 Mass. at 419. The judge awarded $6,000 actual damages. *See NPS, LLC v. Minihane*, 451 Mass. at 419 n.4.

NPS appealed. Taking the case on direct appellate review, the Supreme Judicial Court reversed, citing *Cummings*. Writing for a unanimous court, Justice Cowin applied the *Kelly v. Marx* two-part test and determined the following: first, that damages at the time of formation were difficult to estimate, given the variable and unknowable demand for luxury seats; and second, that the total amount Minihane would have paid under the license agreement was not grossly disproportionate to potential actual damages in the event of breach. *See NPS, LLC v. Minihane*, 451 Mass. at 422. Justice Cowin acknowledged that the clause was based upon a worst case scenario, namely, that NPS would be unable to re-license the luxury seats at any time during the ten-year term of the lease. However, under the holding of *TAL Financial Corp. v. CSC Consulting, Inc.*, it was Minihane's burden to show that the sum stipulated as damages was "unreasonably and grossly disproportionate to the real damages from a breach" or "unconscionably excessive." *NPS, LLC v. Minihane*, 451 Mass. at 421, (quoting from *TAL Fin. Corp. v. CSC Consulting, Inc.* 446 Mass. 422, 423 (2006)). He had failed.

The court also took up the dangling issue from *Cummings*, an issue not argued on the appeal by either party, but "raised (albeit obliquely) in the defendant's amended answer," namely, the issue of mitigation. *See NPS, LLC v. Minihane*, 451 Mass. at 423. In what appears to have been a matter of first impression in Massachusetts, the court held that "in the case of an enforceable liquidated damages provision, mitigation is irrelevant and should not be considered in assessing damages." *NPS, LLC v. Minihane*, 451 Mass. at 424. Justice Cowin anchored this holding with citations to foreign authorities as well as commentary. *See NPS, LLC v. Minihane*, 451 Mass. at 423 (citing *Barrie School v. Patch*, 401 Md. 497, 933 A2d 382 (2007); *Federal Realty Ltd. Partnership*, 289 A.2d 439, 735 N.Y.S.2d 159 (N.Y. 2001); *Lake Ridge Academy v. Carney*, 66 Ohio St. 3d 376, 613 N.E.2d 183 (1993); *Cady v. IMC Mtge. Co.*, 862 A2d 202 (R.I. 2004) (applying Florida law); Williston, *Contracts* § 65.31 at 364 (4th ed. 2002)). As a matter of policy, she stated that a contrary rule would defeat certain accepted purposes of liquidated damages clauses, including "peace of mind and certainty of result." *NPS, LLC v. Minihane*, 451 Mass. at 423 (citing *Kelly v. Marx*, 428 Mass. 877 (1999) (quoting Justice Spina's dissent from *Kelly v. Marx*, 44 Mass. App. Ct. 825, 833 (1998))). Consequently, even if NPS had relicensed the seats by the time of trial, or could reasonably have done so, such evidence would have had no bearing on the case. Minihane owed $65,500 plus interest and costs.

CHAPTER 11

An Evaluation of the Law in the Wake of *Cummings* and *Minihane*: How Can the Court Avoid Marginalizing or Submerging the Compensatory Principle?

Gary L. Monserud, Esq.
New England Law | Boston

§ 11.1   Introduction 11–1

§ 11.2   The Advantages of *Cummings* and *Minihane* 11–2

    § 11.2.1   Logical Extensions of *Kelly v. Marx* 11–2

    § 11.2.2   Economic Benefits 11–3

    § 11.2.3   Predictability and Security 11–3

    § 11.2.4   Preventing Bargaining Abuse 11–4

    § 11.2.5   Acceleration Clauses 11–4

    § 11.2.6   Freedom of Contract 11–7

    § 11.2.7   Summation 11–8

§ 11.3   The Need for a Limiting Principle 11–8

    § 11.3.1   The Inherent Danger of Overcompensation under Acceleration Clauses 11–8

    § 11.3.2   Specific Performance 11–9

    § 11.3.3   Accelerated Rent for Real Estate: An Analogy to Specific Performance 11–9

§ 11.3.4   The Potential Problem of Overcompensation 11–10

§ 11.3.5   *Panagakos v. Collins*, 80 Mass. App. Ct. 697
           (2011)..11–13

CHAPTER 11

An Evaluation of the Law in the Wake of *Cummings* and *Minihane*: How Can the Court Avoid Marginalizing or Submerging the Compensatory Principle?

Gary L. Monserud, Esq.
New England Law | Boston

Scope Note

This chapter discusses *Cummings* and *Minihane* in light of the compensatory principle and points out positive implications of the holdings in these cases. It also makes an argument for a limitation on the application of these holdings to prevent acceleration clauses from becoming oppressive and abusive.

§ 11.1   INTRODUCTION

While the *Minihane* decision did bring forth spirited criticism in a student authored law review article published in the *Hofstra Law Review*, Lisa A. Fortin, "Why There Should be a Duty to Mitigate Liquidated Damages Clauses," 38 *Hofstra L. Rev.* 285 (2009–2010), neither *Cummings* nor *Minihane* generated a publicly hostile response from the bar like *Shapiro* did in 1989. Yet these cases merit further close scrutiny because they changed the trajectory of the law of liquidated damages in Massachusetts. While each decision *may* have been justifiable on its facts, in combination they have set the law on a course that will marginalize or submerge the compensatory principle if the Supreme Judicial Court does not rechart its course. On the other hand, the *Cummings* and *Minihane* holdings do advance some desirable policies. This section explores the positive side of the *Cummings* and *Minihane* decisions and warns of the dangers if the holdings in these cases are applied without limitations.

§ 11.2   THE ADVANTAGES OF *CUMMINGS* AND *MINIHANE*

§ 11.2.1   Logical Extensions of *Kelly v. Marx*

Although the results—especially in *Minihane*—may seem harsh, on a theoretical level both decisions are logical extensions of the single look rule articulated in *Kelly v. Marx*.

In theory, the results reached are arguably consistent with the compensatory principle. Honoring the compensatory principle implies protection of an aggrieved party's expectation interest, if possible. The expectation interest is the aggrieved party's interest "in having the benefit of his bargain by being put in as good a position as he would have been in had the contract been performed." *Restatement (Second) of the Law of Contracts* § 344(a) With respect to the lease in *Cummings*, or any lease, the lessor's expectation interest is the rent for the agreed term, without any extra expense in collecting it. Assuming a worst case scenario, there may be no market for releasing on comparable terms, or on any terms, if a lessee defaults. Therefore, it must be granted that at the point of contract formation, an acceleration clause for the full term of a lease does not *necessarily* overshoot the lessor's expectation interest, and can conceivably constitute a sensible ex ante estimate of damages, if one assumes zero costs saved by the lessor. *Cummings* and *Minihane* are distinguishable from cases where stipulated damages necessarily outrun possible actual losses. An example of such a case is *Lake River Corp. v. Carborundum Co.*, 769 F.2d 1284 (7th Cir. 1985), Judge Posner's famous case, wherein the damages contractually agreed upon *necessarily* overshot potential losses under all conceivable scenarios no matter when a breach occurred. So, while lessees and licensees may grumble, acceleration clauses are not inherently punitive, and are consistent with awarding lost expectancies under worst case scenarios.

Practice Note

While the *Restatement (Second)* recognizes the expectation, reliance, and restitution interests in Section 344, the preferred goal is to give the party aggrieved by a breach his or her lost expectations or the benefit of the bargain, as explicitly acknowledged in Section 347. Justice Cordy recognized this in *Perroncello v. Donahue*, 448 Mass. 199 (2007), stating "[t]he law of contracts is intended to give an injured party the benefit of the bargain, not the benefit of the bargain and a windfall." *Perroncello v. Donahue,* 448 Mass. at 206.

§ 11.2.2   Economic Benefits

On the practical side, the rules adopted in *Cummings* and *Minihane* serve an important economic interest, namely, financially undergirding the development of properties for leasing or licensing. A responsible lender will be concerned about advancing money for land acquisitions or for construction or rehabilitation of any office building, warehouse, mall, stadium, apartment complex, or any other improvement to real property without some assurance of the economic viability of the intended enterprise. Holding a first mortgage will be small comfort if there is no realistic expectation of an income stream from the property sufficient to make loan payments in a timely manner. By approving and enforcing acceleration clauses, even clauses that appear harsh, the Supreme Judicial Court has gone some distance toward providing security to lenders, thereby advancing an important goal of encouraging commercial and residential real estate development. Quite apart from lenders, any entrepreneur entertaining a plan to develop real estate for lease might well be more motivated to go forward if advised that the expected revenue stream will likely gain judicial protection. Thus, from the standpoint of lenders and developers, the rules adopted in *Cummings* and *Minihane* make good sense. Along with security deposits, personal guaranties, and letters of credit, enforceable agreed-upon damages clauses for the expected income for a term can help to maximize the security of an investment.

§ 11.2.3   Predictability and Security

The holdings in *Cummings* and *Minihane* arguably enhance predictability and security. During the bargaining phase, one party's acceptance of a steep monetary consequence in the event of breach augments the security of the other party. If a knowledgeable lessee, aware of an acceleration clause and advised of a high probability of enforcement, nonetheless signs a lease, the lessor can be reasonably confident of a serious intent to perform. Judge Posner has observed that if someone agrees to a contract with a hefty liquidated damages clause, the agreement operates "as a signal that the party subject to it is likely to perform his contract promises. This makes him a more attractive contract partner, since if he doesn't perform, he will be punished severely." *See XCO Int'l, Inc. v. Pac. Scientific Co.,* 369 F.3d 998, 1001 (7th Cir. 2004), *rehearing denied* and *rehearing en banc denied,* June 24, 2004. An in terrorem mindset in the business world can be a good thing, if we assume avoidance of breaches and completion of contracts are desirable ends. (It should be noted, however, that Judge Posner is aware that the enforcement of stiff liquidated damages clauses may discourage efficient breaches, an effect not wholly positive in his worldview. *See XCO Int'l, Inc. v. Pac. Scientific Co.*, 369 F.3d at 998.) Moreover, if there is a breach by a lessee and litigation, a presumption in favor of enforcing a rent acceleration clause, *even if a clause seems harsh,* will save considerable costs by encouraging settlement and by raising the probability of disposition by pretrial motions.

§ 11.2.4   Preventing Bargaining Abuse

The law provides safeguards to prevent abuse in the bargaining process. Economic duress, mistake, and varying degrees of misrepresentation are available as grounds for relief. The newer doctrine of unconscionability, *see* U.C.C. § 2-302; *Restatement (Second) of the Law of Contracts* § 208, can be brought to bear against any acceleration clause that is substantively oppressive and was entered into by sharp practices. If the long line of cases in which stipulated damages clauses have been invalidated was expunged by legislation or judicial decision, the truly oppressed party would still have some ammunition for an attack on an egregiously onerous clause. That being the case, thoughtful lawyers can reasonably argue that when nothing is foul in the making of bargains with acceleration clauses, these clauses should be enforced without any special scrutiny.

§ 11.2.5   Acceleration Clauses

Due to the weight of old case law pertaining to leases, enforcement of acceleration clauses may be desirable (or necessary) in Massachusetts to prevent serious economic injustices to lessors. Without an acceleration clause, a lessor may be compelled to wait for years before a court will fix the damages for a lessee's breach. The lessor's dilemma became painfully evident a recent case, *275 Washington Street Corp. v. Hudson River International, LLC.*, 81 Mass. App. Ct. 418 (2012). On April 13, 2006, the lessor (275 Washington Street Corp.) agreed to lease commercial property in Boston to lessee (Hudson River International) for a term of twelve years, ending April 16, 2018. The premises were to be used for a dental practice. The base rent was $16,000 per month, subject to incremental annual increases. The lessee faltered on its obligations after one year. Before the end of the second year, the lessee ceased making any rent payments, whereupon the lessor reentered, effectively terminating the lease and soon after commenced a suit for damages (mainly unpaid rent). The defendant lessee moved to dismiss, "claiming that suit was prematurely brought since the lease term had not yet run and therefore the amount of damages owed was not ascertainable." *275 Wash. St. Corp. v. Hudson River Int'l, LLC,* 81 Mass. App. Ct. at 421. A motion judge denied the motion.

The lease contained an indemnification clause that required the lessee on default to indemnify the lessor "against all loss of rent and other payments which the Landlord may incur by reason . . . of such termination during the remainder of the term." *275 Wash. St. Corp. v. Hudson River Int'l, LLC,* 81 Mass. App. Ct. at 420 (quoting from ¶ 21(h) of the lease). Postbreach events arguably made damages reasonably ascertainable because approximately two years after the lessee abandoned the premises, the lessor entered into a substitute ten-year lease, which overlapped the term of the twelve-year lease that had been breached. Using this substitute rental rate (which was lower than the agreed rent in the lease which was breached), and other data submitted by the parties, a trial judge computed damages (including lost future rents) to be in excess of $1,000,000 and entered judgment accordingly, preserving appeal rights for both parties. Future lost rents were reduced to present value. See *275 Washington Street Corp. v. Hudson River International, LLC,* 81 Mass. App. Ct. at 419 n.4 for an overview of the damages stipulated by the parties.

On appeal, in an opinion authored by Justice Fecteau, the Appeals Court sustained the finding of liability for breach of the lease, but further held that "[t]he part of the judgment assessing damages is vacated, and the case is remanded to the Superior Court for calculation of damages due to the landlord as of the time it recovered possession of the premises . . . ." *275 Wash. St. Corp. v. Hudson River Int'l, LLC,* 81 Mass. App. Ct. at 427–28. The court reversed as to damages incurred after the lessor recovered possession on the basis of case law which required that "[r]ecovery under an indemnity clause of a lease cannot be had until the specified term of the lease has ended." *275 Wash. St. Corp. v. Hudson River Int'l, LLC,* 81 Mass. App. Ct. at 423 (quoting from *Zevitas v. Adams,* 276 Mass. 307 (1931)). Therefore, the lessor would be obliged to wait until 2018 (the end of the twelve-year term) to collect its posttermination losses, providing intervening events did not eradicate or reduce the lessor's possibilities of collecting a judgment. Justice Fecteau noted the absence of any liquidated damages clause. *See 275 Wash. St. Corp. v. Hudson River Int'l, LLC,* 81 Mass. App. Ct. at 422 n.4.

The Supreme Judicial Court took the case on further appellate review to answer three questions:

> First, after a breach of a commercial lease by the tenant and termination of the lease by the landlord, does an indemnification clause in the lease, in the absence of specific language so providing, allow the landlord to recover before the end of the lease term the present value of lost future rent once the landlord relets the property to another tenant for the duration of the lease? Second, in the absence of a clause in the lease

specifically so providing, does our common law allow a landlord to recover contract damages for the present value of lost future rent after the termination of the lease? Third, does the liability of the guarantor here exceed the liability of the tenant?

275 Wash. St. Corp. v. Hudson River Int'l, LLC, 465 Mass. 16, 17 (2013).

To each of these questions the court answered "no." The opinion, authored by Justice Gants, rests upon a careful examination of precedent as well as policy-based arguments against retention of the common law rule requiring computation of a lessor's indemnification claim to await the end of the agreed-upon term. The court did not find the "common-law rule to be broken" and consequently discerned "no reason to fix it." *275 Wash. St. Corp. v. Hudson River Int'l, LLC*, 465 Mass. at 29–30. In a sense, the court pushed the burden of protecting lessors unto the bar, stating: "[t]he parties are free to set forth in a lease when indemnification comes due and in what amount, but where, as here, the lease does not specify when indemnification is due, indemnification under our common law does not become due until the end of the original lease term, when damages may be 'wholly ascertained.'" *275 Wash. St. Corp. v. Hudson River Int'l, LLC*, 465 Mass. at 24 (citing *Gardiner v. Parsons*, 224 Mass. 347, 350 (1916), and *Zevitas v. Adams*, 276 Mass. 307, 317 (1931)). Furthermore, "[i]f the landlord wants the indemnified amount to become due once the property is relet, it may insist that the lease so provide and identify the means to calculate the amount of indemnified loss." *275 Wash. St. Corp. v. Hudson River Int'l, LLC*, 465 Mass. at 26.

The foregoing language makes leasing risky for lessors without ironclad contractual protections and puts a high premium on good drafting. Matters would have been vastly simplified if the parties had agreed upon an enforceable acceleration clause, or alternatively, a carefully drafted indemnity clause, delineating with exactitude posttermination rights agreed upon by the parties. The *Cummings-Minihane* holdings can help solve a problem created by old case law that bars a suit for future damages in cases such as *25 Washington Street Corp*. The *Cummings-Minihane* holdings can help to solve a problem created by old case law which bars suits for future damages under an indemnification clause in cases arising from broken leases.

Practice Note

The Practitioner must beware that the Supreme Judicial Court has held that a commercial lease "is a contract rather than a conveyance of property." *See 275 Wash. St. Corp. v. Hudson River Int'l, LLC*, 465 Mass. 16, 27 (citing *Humphrey v. Byron*, 447 Mass. 322, 326 (2006), and *Wesson v. Leone Enters., Inc.*, 437 Mass. 708, 720 (2002)). Yet, the court has been equally clear that breach of a commercial lease does not allow the landlord to collect benefit-of-the-bargain damages; rather, "[i]t is well settled in the Commonwealth that when a landlord terminates a lease following the default of a tenant, the tenant is obligated to pay the rent due prior to the termination but has no obligation to pay any rent that accrues after the termination unless the lease otherwise provides." *275 Wash. St. Corp. v. Hudson River Int'l, LLC*, 465 Mass. at 21 (citing *Krasne v. Tedeschi & Grasso*, 436 Mass. 103, 109 (2002)). Consequently, if a lessor (landlord) expects to collect any posttermination "damages," the lease must have an enforceable acceleration clause or an indemnity clause that will pass judicial muster. Drafting an indemnity clause that will survive scrutiny could be tricky. This makes the clarification of the law pertaining to acceleration clauses a matter of some importance.

§ 11.2.6   Freedom of Contract

This brings us to the last point commonly reiterated and often strenuously insisted upon by supporters of virtually unfettered stipulated damages clauses: that freedom of contract requires a judicial hands-off treatment of liquidated damages clauses, especially where commercial entities agree upon such clauses. As stated by Judge Posner writing for the 7th Circuit in *XCO International, Inc. v. Pacific Scientific Co.* in 2004:

> Where both parties are substantial commercial enterprises . . . and where damages are liquidated for breach by either party, making an inference of fraud or duress implausible, it is difficult to see why the law should take an interest in whether the estimate of harm underlying the liquidation of damages is reasonable. Courts don't review other provisions of contracts for reasonableness; why this one?

XCO Int'l, Inc. v. Pac. Scientific Co., 369 F.3d 998, 1001 (7th Cir. 2004).

Competent people are at liberty to make foolish bargains. Hence, it is argued, people should be equally at liberty to agree on damages that at a later time may seem foolish, harsh, or excessive in light of actual losses suffered. In *Cummings*, Justice Cordy cited Judge Posner's opinion in *XCO International, Inc.* to make the point that contract law is moving toward greater freedom with regard to stipulated damages, and that the traditional limitations are increasingly seen as an anachronism. *See Cummings Props., LLC v. Nat'l Communications Corp.*, 449 Mass. 490, 495 (2007).

§ 11.2.7   Summation

There are good things to say about the rules adopted in *Cummings* and *Mini-hane*. But, the advantages of these holdings should not obscure their potential for harm. In combination with *Kelly v. Marx*, taking particular notice of the rule from *Minihane* that eliminates any consideration of mitigation, these cases have the potential to prevent the courts from addressing serious injustices. As with purchase and sale agreements, both a limiting principle on the enforcement of acceleration clauses, and exceptions for unusual cases should be explored.

§ 11.3   THE NEED FOR A LIMITING PRINCIPLE

§ 11.3.1   The Inherent Danger of Overcompensation under Acceleration Clauses

The need for a limiting principle can be illustrated by reference to the fact pattern from *275 Washington Street Corp.,* wherein the parties entered into a twelve-year lease in 2006, and the lessee promised to pay $16,000 per month. Suppose the parties had agreed upon an acceleration clause, declaring the rent for the remainder of the term due and payable as liquidated damages upon the lessee's default. Default occurred before the first two years of the term were up, meaning there were approximately ten years remaining on the lease. For those ten years, the total rent payments (without any incremental adjustments) would have been $1,920,000, and that presumably would have been the lessor's claim under an acceleration clause. But, for eight of the ten years remaining, the lessor made a substitute lease, albeit for a lower rent, as the record makes clear. *For purposes of argument,* assume the rent was eighty percent of the original lease, or $12,800 per month. This would yield $153,600 per year which adds up to $1,228,800 over eight years. Therefore, if an acceleration clause for the rent had been agreed upon *and enforced,* and all evidence of a mitigating reletting had been precluded in light of *Minihane,* the lessor would have had a gain of $1,228,800, minus whatever expenses were involved in making the second rental, as a result of the lessee's breach.

If the rental price had been increased by twenty percent over the last eight year period, then the lessor would have received $19,200 per month, $230,400 per year, which yields a total gain of $1,843,200 for the eight-year period, beyond the liquidated rental sums as per the original agreement. Thus, when evidence of mitigation or possible mitigation is disallowed, and no second look is allowed, any lessor capable of releasing at a decent rent can quite literally *double his or her initial expectations* by enforcement of an acceleration clause. By a long and tortured route, we have come unwittingly to a point in history where the courts—following precedent—will protect economic consequences similar to those that gave rise to the limits on penal bonds in England and in nineteenth century Massachusetts.

§ 11.3.2   Specific Performance

When an acceleration clause for rent remaining on a term is enforced, the lessor's remedy is analogous to specific performance for a seller under a purchase and sale agreement. Consider: if a seller and buyer enter into a purchase and sale agreement on real property for $1,000,000 (with a 5 percent deposit designated as liquidated damages) and the buyer defaults, in accord with *Perroncello*, the seller would be entitled to either specific performance whereby seller gains the full purchase price in exchange for a deed, or liquidated damages, *but not both.* As stated by Justice Cordy, to allow both would overcompensate the seller, whose expectation interest was the purchase price. What goes unsaid (it being obvious) is that if the seller forgoes the liquidated damages and obtains a judgment for the purchase price, the seller of necessity must tender the deed. It is self-evident, hence unsaid, that no court would seriously entertain an argument that the buyer should be ordered to pay the full price *and at the same time allow the seller to retain title.* The rules are analogous in sales of goods under U.C.C. § 2-709.

§ 11.3.3   Accelerated Rent for Real Estate: An Analogy to Specific Performance

Matters become blurred in lease cases when rent for real estate is accelerated. Suing for accelerated rent is similar to a suit for specific performance by a seller on a purchase and sale agreement because the lessor sues for the total consideration agreed upon. Yet in cases arising from leases, such as *Cummings,* the lessee is dispossessed, usually by summary process, meaning the leasehold reverts to the lessor, and the lessor obtains a judgment for the accelerated rent for the term. The lessee is deprived of any and all interest in the leasehold. This is analogous to a seller winning specific performance (the agreed price) and being at liberty to sell the real estate to a third party without sharing any proceeds with the buyer who paid the full price. The potential for excessive recoveries, as least compensation far outrunning a lessor's expectation interest, is inherent in the allowance of dispossession and the enforcement of acceleration clauses, especially when mitigation evidence is precluded.

§ 11.3.4   The Potential Problem of Overcompensation

The problems arising from the enforcement of an acceleration clause when property is relet were explored thoroughly in Chief Judge Feeney's Bankruptcy Court decision in *In re Admetric Biochem, Inc.*, 284 B.R. 1 (2002); (motion for vacatur denied, 300 B.R. 141 (2003)), a case involving Cummings Properties, LLC, issued in September 2002. In August 2000, Admetric entered into a commercial lease with Cummings for approximately 12,000 square feet of office space in Medford. The term was for five years, beginning October 1, 2000. The annual rent was $438,000 or $36,500 per month. Upon the lessee's substantial breach and failure to cure within ten days of notice, the lease provided for an acceleration of rent remaining for the entire term. *See In re Admetric Biochem, Inc.*, 284 B.R. at 3–4 (quoting § 20 of the lease). A paragraph adopted in a Rider injected an element of mercy, allowing cure up to final judgment. *See In re Admetric Biochem, Inc.*, 284 B.R. at 4 (quoting ¶ K, Rider to the lease).

Less than one year into the lease term, Admetric encountered financial difficulties and defaulted on its monthly rent payment and other charges. Cummings gave notice of breach. Admetric failed to cure, whereupon Cummings commenced an action in District Court seeking, inter alia, possession of the leased premises, pretermination rent, and accelerated rent in the sum of $1,824,000, plus miscellaneous charges. The accelerated rent was approximately 80 percent of the total rent for the five-year term of the lease. Soon after commencement of the lawsuit, the parties agreed that judgment would enter for Cummings for possession only, without prejudice to Cummings's damage claim or Admetric's defenses thereto. *See In re Admetric Biochem, Inc.*, 284 B.R. at 4. On October 30, 2001, Admetric filed a voluntary Chapter 7 bankruptcy petition. The Trustee removed the District Court action (summary process proceedings) to the Bankruptcy Court where the enforceability of the acceleration clause was litigated under the *Kelly v. Marx* test.

Cummings's lawyers realized that the claim for accelerated rent would be limited in the Bankruptcy Court by virtue of 11 U.S.C. § 502(b)(6). In substance, Section 502(b)(6) limits the lessor's claim to the greater of one year's rent, or 15 percent of the rent for the term remaining, not to exceed three years. Since one year's rent exceeded 15 percent of the term remaining, the statutory cap amounted to $437,691, which was the amount Cummings claimed on a motion for summary judgment. By cross motion, the Trustee claimed that the acceleration clause was unenforceable under *Kelly v. Marx* because it allowed damages "grossly disproportionate to a reasonable estimate of actual damages made at the time of contract formation." *In re Admetric Biochem, Inc.*, 284 B.R. at 2. Thus, the Trustee challenged the liquidated damages clause under the ex ante test articulated in *Kelly v. Marx*.

Practice Note

Title 11, Section 502 of the U.S.C. provided an allowance for certain creditors' claims within statutorily set limits. The limit on a creditor-lessor's claim against a debtor was set forth in Section 502(b)(6), which required the following:

> If such objective to a claim is made, the court, after notice and hearing, shall determine the amount of such claim in lawful currency of the United States as of the date of the filing of the petition, and shall allow such claim in such amount, except to the extent that . . . if such claim is the claim of a lessor for damages resulting from the termination of a lease of real property, such claim exceeds
>
> (A) the rent reserved by such lease, without acceleration, for the greater of one year, or 15 percent, not to exceed three years, of the remaining term of such lease, following the earlier of—
>
>   (i) The date of the filing of the petition; and
>
>   (ii) the date on which the lessor repossessed, or the lessee surrendered, the leased property; plus
>
> (B) any unpaid rent due under such lease, without acceleration, on the earlier of such dates. 11 U.S.C. § 502(b)(6).

Cummings's lawyers argued that the Trustee could not meet her burden of proving that the computation of accelerated rent was an unreasonable estimate of damages at the time the lease was agreed upon. Concentrating on the first prong of the ex ante test, the Trustee countered that damages were not difficult to ascertain in advance because "one could reasonably estimate Cummings's damages as the sum of (a) unpaid rent as of the date of breach; (b) monthly rent until a replacement tenant is found; and (c) Cummings' expenses in reletting the premises—less any rental increase that Cummings would receive from the replacement tenant." *In re Admetric Biochem, Inc.*, 284 B.R. at 6. This argument drove the analysis deep into the *Kelly v. Marx* ex ante test, and the arguments became more subtle. The meaning of the first prong of *Kelly v. Marx* (whether damages were difficult to estimate ex ante) is not self-evident. This question could mean:

- that the *amount of actual damages*, in the event of breach, was difficult to estimate at the time of contracting; or

- that at the time of contracting it was foreseeable that the amount of damages *would be difficult to determine* postbreach. See Prof. Melvin Eisenberg, "The Limits of Cognition and the Limits of Contract," 47 *Stan. L. Rev.* 211, 230 (1995) for insight into the ambiguity of the first prong of the ex ante test.

Cummings's lawyers argued on the basis of the first meaning. The Trustee's argument assumed the second meaning, or tended in that direction. It is not clear whether Judge Feeney chose between the competing interpretations of the first prong, but she did agree with the Trustee about the unreasonableness of the estimate, finding it "highly unlikely that any particular rental space managed by Cummings remains vacant for three or four years at a stretch, which is the assumption implicit in the accelerated rent/liquidated damages provision." *In re Admetric Biochem, Inc.*, 284 B.R. at 9. Looking at it from a different angle, damages could be computed by ascertaining lost rental payments and expenses incurred; therefore, viewing the matter prospectively, damages were not impossible or extremely difficult to estimate.

Judge Feeney's assessment of the acceleration clause was probably influenced by evidence establishing that a new tenant had subsequently entered into a five-year lease for the space vacated by Admetric at an annual rent of approximately $584,000, meaning the second lease generated more than $500,000 above the total lease price in the Cummings-Admetric lease for Cummings over its five-year term. Realizing the difficulty posed by this evidence, counsel for Cummings advanced an argument that as lessor with space to spare his client was in a situation analogous to a lost volume seller who makes out an entitlement to lost profits under U.C.C. § 2-708(2). Judge Feeney was not persuaded. *See In re Admetric Biochem, Inc.*, 284 B.R. at 10–11. Consequently, she determined that the liquidated damages clause was unenforceable and found instead that the lessee's $146,000 security deposit, representing approximately four months' rent, was a reasonable ex ante estimate of Cummings's damages attributable to Admetric's default. *See In re Admetric Biochem, Inc.*, 284 B.R. at 8.

Viewed in light of the compensatory principle, Judge Feeney's decision seems right. Of course, her analysis turned in part on her recognition that the premises were relet for a five-year term at a higher price, evidence of mitigation not allowable under *Minihane*. Therefore, if the enforceability of the liquidated damages clause had been adjudicated in the state courts after *Cummings* and *Minihane*, the result would with little doubt have been opposite. Cummings would have been able to collect roughly double what it would have collected for rental of the property but for Admetric's financial difficulties and consequent breach. Doubling a party's expectation interest due to the other's breach, however described, offends the compensatory principle. Reflection upon the real possibility of allowing an aggrieved party an award that doubles its expectancy can make a thoughtful observer uneasy about the trajectory of the law.

§ 11.3.5   *Panagakos v. Collins*, 80 Mass. App. Ct. 697 (2011)

Justice Hanlon, writing for the Appeals Court, expressed her uneasiness with our law of liquidated damages when the court decided *Panagakos v. Collins*, 80 Mass. App. Ct. 697 (2011). The case arose from a commercial lease. In 1995, Panagakos leased real estate to McWal, Inc. for the operation of a restaurant in Dartmouth. Walter Collins (McWal's president) guaranteed payment of the rent. A second renewal of the lease ran from January 2006 through December 31, 2010, at an annual base rent of $133,000. A rent acceleration cause was agreed upon as lessor's liquidated damages in the event of the lessee's default. The acceleration clause provided that accelerated rent would be reduced by rent received on a subsequent reletting in the event of lessee's default. (See *Panagakos v. Collins*, 80 Mass. App. Ct. at 700 for a full description of the clause.) A little more than one year into the lease, McWal failed to pay the rent, whereupon Panagakos initiated summary process to regain possession under G.L. c. 239. Being in a difficult situation, Collins decided that he would try to sell his restaurant business and hired a broker to find a suitable buyer. On being informed of his lessee's intentions, Panagakos "indicated that he would agree to an assignment provided McWal (lessee) remain current on the rental payments until an assignment could be made." *Panagakos v. Collins*, 80 Mass. App. Ct. at 699. The broker turned up a responsible and willing buyer; however, Panagakos refused to either make necessary repairs to enable the prospective buyer to operate a restaurant, or to allow a lease beyond three and one-half years (the remainder of the lease term), so that a buyer could make the repairs and have sufficient time to recoup the investment. *See Panagakos v. Collins*, 80 Mass. App. Ct. at 700 n.7 (broker testified that to make an investment in the restaurant financially feasible the lessee would require a twenty- to twenty-five-year lease). Consequently, the prospective buyer lost interest. Collins gave up, and McWal defaulted on further rent payments.

Panagakos sought damages against Collins in his capacity as guarantor, including damages based upon the rent acceleration clause. A trial judge heard evidence, but only allowed two month's future rent (posttermination rent) because he concluded that "he [Panagakos] was under an affirmative duty to make reasonable efforts to mitigate those future damages . . . includ[ing] ensuring that the premises are in repair as well as leasing for a term of sufficient length to attract a worthwhile tenant." *Panagakos v. Collins*, 80 Mass. App. Ct. at 701. Finding that Panagakos had failed to use reasonable efforts to mitigate damages, the acceleration clause was not enforceable, according to the trial judge. Panagakos appealed, arguing principally that in light of *Cummings* and *Minihane*, "the presence of a default/acceleration clause, such as the one contained in the lease, makes irrelevant the issue of mitigation of damages, because an acceleration clause is an enforceable liquidated damages provision." *Panagakos v. Collins*, 80 Mass. App. Ct. at 702.

Writing for the Appeals Court, Justice Hanlon carefully parsed *Cummings* and *Minihane*, and concluded:

> The combined force of these cases *constrains us to conclude* that the trial judge erred when he considered Panagakos's failure to mitigate in his assessment of damages from Collins's acknowledged breach of the lease .We therefore vacate the damages award and remand for further proceedings consistent with this opinion. At any further proceeding, Collins shall bear the burden of proving that the accelerated rental figure constitutes a penalty by reason of its disproportionality to a reasonable estimate of actual damages.

Panagakos v. Collins, 80 Mass. App. Ct. at703 (emphasis added).

The observation that the court was *constrained to conclude* sends a distress signal. The Appeals Court decided, albeit reluctantly, that the failure to mitigate was irrelevant. Hence, the lessee was required to shoulder the burden of proving that from the vantage point of formation, the estimate was unreasonable, a burden nobody seems able to meet in the wake of *Cummings* and *Minihane*. The stress engendered by the transfer of the single look rule to leases, and the barring of evidence bearing upon mitigation, is real and immediate. *Panagakos* demonstrates that all is not well with the expansion of *Kelly v. Marx* into leases and licenses, especially after the categorical exclusion of evidence pertaining to mitigation in *Minihane*. It is time to rechart the path for the future. If some adjustments are not made, lessors will routinely be able to collect sums far exceeding lost expectancies, thereby violating the compensatory principle.

CHAPTER 12

An Argument for a Limiting Principle on the Use of Acceleration Clauses in Leases and Licenses

Gary L. Monserud, Esq.
New England Law | Boston

§ 12.1   Introduction 12–1

§ 12.2   Excluding Choices of Lesser Merit 12–1

    § 12.2.1   Should the Single Look Rule Be Refined? 12–2

    § 12.2.2   Should Evidence Pertaining to Mitigation
    Be Allowed? 12–3

§ 12.3   A Proposal for an Imposed Limitation on Acceleration
Clauses in Leases and Licenses 12–4

    § 12.3.1   Sales versus Leases: Critical Distinctions 12–5

    § 12.3.2   Establishing a Baseline: A Modest Proposal 12–7

    § 12.3.3   Balancing the Equities 12–7

§ 12.4   What Should Happen When Acceleration Clauses
Exceed an Established Norm? 12–8

CHAPTER 12

An Argument for a Limiting Principle on the Use of Acceleration Clauses in Leases and Licenses

Gary L. Monserud, Esq.
New England Law | Boston

Scope Note

This chapter discusses the challenges of finding a way to limit the application of acceleration clauses to avoid undermining the compensatory principle while at the same time protecting the legitimate interests of lessors and licensors. After casting aside choices of lesser merit, the chapter sets forth an argument for a limitation on acceleration clauses similar to the limitation set by Congress in the Bankruptcy Code.

§ 12.1   INTRODUCTION

Because the problem that has emerged in recent case law is the undermining of the compensatory principle, the quest for a solution should involve reflection upon the case law in which the compensatory principle was honored. Assuming that the single look rule adopted in *Kelly v. Marx* will be the law for the foreseeable future, the challenge is to find a path forward consistent with that rule. Charting a path for the future requires the avoidance of imprudent choices as well as envisioning a path that is workable.

§ 12.2   EXCLUDING CHOICES OF LESSER MERIT

Working with the single look rule in mind, three adjustments in the case law that might better protect lessees can be envisioned:

- the single look rule could be applied in a manner that makes acceleration clauses less likely to survive scrutiny;

- the Supreme Judicial Court could reopen the door to evidence pertaining to mitigation that could reduce recoveries under liquidated damages clauses; or

- the legislature or the courts could devise a way of setting limits to the acceleration clauses, routinely enforcing clauses within limits while subjecting more onerous clauses to serious scrutiny.

While the first two choices have some appeal, each is problematic. Consider the pitfalls in cases involving leases, realizing that the arguments pertain to licenses as well.

§ 12.2.1   Should the Single Look Rule Be Refined?

As to refining the single look rule, consider again the Trustee's argument in *Admetric*, wherein she focused upon the first prong of the two-part test, which asks from the vantage point of formation whether "actual damages are difficult to ascertain." *See In re Admetric Biochem, Inc.*, 284 B.R. 1, 6. If the question asks whether the dollar amount of damages is subject to prospective ascertainment, the party challenging the clause, bearing the burden of proof, will nearly always lose because nobody can reasonably ascertain the damages for breach of a lease in advance. Market conditions for a substitute future lease will be uncertain, and the longer the lease, the higher the uncertainty. On the other hand, if the question asks whether the dollar amount of damages will be reasonably susceptible to ascertainment at a future date in the event of beach, the challenger will often win, because after breach, the time remaining will be certain and market conditions reasonably provable. The courts, in Massachusetts and elsewhere, without articulating the distinction, usually take the first view, so that the challenger loses. An adoption of the second view, which would be a refinement of *Kelly v. Marx* in its application to leases, has an appeal. It would put some teeth into the first prong of the prospective test.

The problem is that this manner of applying the single look rule, if adopted, would tend to render most acceleration clauses unenforceable because the manner of computing future losses would be readily foreseeable to anyone familiar with the computations of damages after a lessee's default in the absence of an acceleration clause. Consequently, such a refinement would commonly leave lessors in the predicament demonstrated in *275 Washington Street Corp. v. Hudson River International*, where (in the absence of an acceleration clause) the lessor had no remedy for future rents until the expiration of the term. Routine nonenforcement of acceleration clauses would inevitably lead to increased litigation as lessors struggled to prove posttermination damages, sometimes years after a default. Therefore, refining the single look test so that acceleration clauses would be normally unenforceable would be a questionable move. It might make good sport for lessees' lawyers, but it would probably be too harsh on lessors.

§ 12.2.2 Should Evidence Pertaining to Mitigation Be Allowed?

Reopening the door to mitigation evidence, including a lessor's failure to use reasonable efforts to mitigate losses, as allowed by the trial judge in *Panagakos* might seem to be a viable choice if the Supreme Judicial Court were writing on a clean slate. However, this path seems improbable inasmuch as the court would need to overrule *Minihane* or greatly limit its application in cases arising from leases and licenses. If *Minihane* were overruled, then logically mitigation evidence would be admissible after breach of purchase and sale agreements, a result that would undermine the application of the single look rule in those cases. In any event, since the earliest decisions in Massachusetts, stipulated damages clauses have either been enforced, or not enforced—such clauses have not been partially enforced—which would be the intent of allowing evidence of mitigation. On the other hand, if *Minihane* were limited so that its proscription of mitigation evidence did not pertain to leases, virtually every defaulting lessee would have good reason to litigate about mitigation, rendering acceleration clauses of negligible value. The most honorable players in the marketplace would likely adjust to this change, and work out settlements taking account of mitigation obligations, but opening the door to evidence about mitigation would be an abrupt turnabout so soon after *Minihane*. Security, peace of mind, and efficiency—values protected by the law of liquidated damages—might be seriously compromised. Moreover, a principled way of allowing mitigation evidence after some breaches and excluding mitigation evidence after others, when liquidated damages clauses have been agreed upon, would likely prove elusive, though I think the door to the law on mitigation might reasonably remain ajar.

Practice Note
The notion of admitting evidence that damages were avoided, or could reasonably have been avoided, and allowing such evidence to reduce liquidated damages (rather than to invalidate a stipulated damages clause) was a main point argued by Lisa A. Fortin in "Why There Should be a Duty to Mitigate Liquidated Damages Clauses," 38 *Hofstra L. Rev.* 285 (2009–2010), an article written in the wake of *Minihane*. While case law has not moved in that direction, the author's arguments merit serious consideration, especially when acceleration

clauses in leases or licenses allow a lessor or licensor to collect double, or nearly double the original expectation interest. Advocates might press the point in an attempt to limit the effect of *Minihane* when evidence of loss avoided, or cavalier rejection of attempts to avoid reletting are provable. The Supreme Judicial Court might consider carving out an exception to the ironclad rule that a valid liquidated damages clause precludes evidence of mitigation, thereby protecting the compensatory principle. Counselors representing lessees might consider negotiating for indemnification clauses that cover rent owing on lessee's default, the lessor's rent lost before mitigation was possible, and finally, the difference between the contracted-for rent in the breached lease and the rent either agreed-upon in a mitigating lease, or available in the market a stipulated time after the lessee's breach. The third item would be (in legal effect) a formula for liquidating future damages, one that should survive scrutiny and would require some limited factfinding. Making the future damages "liquidated by agreement" would avoid the harsh result for the lessor made evident in *275 Washington Street Corp.,* and at the same time would protect the lessee. Were such combinations of indemnification and liquidated damages to come before the appellate courts, one would hope that the courts would approve them inasmuch as they would certainly be reasonable estimates of damages likely to be suffered, would contractually give lessors meaningful protection hard to achieve by indemnification agreements alone, and would give a lessee reasonable protection not now available under acceleration clauses in light of *Minihane.*

§ 12.3   A PROPOSAL FOR AN IMPOSED LIMITATION ON ACCELERATION CLAUSES IN LEASES AND LICENSES

In light of our case law, the choice that seems most viable is to fix a limit for acceleration clauses agreed upon as liquidated damages. I have argued for a percentage limit on liquidated damages clauses in purchase and sale agreements. *See Law of Liquidated Damages in Massachusetts,* § 9.2 (MCLE, Inc. 2013). There should be a corresponding reasonable limit on the length of time allowable for acceleration clauses designated as liquidated damages. This is precisely what Congress accomplished to protect creditors in bankruptcy cases. 11 U.S.C. § 502(b)(6). The question then becomes: What is a reasonable limit?

In her opinion in *Admetric*, Chief Judge Feeney compared the 5 percent deposit approved in *Kelly v. Marx* with the percentage claimed by Cummings pursuant to its lease, and noted that the percentage claimed was "far higher than that considered by the court in *Marx.*" *In re Admetric Biochem, Inc.*, 284 B.R. at 9. The correctness of her observation seems indisputable, but it is proves unsatisfactory to borrow percentages allowable in sales contracts to govern acceleration clauses in lease agreements.

§ 12.3.1 Sales versus Leases: Critical Distinctions

A comparison between a sale and a lease will make the point. Assume parties enter into a contract for the purchase and sale of a commercial building for $1,000,000 with a 5 percent ($50,000) deposit designated as liquidated damages. Unless the relevant market drops precipitously, the seller will probably fare reasonably well on retaining the deposit if the buyer defaults. On the other hand, assume a commercial property is leased for five years (sixty months) for a total rent of $1,000,000 which breaks down to $200,000 annually ($16,666.00) monthly. Assume the same 5 percent of the lessee's total consideration ($50,000) is stipulated as liquidated damages, as opposed to an acceleration clause for the rent remaining for the term at the time of breach. If the lessee defaults after two years, having paid $400,000, and the lessor can relet within three months or less, with no substantial additional expenses, the $50,000 will more or less cover the damages. In *Admetric,* four months accelerated rent may have been a realistic award, considering market demand and the undisputed evidence of a reletting at a higher rent. But, if markets for rental space have gone sour, and reletting takes longer, or reletting is only possible at a reduced rent, or if substantial renovations are required to relet at a comparable rent, the 5 percent will prove to be unrealistic.

The need for higher liquidated damages provisions in leases, as opposed to sales, is grounded in the nature of the lease transaction. Unless a seller acts as a lender, a seller obtains the consideration for the sale on closing. A lease is not, in the normal course, structured for the lessor to recoup during the lease term the whole of the lessor's investment in the property. On the contrary, the lessor must assume there will be value in the reversionary interest in the property, and must often take account of upstream obligations, including obligations to lenders, during and after the lease term. While a sale of real estate commonly rests upon an assumption that the seller will pay creditors from the sale proceeds, rent from a lease may be calculated to make minor indents in a lessor's long-term obligations, leaving the lessor vulnerable to creditors' claims if there is a lengthy period without expected (contracted for) occupancy. Taking account of the legitimate interests of lessors, and their creditors, a rule must be sought that will simultaneously honor the compensatory principle and protect lessors.

In *Admetric,* Judge Feeney was searching for such a principle, and excoriated Cummings's lawyers for not assisting her in finding one:

Cummings, in response to the Trustee's arguments, failed to submit evidence of the turnaround time for leasing vacant space. Cummings did not attribute its 10% vacancy rate to defaults by tenants, and the vacant space in its real estate portfolio could be attributable to space available as a result of the expiration of leases at the end of their fixed terms, as well as space available as a result of defaults by tenants. *A reasonable estimate of Cummings' damages could be and should have been tied to the average time it takes Cummings to relet space after it becomes available.* While Cummings may always have a vacancy rate of about 10%, a realistic estimate of its damages would be tied to the amount of time that space, comparable to the space occupied by Admetric, remained vacant and the average rent per square foot attributable to that space. The Court finds it highly unlikely that any particular rental space managed by Cummings remains vacant for three or four years at a stretch, which is the assumption implicit in the accelerated rent/liquidated damages provision.

In re Admetric Biochem, Inc., 284 B.R. at 8–9 (emphasis added).

Judge Feeney was suggesting, perhaps, that for an acceleration clause to be a valid ex ante estimation of probable damages, it should be tailor-made. Indeed, requiring a process of honest deliberation about probable damages after breach might produce honest and reliable estimates of future losses. But, making enforcement contingent upon evidence of such a process invites litigation about the process behind the clause. Given the reality of form lease agreements proffered by lessors, evidence about the agreement process would not likely establish much more than an awareness of clauses to which lessees acquiesce. There is a need for a norm as to what is reasonable for acceleration clauses in commercial leases. It would be advisable if the norm were legislatively fixed after factfinding, which should include the views of economists familiar with this sector of the economy. In the absence of any limits legislatively set, it would be advisable for the Supreme Judicial Court to remand an appropriate case to a trial court for factfinding to fix a reasonable limit for acceleration clauses for commercial leases. There may well be justifications for treating residential leases differently, though the proposal herein contained would probably be workable for residential as well as commercial leases.

§ 12.3.2 Establishing a Baseline: A Modest Proposal

Fixing a baseline is a vexing problem. The case law does not provide data from which a reasonable baseline can be derived. The Bankruptcy Code formula was designed for nationwide applicability to protect creditors, not as a solution to a local problem about acceleration clauses agreed upon as liquidated damages. It would be preferable if persons trained in accounting and economics would be involved in forging a good baseline rule, sufficient to minimally protect lessors while preventing overreaching against lessees. Nonetheless, taking into account the formula from 11 U.S.C. § 502(b)(6), in the absence of state legislative intervention, a judicially imposed rule such as the following would probably be workable: on a lessee's default, a lessor should be allowed accelerated rent for the remainder of the lease term, limited to a maximum of 20 percent of the lease term, or one year, whichever is shorter. On a ten-year lease (120 months), 20 percent would be twenty-four months, so liquidated damages would be limited to one year's accelerated rent. On a five-year lease (sixty months), 20 percent would be twelve months, so again there would be the one-year limit. On a three year lease (thirty-six months), the liquidated damages allowed under an acceleration clause would be limited to 20 percent or rent for 7.2 months. On a two-year lease (twenty-four months), the limit would be rent for 4.8 months, assuming that many unpaid months were left on the lease. On a one-year lease, 20 percent would allow a lessor a maximum of accelerated rent for 2.4 months.

§ 12.3.3 Balancing the Equities

To some, this might seem unduly generous to lessors, to others, too stingy. It would seem harsh if applied to the facts underlying *Cummings Properties, LLC v. National Communications Corporation. See Cummings Props., LLC v. Nat'l Communications Corp.*, 869 N.E. 2d 617 (Mass. 2007). When the lessee defaulted in August 2003, there were thirty-two months remaining on the five-year lease. The accelerated rent ultimately allowed by the Supreme Judicial Court amounted to $525,000 (rounded), more than 50 percent of the rent calculated for a full five-year term. If a 20 percent/one-year limit had been imposed, the lessor would have been limited to about $197,112. That may seem harsh for the lessor; indeed, the justice of this limit presumes that within that time period Cummings, or any lessor similarly situated, could have relet the space at a reasonable rent, or used the space constructively for some other purpose. Given the fact that a district judge computed actual damages at $492,000, a one-year limit would seem unfair to the lessor; but then again, it is not clear how mitigation figured into the computation. See *Cummings Properties, LLC v. National Communications Corporation*, 449 Mass. 490, 493 (2007), for Justice Cordy's explanation for the computation. It seems plain that any limit fixed will be deemed unfair by some lessors. Yet it is advisable and necessary to develop some rational norm around which lessors and lessees can draft and plan in order to take the hard edge off of awards that either dishonor the compensatory principle or discourage mitigation, or both. Fixing a rational norm would provide guidance to scriveners laboring to draft acceleration clauses that would survive serious judicial scrutiny. An accepted norm would serve as a self-evident motivation for mitigation in cases involving commercial leases. Clauses drafted to fit into an established norm should be routinely enforced. If clauses honoring an established norm were enforced in the normal course, drafters would be motivated to redraft leases and licenses to conform to the norm. If such a norm caused slight rent increases, so be it. Without some norm to limit the damages collectible under acceleration clauses, the law will serve as a springboard for routine offenses against the compensatory principle and will provide no incentive for mitigation by prudent efforts to make use of vacant properties.

Practice Note

It may also be prudent for the Supreme Judicial Court to approve of acceleration clauses of unlimited length, if such clauses contain a built-in reduction of the lessee's liability with reference to income from a reletting. This would not solve the problem made evident in *Panagakos v. Collins*, where the lessor refused to use reasonable efforts to mitigate, but it would preclude collection of both accelerated rents and equal or greater amounts on a reletting. Any clause allowing for a reduction of accelerated rents by the lessor's gain from a reletting (with adjustments for the lessor's costs of reletting, if any) should be given judicial approval. The formula would demonstrate a good-faith attempt ex ante to measure damages likely to be incurred with a much greater degree of refinement than an acceleration clause without any recognition of avoidable damages due to a reletting.

§ 12.4   WHAT SHOULD HAPPEN WHEN ACCELERATION CLAUSES EXCEED AN ESTABLISHED NORM?

If the stipulated damages in any lease or license, computed under an acceleration clause, were found to outrun any hereafter established norm, and litigation ensued, the trial judge should be empowered to have a second look because acceleration clauses outside of any norm (such as one year or 20 percent) might well be justified in rare cases. If a clause outran the accepted norm, the burden should be shifted to the lessor trying to enforce the clause. The lessor should be required to establish:

- that the clause was knowingly agreed upon;

- that particular circumstances justified a departure from the norm when the contract was made;

- that the lessor suffered a net economic loss attributable to the lessee's breach; and

- that the accelerated rent is not grossly disproportionate to the raw actual damages flowing from the lessee's breach.

Factors involved in proving that a clause was knowingly agreed upon were discussed earlier. *See Law of Liquidated Damages in Massachusetts* ch. 9 (MCLE, Inc. 2013). As to the second requirement, at least two circumstances would justify an exception to any norm established: cases where a lessee is an anchor tenant and cases wherein a lessor makes substantial renovations or modifications requiring significant outlays in order to meet the needs of a particular lessee. Both situations are illustrated in *Kimco of New England, Inc. v. Cliftex Corp.*, 1998 WL 409003, relied upon by Cummings's lawyer in making a claim in the Bankruptcy Court against Admetric. *See In re Admetric Biochem, Inc.*, 284 B.R. at 9.

Cliftex (lessee) entered into leases for retail space with two different lessors. Both leases had acceleration clauses. The first lease was made with Rockingham 620, Inc. (Rockingham) for 3,600 square feet in the Rockingham Mall for a term of approximately five years. The second lease was made with Kimco of New England, Inc. (Kimco) for space in the Searstown Mall. The term was slightly under eleven years. Business did not go well for Cliftex, so its agents gave notice of intent to vacate the stores leased in both locations. Cliftex ceased operations and vacated both stores in January, 1997. Both lessors commenced summary eviction proceedings, which resulted in settlements by the terms of which Cliftex acknowledged termination and agreed to the lessors' retaking of the premises. Both lessors demanded liquidated damages under acceleration clauses allowing unpaid rent for the remaining terms of the leases. Cliftex objected, contending that the acceleration clauses constituted penalties.

A Superior Court Judge determined that the acceleration clauses were enforceable and granted summary judgment for the lessors accordingly, thereby allowing accelerated rent for more than eight years on the Searstown Mall lease and for more than three years on the Rockingham Mall lease. Needless to say, these awards far exceed what would have been computed with a 20 percent or one-year cap on accelerated rent, as suggested above. Yet the awards may have been justified on the facts of these cases. As the motion judge, Judge Fremont-Smith stated:

> In the case at bar, both at the time of contracting and
> at the time of defendant's default, it was difficult or
> impossible for the parties to forecast reasonably the
> amount of actual damages which would be sustained
> by the plaintiffs as a result of a default. Not only had
> Kimco refurbished the Searstown Store for $105,576
> for Cliftex before it took possession, but stores in a
> shopping mall are interdependent for profitability, so
> that the vacancy of one store may be expected to af-
> fect the profitability of other stores in the mall and the
> amount of rental income to the plaintiffs from those
> stores.

Kimco of New England, Inc. v. Cliftex Corp., 1998 WL 409003 (Mass. Superior).

The reasoning is sound: either a lessor's investments to modify space for a particular tenant or the interdependency of tenants, as in a shopping mall, or a combination of such circumstances, can justify stipulated damages well beyond one
year's accelerated rent. An exception to any norm adopted is justified in such
circumstances because lessors would find it practically difficult, or impossible,
to compute consequential damages either at the time of contracting or the time
of breach. The remaining criterion, proportionality, is a matter bound to be deli-
cate when actual damages are especially difficult to prove. A trial judge should
only demand a good-faith showing that the accelerated sums are not grossly
disproportionate to raw actual damages.

The analytical pathway suggested for evaluating acceleration clauses beyond
established norms for leases and licenses would allow not only a second look in
some cases, but also would allow evidence of what might constitute mitigating
events, or a failure to mitigate. The objection will be that *Minihane* proscribes
evidence of mitigation, hence, any second look exceptions undercut *Minihane*.
But, evidence is commonly allowable for one purpose, not for another. There is a
way of considering postbreach evidence of economic consequences apart from
using it to show mitigation or the absence of reasonable efforts to mitigate. Rather, postbreach evidence of actual consequences should be allowable simply to
test the reasonableness of that upon which the parties agreed, when agreements
outrun a norm. Without allowing evidence of real consequences, in cases where
a particular scrutiny is warranted, a meaningful judicial review is difficult to
envision.

Finally, perhaps controversially, damages awards based upon acceleration clauses should be reduced to present value. This was done by the trial judge in awarding future lost rents in *275 Washington Street Corp. v. Hudson River International, LLC,* 81 Mass. App. Ct. 418, 419 n.4 (Mass. App. 2012). The case was

reversed on appeal because under the case law the lessor was required to wait until the end of the lease term to compute damages, but there was no negative comment on reduction of future damages to present value. There is no sound reason for allowing accelerated rent on a long-term lease without a reduction to present value; the lessor would not have had use of the money until it was paid had the lease not been breached.

CHAPTER 13

What's at Stake? A Collision of Jurisprudential Views

Gary L. Monserud, Esq.
New England Law | Boston

§ 13.1   Introduction 13–1

§ 13.2   Judge Richard Posner and His Views on Liquidated
         Damages Clauses 13–2

§ 13.3   Professor Melvin Eisenberg: The Limits of Cognition
         and the Relevance of Those Limits to Liquidated
         Damages Clauses 13–4

§ 13.4   The Relevance of the Limits of Human Cognition
         to Liquidated Damages Clauses 13–7

CHAPTER 13

What's at Stake? A Collision of Jurisprudential Views

Gary L. Monserud, Esq.
New England Law | Boston

Scope Note

This chapter sharpens up the issues surrounding the judiciary's role in policing clauses where damages are stipulated. It presents two opposing principles, judicial deference to stipulated damages clauses versus judicial scrutiny of such clauses in the interest of protecting the compensatory principle.

§ 13.1   INTRODUCTION

In our era there are many conflicting jurisprudential views. The law of liquidated damages is one arena in which a clash of jurisprudential views is being played out in Massachusetts and elsewhere. What is at stake is the role of the judiciary in policing clauses where damages are stipulated in advance. One view is represented by the thinking of Judge Richard Posner of the Seventh Circuit. This view is libertarian and was adopted—or at least given some weight—in Justice Cordy's opinion in *Cummings Properties, LLC v. National Communications Corp.*, 449 Mass. 490 (Mass. 2007). According to this view, courts should defer to the agreements of the parties as to stipulated damages, much as the courts should respect any other clauses agreed upon. A competing view favors a close and continuing judicial scrutiny of stipulated damages clauses in order to guard the compensatory principle. This view underlay the result in *Perroncello v. Donahue*. A chief proponent of continuing judicial scrutiny of liquidated damages clauses is Professor Melvin Eisenberg, University of California, Berkeley, who has written extensively on current issues in Contracts law.

§ 13.2   JUDGE RICHARD POSNER AND HIS VIEWS ON LIQUIDATED DAMAGES CLAUSES

At this point, with jurisprudential concerns in mind, I want to recall a few points from Justice Cordy's analysis in *Cummings*, noting especially his favorable reference to Judge Posner's views. Justice Cordy began with the baseline rule "that a contract provision clearly and reasonably establishing liquidated damages should be enforced so long as it is not so disproportionate to anticipated damages as to constitute a penalty." *Cummings Props., LLC v. Nat'l Communications Corp.*, 449 Mass. at 494 (citing *Tal Fin. Corp. v. CSC Consulting, Inc.*, 446 Mass. 422 (2006)). He then moved to the doctrine that a rent acceleration clause "may constitute an enforceable liquidated damages provision so long as it is not a penalty," citing *Commissioner of Insurance* and three appellate opinions from neighboring jurisdictions. *See Comm'r of Ins. v. Mass. Accident Co.*, 499 Mass. at 495 (1942). *See also Ganary v. Linker Realty Corp.*, 131 N.J.L. 317, 36 A2d 405 (1944); *Fifty States Mgmt. Corp. v. Pioneer Auto Parks, Inc.*, 46 N.Y. 2d 573, 389 N.E.2d 113 (1979); *Pierce v. Hoffstot*, 211 Pa. Super. 380, 236 A.2d 828 (1967). Justice Cordy next turned to Cummings's appeal which "urges us to update our jurisprudence in light of the near unanimous trend toward upholding liquidated damages clauses in agreements between sophisticated parties, and to adopt a presumption against interpreting such clauses as penalties." *Cummings Props., LLC v. Nat'l Communications Corp.*, 449 Mass. at 495.

The invitation to adopt a presumption was unnecessary, for in fixing the burden of proof, the court had already adopted a presumption of enforceability in *TAL Financial. Corp.* In any event, Cummings's urging went beyond a quest for a presumption; it was a request for a hands-off approach when parties are sophisticated. Justice Cordy's opinion indicates a favorable view of Cummings's request: "[w]e agree that '[t]he rule against penalty clauses, though it lingers, has come to seem rather an anachronism, especially in cases in which commercial enterprises are on both sides of the contract.'" *Cummings Props., LLC v. Nat'l Communications Corp.*, 449 Mass. at 495 (quoting *XCO Int'l, Inc. v. Pac. Scientific Co.*, 369 F.3d 998, 1002 (7th Cir. 2004)). The case citations underpinning this viewpoint began with *XCO International, Inc. v. Pacific Scientific Co.*, a case whose opinion was authored by Judge Posner.

Judge Posner's opinion in *XCO International* is a mini-treatise on liquidated damages. XCO International assigned certain U.S. and foreign (mainly European) patents to Pacific Scientific (PacSci) for a consideration. The agreement provided that PacSci "would be 'responsible for all expenses of any kind relating to' the patent rights that it was buying, including the fees charged by European patent authorities to maintain patents in effect." *XCO Int'l, Inc. v. Pac. Scientific Co.*, 369 F.3d at 999. PacSci defaulted on its obligation to maintain the patents, letting some lapse. XCO declared breach and terminated the contract (as it was allowed to do) and then sought the lump sum of $100,000 per year as liquidated damages under the terms of the agreement. A federal district judge in Illinois refused to enforce the liquidated damages clause.

On appeal, one of PacSci's main arguments against enforcement was that the clause failed "to differentiate between different *kinds* of breach, some more serious than others. . . ." *XCO Int'l, Inc. v. Pac. Scientific Co.*, 369 F.3d at 1004. This was the argument rejected in *Cummings*. In *XCO*, Judge Posner took that argument seriously, *see XCO Int'l, Inc. v. Pac. Scientific Co.*, 369 F.3d at 1004, but rejected it, displaying a willingness to *reform the clause*, if necessary, to salvage it. (See *XCO International, Inc. v. Pacific Scientific Co.*, 369 F.3d at 1004 for Judge Posner's full explanation.) This willingness to intervene in order to salvage a stipulated damages clause derives from Judge Posner's deep suspicion of using judicial power to invalidate such clauses as his opinion in XCO International makes clear:

> Yet it is the rule of the common law of contracts, in Illinois as elsewhere, that unless the parties' ex ante estimate of damages is reasonable, their liquidated damages provision is unenforceable, as constituting a penalty tending to "force" performance. [citations omitted] The reason for the rule is mysterious; it is one of the abiding mysteries of the common law. At least in a case such as this, where both parties are substantial commercial enterprises . . . and where damages are liquidated for breach by either party, making an inference of fraud or duress implausible, it is difficult to see why the law should take an interest in whether the estimate of harm underlying the liquidation of damages is reasonable. *Courts don't review other provisions of contracts for reasonableness; why this one?*

XCO Int'l, Inc. v. Pac. Scientific Co., 369 F.3d at 1001 (emphasis added).

This is Judge Posner's view in a nutshell: that stipulated damages clauses should be not be given any more rigorous examination than any other contract terms agreed upon, especially if agreed upon by sophisticated parties (although, in all fairness Judge Posner does leave room for special scrutiny in some consumer cases, *see XCO Int'l, Inc. v. Pac. Scientific Co.*, 369 F.3d at 1002). This is the jurisprudential viewpoint to which the law of Massachusetts is linked through Justice Cordy's opinion in *Cummings*. This sharpens up the issue: is there a sound reason for courts in the absence of any blameworthy behavior to scrutinize clauses for stipulated damages more closely than other clauses freely agreed upon? There is an answer to this question, and it is anchored in recent scholarship that bridges the gap between social sciences and contract law.

§ 13.3   PROFESSOR MELVIN EISENBERG: THE LIMITS OF COGNITION AND THE RELEVANCE OF THOSE LIMITS TO LIQUIDATED DAMAGES CLAUSES

Professor Melvin Eisenberg has sought to bridge the gap between contract law and current findings in the psychology of human cognition. An article that directly addresses this point is entitled "The Limits of Cognition and the Limits of Contract," published in the *Stanford Law Review* in 1995. *See also* Melvin Aron Eisenberg, "The Emergence of Dynamic Contract Law," 88 *Cal. L. Rev.* 1743, 1783–90 (Dec. 2000). My review will of necessity be abbreviated, but since he hones in on liquidated damages clauses and the limits of cognition, some minimal understanding of his thinking seems imperative.

Professor Eisenberg begins with a recognition of what he terms the *bargain principle*, meaning the foundational principle of contract law that "bargains are enforced according to their terms." Melvin Eisenberg, "The Limits of Cognition and the Limits of Contract," 47 *Stan. L. Rev.* at 211 n.1. A set of social propositions underlie our general acceptance of the bargain principle: enforcing bargains enables people to plan their futures, allocates resources to their highest-valued use, and facilitates the creation of whatever is valued by bargaining parties. Many of the rules of contract law advance the making and enforcement of bargains. On the other hand, there are exceptions to the bargain principle, many grounded in blameworthy behavior, such as duress, misrepresentation, and unconscionability. There are other exceptions to the bargain principle, not grounded in blameworthy behavior, but rather in *presumed limits of human cognition.* Infants are presumed to have limited intellectual capacities; hence, there is a body of law allowing disaffirmation by persons who have not attained the age of majority. *See, e.g., Restatement (Second) of the Law of Contracts* § 14. Similarly, persons with mental deficits or illnesses may in some circumstances avoid bargains under recognized cognitive or volitional tests. *See, e.g., Restatement (Second) of the Law of Contracts* § 15. From these doctrines, wherein presumed limits on capacity are explicitly acknowledged, Professor Eisenberg asserts that other doctrines limiting the bargain principle are best understood as being *implicitly based* on the limits of human cognition. The rules surrounding stipulated damages are best understood as implicitly based on such limits.

The limits of human cognition in the bargain context are rooted in the fact that a bargain arises from one or more promises. A promise is a manifestation of an intention to act, or to refrain from acting, at some point in the future. *See, e.g., Restatement (Second) of the Law of Contracts* § 2. The future is uncertain. Therefore, the act of committing to do or not to do anything in the future necessarily involves some level of uncertainty. *See* Melvin Eisenberg, "The Limits of Cognition and the Limits of Contract," 47 *Stan. L. Rev.* at 213. Rational choices require evaluations of probabilities in the midst of uncertainties. The costs of researching and processing information about all of the probabilities bearing upon promises is generally beyond the reach of bargaining parties; consequently, "human rationality is normally bounded by limited information and limited information processing. Actors normally do not try to make optimal substantive decisions, but only satisfactory substantive decisions." Melvin Eisenberg, "The Limits of Cognition and the Limits of Contract," 47 *Stan. L. Rev.* at 214. Thus, actors (promisors) operate with a *bounded rationality*, meaning "that actors will adopt selective research and processing procedures." Melvin Eisenberg, "The Limits of Cognition and the Limits of Contract," 47 *Stan. L. Rev.* at 214. The concept of bounded rationality does not imply that actors with less than complete information or information processing uniformly tend to make irrational decisions, but according to Professor Eisenberg, "two bodies of empirical evidence show that under certain circumstances, actors are often systematically irrational; that is, they fail to make rational decisions even within the bounds of the information they have acquired." Melvin Eisenberg, "The Limits of Cognition and the Limits of Contract," 47 *Stan. L. Rev.* at 216.

The first body of empirical research to which he refers shows that as a systematic matter, people tend to be unrealistically optimistic. Many examples he cites from research are comical. For example, nearly 90 percent of drivers believe they drive better than average. *See* Melvin Eisenberg, "The Limits of Cognition and the Limits of Contract," 47 *Stan. L. Rev.* at 216. Similarly, peoples' estimates of their own chances for personal and professional success tend to be wildly optimistic. *See* 47 *Stan. L. Rev.* at 217. In one survey, although persons about to be married correctly estimated the divorce rate at 50 percent, respondents tended to rate their own chance of divorce as zero. *See* 47 *Stan. L. Rev.* at 217. The data suggests that an amazingly positive view of the future dominates most people's mental lives. Perhaps this bodes well for our mental health and survival. On the other hand, unrealistic optimism does not bode well for rational decision making. Irrational optimism, however, is not Professor Eisenberg's major point of concern. Rather, he focuses upon certain ingrained and demonstrable defects in decision making and concludes: "in the last thirty years cognitive psychology has established that real people use certain decisionmaking rules (heuristics) that yield systematic errors, and that other aspects of actors' cognitive capabilities are also systematically defective." Melvin Eisenberg, "The Limits of Cognition and the Limits of Contract," 47 *Stan. L. Rev.* at 218.

For example, there is the concept of *invariance*, meaning that a decision maker's preference between two possibilities should not depend on how the choice is framed. Yet surveys show that the framing of questions tends to be outcome-determinative, meaning that sophisticated and naive persons alike make irrational choices based upon the manner in which choices are presented. *See* 47 *Stan. L. Rev.* at 218–19. More importantly for contract law, Professor Eisenberg examines four systematic defects on capability that have effects on contract law, namely: "defects associated with the heuristics known as availability and representativeness, defective telescopic faculties, and defective risk assessment faculties." *See* 47 *Stan. L. Rev.* at 221. The heuristic (decision-making rule) known as availability means that when any actor must make a decision that requires a judgment about the future, he or she judges probabilities on the basis of data and scenarios *immediately available in memory or imagination.* This heuristic leads necessarily to systematic biases as to the database. Closely related is the heuristic of representativeness, meaning actors seldom collect all relevant data; rather, "they usually make decisions on the basis of some subset of the data that they judge to be representative." *See* 47 *Stan. L. Rev.* at 222. The phenomenon of faulty telescopic faculties means that "[a]ctors systematically give too little weight to future benefits and costs compared to present benefits and costs." *See* 47 *Stan. L. Rev.* at 222. As the term implies, "faulty risk estimate faculties" means simply that actors are disinclined to think about or take seriously low-probability hazards, a factor that relates to the widespread tendency toward unjustified optimism about personal and business success. In conclusion, Professor Eisenberg writes:

> The defects in cognition discussed above are closely related and interactive. For example, people may underweigh future costs in part because the future involves a great number of risks, and actors underestimate risks, and in part because the present is vivid, concrete, and instantiated, while the future is pallid, abstract, and general. Conversely, people may underestimate risks in part because risks are often pallid, abstract, and general, and in part because risks relate to the future, and actors give too little weight to future costs.
>
> These defects in cognition are also closely related to and interact with the dispositional problem of unrealistic optimism: If actors are unrealistically optimistic, they will systematically underestimate risks. If actors

systematically underestimate risks, they will be unrealistically optimistic.

Melvin Eisenberg, "The Limits of Cognition and the Limits of Contract," 47
Stan. L. Rev. at 224.

§ 13.4 THE RELEVANCE OF THE LIMITS OF HUMAN COGNITION TO LIQUIDATED DAMAGES CLAUSES

Having identified limits of cognition as demonstrated in recent research, Professor Eisenberg moves on to show the application of these insights to discrete are-
as of contract law, the first of which is liquidated damages law. *See* 47 *Stan. L.
Rev.* at 224. He begins with the observation that liquidated damages clauses have
generally been reviewed with special scrutiny, and generally have not been enforceable in the same way most bargained-for terms are enforceable. He
acknowledges criticism of this special scrutiny, citing Judge Posner's critique in
Lake River Corp. v. Carborundum Co. See 47 *Stan. L. Rev.* at 226 (citing *Lake
River Corp. v. Carborundum Co.*, 769 F. 2d 1284 (7th Cir. 1985)). In criticizing
the special treatment afforded liquidated damages clauses, Judge Posner, and
others, assume that the special treatment of stipulated damages clauses has been
justified because such clauses present a special potential for blameworthy exploitation. The critics assume, therefore, that if the likelihood of exploitation can
be diminished or eliminated, any justification for special scrutiny will likewise
be gone. While acknowledging that courts have sometimes used rhetoric that
justifies this critique, Professor Eisenberg succinctly responds: "In fact, however,
the justification for the special scrutiny is not that liquidated damages provisions
are specially amenable to advantage taking and oppression, but that such provisions *are systematically more likely to be the products of limits of cognition than
performance terms, that is terms that specify the performance each party is to
render.*" Melvin Eisenberg, "The Limits of Cognition and the Limits of Contract,"
47 *Stan. L. Rev.* at 226 (emphasis added).

He then gives two examples from case law. The first is the famous English case
Kemble v. Farren, wherein the performer and her employer agreed upon contract
terms spelled out in great detail, and at the end of the written agreement provided that for any failure to fulfill the agreement, or any part thereof, the party in
breach would owe the other 1,000 pounds. *See* 47 *Stan. L. Rev.* at 228 (citing
Kemble v. Farren, 19 Eng. Rep. 71 (C.P. 1829)). The court determined that the
clause was not enforceable, viewing it as a penalty if applied to minor breaches,
as it by its terms could be applied. Professor Eisenberg does not take issue with
the holding but offers an explanation not enunciated by the court, namely, "it is

almost certain that as a result of the limits of cognition, the parties failed to think through the scenarios under which the provisions would apply." Melvin Eisenberg, "The Limits of Cognition and the Limits of Contract," 47 *Stan. L. Rev.* at 229. He persuasively makes a similar claim about the parties' liquidated damages clause, struck down in *Lake River Corp. See* 47 *Stan. L. Rev.* at 229. Thus, the longstanding judicial practice of scrutinizing liquidated damages more carefully than a court would scrutinize considerations exchanged *is justified on the basis of cognitive psychology.*

Examining both the single look and second look rules, Professor Eisenberg comes down firmly in favor of an after-the-breach look as being more consistent with what is known about the limits of cognition than is the single look rule. His recommendation in summary form is:

> Under the cognitive approach to the liquidated damages principle, therefore, courts should formulate and apply the principle as follows: If, in the breach scenario that has actually occurred, liquidated damages are significantly disproportional to real losses (that is, losses in fact, not simply legal damages), the provision is unenforceable unless it is established that the parties had a specific and well-thought-through intention that the provision apply in a scenario like the one that actually occurred.

Melvin Eisenberg, "The Limits of Cognition and the Limits of Contract," 47 *Stan. L. Rev.* at 234–35.

Due to limits of cognition as well-established by research, Professor Eisenberg advises that the parties' intent should be regarded as immaterial, and that the difficulty of estimating damages at the time of formation should be discarded, but that "courts should normally take a less searching look at liquidated damages provisions that take the form of an advance deposit." Melvin Eisenberg, "The Limits of Cognition and the Limits of Contract," 47 *Stan. L. Rev.* at 235. Deposits by their very nature do not involve cognitional problems to the same extent as other clauses, since the very act of putting down the money tends to focus the mind. *See* 47 *Stan. L. Rev.* at 235.

Winding up his case for a fresh approach to liquidated damages clauses in light of established limits of cognition, Professor Eisenberg concludes:

> The blameworthiness rationale of the liquidated damage principle is difficult to support. Because that rational is weak, if not incorrect, the case law is often

incoherent: Like cases are often decided differently, and results are often difficult to predict. The cognitive justification of the liquidated damages principle drives to the surface the real reason to give special scrutiny to liquidated damages provisions, and prescribes the form that scrutiny should take.

Melvin Eisenberg, "The Limits of Cognition and the Limits of Contract," 47 *Stan. L. Rev.* at 236.

I have included this excursus on cognitive limits, not to urge a wholesale adoption of Professor Eisenberg's approach in a manner that would override precedent in Massachusetts, but rather to justify limitations on the application of the single look rule adopted in *Kelly v. Marx and to justify the second look in exceptional situations.* I also aim to rebut the libertarian theory advanced by Judge Richard Posner which has been implicitly accepted—or at minimum given a favorable rating—in Massachusetts case law, particularly in *Cummings* when the single look rule was transferred from sales to leases. What Professor Eisenberg brings to the debate are insights about human cognition that sustain ancient wisdom: all persons, simple and sophisticated, can focus much more realistically upon performance obligations and expectations than upon the more distant consequences of possible breach. At the time of formation there are built-in cognitive limitations that tend to limit actors' (promisors') abilities rightly to judge what should be agreed upon as fair remedies in the event of breach. That being the case, there is a justification in cognitive psychology for imposed limits on stipulated damages clauses [plural] and for the second look in cases where sensible norms are ignored.

CHAPTER 14

The Challenge: Recharting the Law of Liquidated Damages in Massachusetts

Gary L. Monserud, Esq.
New England Law | Boston

§ 14.1   **Reflections on the Long History of Liquidated Damages in This Jurisdiction** 14–1

§ 14.2   **A Reasonable and Necessary Recharting of the Law** 14–3

The Challenge: Recharting the Law of Liquidated Damages in Massachusetts

Gary L. Monserud, Esq.
New England Law | Boston

Scope Note

Noting a need for limits on stipulated damages clauses in contracts for the sale of real estate, and limits on acceleration clauses in leases and licenses when these are designated as liquidated damages clauses, this chapter sums up the lessons to be gained from a study of history and recommends that the course of the law be recharted to protect the compensatory principle.

§ 14.1 REFLECTIONS ON THE LONG HISTORY OF LIQUIDATED DAMAGES IN THIS JURISDICTION

Sometimes it is prudent and appropriate simply to recall our legal history and to reflect upon it, as it may bear much wisdom from former generations. The law pertaining to liquidated damages in Massachusetts has deep roots in English law and equity wherein penal bonds were struck down when they offended the compensatory principle. The courts in England long divided valid liquidations of damages from penalty clauses, setting up contractual intent as the guide to deciding into which category any clause should fall. Throughout the nineteenth and well into the twentieth century the Massachusetts courts used contractual intent as the criterion for deciding whether or not stipulated damages clauses would be enforceable. Intent was *inferred* from circumstances, including observable consequences.

The *Restatement (First) of the Law of Contracts* abandoned contractual intent as a criterion, substituting instead a two-part inquiry to be made from the vantage point of formation. The courts in Massachusetts eventually adopted this approach. The first *Restatement* did not proscribe a second look in all cases, but allowed consideration of facts determinable postbreach for an assessment of whether or not the clause was mistakenly agreed upon, thereby allowing a second look in exceptional cases. Moreover, apart from the doctrine of mutual mistake, Professor Williston realized that in some cases postbreach facts could show the unreasonableness of an estimate at the time of contracting, and assumed courts would act in some cases on the basis of postbreach facts. *See Law of Liquidated Damages in Massachusetts* § 6.2 (MCLE, Inc. 2013) (citing Samuel Williston, *A Treatise on the Law of Contracts* (rev. ed. by Samuel Williston and George Thompson 1936)).

The *Restatement (Second) of Contracts* § 356 and its illustrations explicitly allow for a second look, with the objective of salvaging clauses that were ex ante unreasonable (but postbreach are reasonable) and to justify nonenforcement in extreme cases, such as cases where no damages whatever are attributable to a breach. After a ten-year flirtation with the second look approach approved by the Massachusetts Appeals Court in *Shapiro v. Grinspoon*, 27 Mass. App. Ct. 596 (1989), the Supreme Judicial Court in *Kelly v. Marx* adopted a single look rule, largely for reasons of policy, but acknowledged that excessive stipulated damages clauses would not be tolerated. The single look rule was transferred from sales to leases in *Cummings* and to licenses in *Minihane*, and in each case an acceleration clause for the entire agreed-upon payment for a term was allowed as liquidated damages based upon the single look rule and the allocation of the burden of proving the requisites of non-enforcement to the challenger. Through two centuries of case law, there was never any doubt that the courts should play a meaningful role in policing stipulated damages clauses.

In *Minihane*, the Supreme Judicial Court for the first time proscribed any inquiry into mitigation, or the possibilities of mitigation, when a clause is upheld using the single look rule. This proscription, combined with the single look rule, has allowed the courts to withdraw from the time-honored judicial role that has kept liquidated damages clauses within reason, namely, a reasonably rigorous scrutiny to prevent clauses from outrunning the compensatory principle. This withdrawal has recently proved to be especially problematic in cases arising from leases and licenses. We have arrived at a point where it is very difficult to prove the grounds for nonenforceability of an acceleration clause since the inquiries are limited to the vantage point of formation. Moreover, evidence that a lessor or licensor is making money on a substitute contract is not admissible. It is quite possible, therefore, for a lessor or licensor to wind up with double his or her expectancy from a bargain due to the effect of cases beginning with *Kelly v. Marx*. Through two centuries of case law in this Commonwealth, there was never any doubt that the courts should play a meaningful role in policing stipulated damages clauses. But, little by little, we have come full circle—back to the jurisprudence where penal bonds allowing double damages were routinely enforced—before the compensatory principle was used as a limitation of agreed-upon damages. We have come to a point where the compensatory principle is in danger of being eliminated because the courts have, step by step, significantly reduced their role in policing stipulated damages clauses; a responsibility that courts in this jurisdiction have assumed as far back as our legal history is reasonably traceable. The courts ought to take up the challenge of policing stipulated damages clauses as jurists so nobly did for two centuries.

§ 14.2   A REASONABLE AND NECESSARY RECHARTING OF THE LAW

It would be helpful if the legislature would set limits on stipulated damages clauses in contracts for the sale of real estate and would also establish limits on acceleration clauses in leases and licenses when these are designated as liquidated damages clauses. Assuming no legislative action, the Supreme Judicial Court should in appropriate cases consider recharting the course of the law. The Supreme Judicial Court might reasonably reevaluate the rule against mitigation evidence, which would require overruling or limiting a holding in *Minihane*. Alternatively, and less problematically, the Supreme Judicial Court could embrace the approach put forth in this book, requiring the single look rule in cases wherein sensible norms are not offended, and mandating a second look under a principled analytical pathway where stipulated damages clauses outrun an established norm.

The approach herein recommended is consistent with the long history of liquidated damages law in this Commonwealth, and is consistent with the insights on the limits of cognition established by cognitive psychology. Judge Posner has put forth his challenge: "[c]ourts don't review other provisions of contracts for reasonableness; why this one?" *XCO Int'l, Inc. v. Pac. Scientific Co.*, 369 F.3d 998, 1001 (7th Cir. 2004). The answer lies in recognizing the wisdom of past generations of jurists and in taking seriously the insights about human nature unearthed by cognitive psychology. Human cognition allows us to evaluate in a rational way the performances to be exchanged; but human cognition does not stretch to an equally rational evaluation of the consequences of breach. The limits on cognition pertain to the sophisticated as well as uninitiated. If the Supreme Judicial Court recharts the course for evaluating liquidated damages clauses in a principled way, in light of history and cognitive psychology, the compensatory principle will again serve its proper role, and the objectives of efficiency, predictability, and security will be advanced as well. A proper balance will have been restored.

TABLE OF CASES

References are to section numbers of this book, unless otherwise indicated.

A

Abrams v. Reynolds Metal Co., 9.1.2
Admetric Biochem, Inc., In re,
 11.3.4, 12.2.1, 12.3, 12.3.1, 12.4
Associated Hat Mfrs. v. Baird United
 Co., 6.2
Astley v. Weldon, 3.1, 10.1
Atkyns v. Kinnier, 4.2.2, 5.3.2
A-Z Servicecenter, Inc. v. Segall, 6.4,
 7.1.1, 7.1.2, 7.1.3, 7.1.5, 7.1.7,
 7.2, 8.1, 8.2, 9.3, 9.3.3, 10.1

B

Banta v. Stamford Motor Co., 6.2
Barell, Ex parte, 5.3.1
Barrie School v. Patch, 10.4
Beck v. Doore, 5.3.3, 9.1.8
Berger v. Victory Realty Trust, 5.3.4

C

Cady v. IMC Mtge. Co., 10.4
Chaffin v. Ramsey, 8.3
Chamberlain Livestock Auction, Inc.
 v. Penner, 8.3
Chase v. Allen, 2.2, 4.2.3, 8.2
Chisholm v. Reitler, 8.3
Clampit v. A.M.R. Corp., 8.3
Coldwell Banker v. Meide & Son,
 Inc., 9.2
Colonial at Lynnfield, Inc. v. Sloan,
 6.3, 7.1.5, 7.1.6, 7.1.7, 7.2, 8.3,
 9.1.4, 9.2, 9.3, 9.3.1, 9.3.2, 9.3.3
Commissioner of Insurance v.
 Massachusetts Accident Co.,
 6.4, 7.1.1, 10.1, 10.2, 10.3, 13.2
Connihan v. Thompson, 8.3

Consumers' Action Network, Inc. v.
 AT&T Broadband of S.
 California, 9.2
Courogenis v. Kerr, 5.2.4
Cummings Props., LLC v. Empire
 Techs., Inc., 10.2, 10.3
Cummings Props., LLC v. National
 Communications Corp., 1.1,
 1.2.4, 1.2.5, 1.3.1, 10.3, 10.4,
 11.1, 11.2.1, 11.2.2, 11.2.3,
 11.2.5, 11.2.6, 11.2.7, 11.3.3,
 11.3.5, 12.3.3, 13.1, 13.2
Curtis v. Brewer, 4.1.1, 4.1.2
Cushing v. Drew, 3.2.4

D

Davis-Hill Co., Inc. v. Wells, 5.2.4
Dean v. Connecticut Tobacco Corp.,
 6.2
De Cordova v. Weeks, 7.1.1, 10.1
Depree v. Bedborough, 5.3.1
Devore v. Good, 5.3.4
DiBella v. Fiumara, 10.1
Donaghue v. Parkman, 5.3.1
Dubinsky v. Wells Bros. Co. of N.Y.,
 5.2.3

F

Factory Realty Corp. v. Corbin-
 Holmes Shoe Co., 1.1
Fifty States Mgmt. Corp. v. Pioneer
 Auto Parks, Inc., 13.2
Fisher v. Schmeling, 9.2
Fisk v. Gray, 2.2, 4.2.2, 6.4, 7.1.1, 10.1

G

Ganary v. Linker Realty Corp., 13.2

Garcin v. Pennsylvania Furnace Co.,
5.2.1, 5.3.1
Gardiner v. Parsons, 11.2.5
Garst v. Harris, 4.2.3, 4.2.4, 5.2.1,
5.3.2, 6.4, 7.1.1
Greenfield Country Estates Tenants
Assn., Inc. v. Deep, 9.1.2
Guerin v. Stacey, 1.3.1, 2.2, 4.2.2,
4.2.3, 4.2.4, 5.2.1, 5.3.2, 7.1.4

H

Hall v. Middleby, 5.2.4
Hastings Assocs., Inc. v. Local 369
Bldg. Fund, Inc., 8.3
Heard v. Bowers, 3.1
Hegner v. Reed, 9.2
Henry v. Davis, 2.2
Higginson v. Weld, 4.1.2, 10.1
Honey Dew Assocs., Inc. v. M & K
Food Corp., 8.3
Howe v. Smith, 5.3.1
Humphrey v. Byron, 11.2.5

I

Illingsworth v. Bushong, 8.3
International Paper Co. v. Priscilla
Co., 7.1.1

J

Jaquith v. Hudson, 1.4

K

Kaplan v. Gray, 5.2.2, 7.2
Keefe v. Fairfield, 5.2.1, 5.3.2
Kellogg v. Curtis, 3.2.4
Kelly v. Marx, 1.2.1, 1.2.2, 1.3.2,
1.3.3, 8.1, 8.2, 8.3, 9.1.1, 9.1.2,
9.1.4, 9.1.5, 9.1.9, 9.1.10, 9.2,
9.3, 9.3.3, 10.4, 11.2.1, 11.2.7,
11.3.4, 11.3.5, 12.1, 12.2.1,
12.3, 13.4, 14.1
Kelly v. Thompson, 5.3.1

Kemble v. Farren, 3.1, 10.1, 13.4
Kimco of New Eng., Inc. v. Cliftex
Corp., 12.4
King v. Milliken, 5.3.3, 5.3.4, 9.1.8
Kothe v. R.C. Taylor Trust, 7.1.1, 10.1
Krasne v. Tedeschi & Grasso, 11.2.5
Kroeger v. Stop & Shop, 1.1

L

Lake Ridge Academy v. Carney, 10.4
Lake River Corp. v. Carborundum
Co., 11.2.1, 13.4
La Valle v. Cataldo, 5.3.4
Lawrence v. Miller, 5.3.4
Lieberman v. Lavene, 5.2.4
Lind Bldg. v. Pacific Bellevue
Developments, 8.1
Lowe v. Peers, 3.1, 3.2.2
Lynch v. Andrew, 1.3.1, 7.1.4, 7.1.5,
7.1.6, 7.2, 8.3, 9.3
Lynde v. Thompson, 4.1.3, 4.2, 4.2.1,
4.2.3, 4.2.5, 8.2

M

Macurdy v. Carver, 5.3.3, 5.3.4
Makletzova v. Diaghileff, 6.4, 7.1.1,
10.1
Manganaro Drywall, Inc. v. Penn-
Simon Constr. Co., 7.1.2
McIlvenny v. Horton, 9.2
McMahon v. McMahon, 8.3
Merrill v. Merrill, 2.2
MetLife Capital Fin. Corp. v.
Washington Ave. Assocs. L.P.,
8.3
Morrison v. Richardson, 4.2.4

N

NPS, LLC v. Minihane, 1.2.5, 8.3,
10.4, 11.1, 11.2.1, 11.2.2, 11.2.3,
11.2.5, 11.2.7, 11.3.1, 11.3.4,
11.3.5, 12.2.2, 12.4, 14.1, 14.2

P

Pacheco v. Scoblionko, 9.2
Panagakos v. Collins, 11.3.5, 12.2.2, 12.3.3
Patterson v. Anderson Motor Co., 9.2
Pay-Saver Corp. v. Vasso Corp., 8.3
Perkins v. Lyman, 3.2.2, 3.2.4
Perroncello v. Donahue, 1.2.3, 1.3.4, 8.3, 9.1.6, 11.2.1, 11.3.2, 13.1
Perry v. Wilson Bros. Inc., 5.2.4
Pierce v. Fuller, 3.2.1, 3.2.2, 3.2.4, 4.1.2
Pierce v. Hoffstot, 13.2
P.J. Carlin Constr. Co. v. New York, 8.3
Putnam Mach. Co. v. Mustakangas, 5.4.5, 6.4, 7.1.1

R

Renda v. Gouchberg, 10.1
Rodriguez v. Learjet, Inc., 8.3
Ropes v. Upton, 4.2.1

S

Schoolnick v. Gold, 6.2
Schrenko v. Regnante, 7.1.6, 7.1.7
Sechrest v. Safiol, 5.3.4
Security Safety Corp. v. Kuznicki, 6.4, 7.1.2, 7.1.5, 9.3
Sentry Ins. v. Firnstein, 10.1
Shallow Brook Assocs. v. Dube, 8.3
Shapiro v. Grinspoon, 7.1.7, 7.2, 8.1, 9.1.2, 9.1.4, 9.2, 9.3.3, 11.1, 14.1
Shute v. Taylor, 2.2, 6.4, 7.1.1
Situation Mgmt. Sys., Inc. v. Malouf, Inc., 1.3.4, 8.3
Slaughter v. La Compagnie Francaises Des Cables Telegraphiques, 8.3
Smith v. Brown, 4.2.1
Smith v. Green, 5.3.3
Smith v. McMahon, 5.3.3, 9.1.8
Space Master Int'l, Inc. v. Worcester, 1.1

Stearns v. Barrett, 3.2.3

T

TAL Fin. Corp. v. CSC Consulting, Inc., 1.2.2, 8.3, 9.2, 9.3, 10.4, 13.2
Thompson v. Gould, 9.1.7
Town Planning & Eng'r Assn., Inc. v. Amesbury Specialty Co., 8.3
275 Washington Street Corp. v. Hudson River Int'l, LLC, 11.2.5, 11.3.1, 12.2.1, 12.2.2, 12.4

U

United Air Lines, Inc. v. Austin Travel Corp., 10.3

V

Vines v. Orchard Hills, 7.1.7

W

Waggoner v. Johnston, 9.2
Wallace v. Smith, 5.3.2
Wallis v. Carpenter, 10.1
Wallis v. Smith, 4.2.2
Warner v. Wilkey, 7.1.3, 7.1.4, 7.1.5, 9.3
Wassenaar v. Panos, 1.1, 8.3, 9.1.3, 9.2, 9.3.3
Watson v. Ingram, 8.1, 9.1.4, 9.2
Wells v. Calman, 9.1.7
Wesson v. Leone Enters., Inc., 11.2.5
Wheaton Bldg. & Lumber Co. v. Boston, 5.2.4
White v. Peabody Constr. Co., 4.1.3

X

XCO Int'l, Inc. v. Pacific Scientific Co., 10.3, 11.2.3, 11.2.6, 13.2, 14.1

Z

Zevitas v. Adams, 11.2.5

TABLE OF STATUTES, RULES, AND REFERENCES

References are to section numbers of this book, unless otherwise indicated.

FEDERAL

UNITED STATES CODE (U.S.C.)
11 U.S.C. § 502, 11.3.4, 12.3, 12.3.2

UNITED STATES CONSTITUTION
art. I § 10, 1.3.1
Fifteenth Amendment, 1.3.1
Fourteenth Amendment, 1.3.1

MASSACHUSETTS

MASSACHUSETTS GENERAL LAWS (G.L. C.)
c. 239, 11.3.5

OTHER JURISDICTIONS

CALIFORNIA
Cal. Civ. Code § 1671, 9.2
Cal. Civ. Code § 1675, 9.2

NORTH DAKOTA
N.D. Code § 9-08-4, 9.2

OKLAHOMA
15 O.S. 1961, § 214, 9.2
15 O.S. 1961, § 215, 9.2

WASHINGTON
RWCA 64.04.005, 9.2

RESTATEMENTS

RESTATEMENT (FIRST) OF CONTRACTS, 5.1, 6.1, 8.2, 14.1
§ 339, 2.2, 5.4.5, 6.1, 6.2, 6.3, 6.4, 7.1.1, 7.1.5, 7.1.7, 9.3
§ 340, 5.4.5, 6.1

RESTATEMENT (SECOND) OF CONTRACTS
§ 14, 13.3
§ 15, 13.3
§ 25, 9.1.5, 13.3
§ 208, 7.1.7, 9.2, 9.3.3, 11.2.4
§ 339, 10.1
§ 344, 1.3.4, 7.1.2, 11.2.1
§ 347, 1.3.4, 11.2.1
§ 348, 1.3.4
§ 356, 2.2, 7.1.7, 7.2, 8.1, 9.2, 9.3, 9.3.3, 14.1

RESTATEMENT (THIRD) OF RESTITUTION AND UNJUST ENRICHMENT
§ 1, 9.1.6

UNIFORM LAWS

UNIFORM COMMERCIAL CODE (U.C.C.)
§ 2-102, 4.1.3, 4.2.4
§ 2-105, 4.1.3, 4.2.4, 6.2
§ 2-205, 9.3.1
§ 2-302, 7.1.7, 9.2, 9.3.3, 11.2.4
§ 2-706, 9.1.2
§ 2-708, 11.3.4
§ 2-709, 11.3.2
§ 2-718, 1.1, 4.2.4, 6.2, 7.1.7, 9.3.3

UNIFORM COMMERCIAL CODE (U.C.C.) *(cont'd)*
§ 2-719, 9.3.3
§ 2A-504, 1.1, 1.2.2, 8.3
Article 2A, 1.2.2, 8.3

UNIFORM LAND TRANSACTIONS ACT, 9.1.2
§ 504, 9.1.2

ADDITIONAL REFERENCES AND RESOURCES

Benfield, Marion W., Jr., "Wasted Days and Wasted Nights: Why the Land Acts Failed," 20 *Nova L. Rev.* 1037 (Spring 1996), 9.1.2

Black's Law Dictionary (9th ed.), 1.1, 8.3, 9.1.5, 9.3.1

Browder, Daniel, "Liquidated Damages in Montana," 67 *Mont. L. Rev.* 361 (2006), 1.4

Corbin, Arthur L., "The Right of a Defaulting Vendee to the Restitution of Installments Paid," XL *Yale L. J.* (May 1931), 9.1.8, 9.2

11 *Corbin on Contracts* (rev. ed. by Joseph M. Perillo, 2005), 1.1, 10.3

Crispi, Gregory Scott, "Measuring 'Actual Harm' for the Purpose of Determining the Enforceability of Liquidated Damages Clauses," 41 *Houston L. Rev.* 1579 (2004-2005), 9.1.3

Daniszewski, Robert & Jeffrey Sacks, "One Look Too Many: Courts Take a 'Second Look' at Liquidated Damages Provisions," 34 *Bos. Bar J.* 12 (March/April 1990), 7.2

Dobbs, Dan B., 1 *Dobbs Law of Remedies* (2d ed.), 9.1.6, 9.1.8

Eisenberg, Melvin Aron, "The Emergence of Dynamic Contract Law," 88 *Cal. L. Rev.* 1743 (Dec. 2000), 13.3

Eisenberg, Melvin Aron, "The Limits of Cognition and the Limits of Contract," 47 *Stan. L. Rev.* 211 (Jan. 1995), 8.1, 11.3.4, 13.3, 13.4

Farnsworth, E. Allan, *Contracts* (4th ed. 2004), 1.1, 1.3.1, 6.2, 7.1.7, 8.3

Fifoot, C.H.S., *Lord Mansfield* (Clarendon Press–Oxford, 1936), 3.1

Fischer, James M., *Understanding Remedies* (LexisNexis, 2d ed.), 9.1.2

Fortin, Lisa A., "Why There Should be a Duty to Mitigate Liquidated Damages Clauses," 38 *Hofstra L. Rev.* 285 (2009-2010), 11.1, 12.2.2

Friedman, Milton R. & James Charles Smith, 2 *Friedman on Contracts and Conveyances of Real Property* (Practising Law Institute, 7th ed. 2011), 5.1, 5.3.4, 8.3

Gilmore, Grant, *The Ages of American Law* (Yale Univ. Press, 1977), 4.1.3

Horwitz, Morton J., "The Historical Foundations of Modern Contract Law," 87 *Harv. L. Rev.* 917 (1974), 2.1

Hovey, William V., "Avuncular Advisor: Breaching Buyers Exposed," *Massachusetts Lawyers Weekly* (June 28, 1993), 7.2, 9.2

Llewellyn, Karl, *The Common Law Tradition—Deciding Appeals* (Little, Brown and Co., 1960), 4.1.3

Lloyd, William H., "Penalties and Forfeitures," XXIX *Harv. L. Rev.* 117 (1915), 2.1

Massachusetts Bar Ass'n of the City of Boston, *Massachusetts Annotations to the Restatement of the Law of Contracts* (American Law Institute Publishers, 1935), 6.2

Murray, John Edward, Jr., *Murray on Contracts* (4th ed. 2001), 1.1

Murray, John Edward, Jr., *Murray on Contracts* (LexisNexis, 5th ed. 2011), 9.1.9

Perillo, Joseph M., *Calamari and Perillo on Contracts* (6th ed.), 1.1

Robbins, Mark D., "Another Look at the 'Second Look' Doctrine: Enforcing Liquidated Damages Clauses Without Hindsight," 44 *Boston Bar. J.* 8 (2000), 4.1.3, 8.2

Simpson, A.W.B., *A History of the Common Law of Contract* (Clarendon Press–Oxford, 1987), 2.1

Talty, Talty and Braunstein, 5 *Massachusetts Practice,* 9.1.7

Teeven, Kevin M., *A History of the Anglo-American Common Law of Contract* (Greenwood Press, 1990), 2.1

Weisfeld, James A., "'Keep the Change!'; A Critique of the No Actual Injury Defense to Liquidated Damages—*Lind Building v. Pacific Bellevue Developments*," 65 *Wash. L. Rev.* 977 (1990), 8.1

Williston, Samuel, 3 *A Treatise on the Law of Contracts* (rev. ed. by Samuel Williston and George Thompson 1936), 1.1, 6.2, 6.3, 10.1, 14.1

24 Williston, *A Treatise on the Law of Contracts* (4th ed. by Richard A. Lord, 2002), 1.1, 1.3.1, 10.4

INDEX

References are to section numbers of this book, unless otherwise indicated.

A

ACCELERATION CLAUSES
As stipulated damages clauses, 10.1
Enforceability of, 11.2.5
Enforced as liquidated damages
clauses, 1.2.4
In leases and licenses, limiting use
of, Ch. 12
Balancing equities, 12.3.3
Established norms, acceleration
clauses exceeding, 12.4
Establishing baseline, 12.3.2
Mitigation of damages, evidence
of, 12.2.2
Overview, 12.1
Sales distinguished, 12.3.1
Single look rule and, 12.2.1
Overcompensation, danger of,
11.3.1, 11.3.4
Real estate, 11.3.3

APPEALS
Prospective nature of, 1.2.1

B

BURDEN OF PROOF
Overview, 1.2.2
Single look rule and, 8.3

C

COMPENSATORY PRINCIPLE,
1.3.4
Freedom of contract versus, 1.4
In English law, 3.1
Penal bonds and, 2.2

CONSEQUENTIAL DAMAGES
Single look rule and, 9.1.3

CONTRACTS
Acceleration clauses (*See*
ACCELERATION CLAUSES)

**DEPOSITS RETAINED
PURSUANT TO,** 5.2
Dubinski v. Wells Bros. Co. of N.Y.,
5.2.3
Garcin v. Pennsylvania Furnace Co.,
5.2.1
Kaplan v. Gray, 5.2.2
Overview, 5.2.4
Freedom of contract
Compensatory principle versus, 1.4
As objective of liquidated
damages, 1.3.1
Single look rule and, 11.2.6
Stipulated damages clauses (*See*
STIPULATED DAMAGES
CLAUSES)

**COVENANTS NOT TO
COMPETE,** 3.2
Overview, 3.2.4
Perkins v. Lyman, 3.2.2
Pierce v. Fuller, 3.2.1
Stearns v. Barrett, 3.2.3

D

DAMAGES
Consequential damages
Single look rule and, 9.1.3
Direct damages
Single look rule and, 9.1.2
Mitigation of
Evidence of, 1.2.5
Acceleration clauses in leases and
licenses, limiting use of, 12.2.2

DEBATE ON LIQUIDATED DAMAGES, Ch. 13
Eisenberg on, 13.3
Human cognition, relevance of limits on, 13.3, 13.4
Overview, 13.1
Posner on, 13.2

DEFERENCE
In stipulated damages clauses, 4.2
Garst v. Harris, 4.2.3
Guerin v. Stacey, 4.2.2
Morrison v. Richardson, 4.2.4
Overview, 4.2.5
Smith v. Brown, 4.2.1

DEFINITION OF LIQUIDATED DAMAGES, 1.1

DEMISE OF SECOND LOOK RULE, Ch. 8
Kelly v. Marx, 8.1
Logical extension of, 11.2.1
Reaction to, 8.2

DEPOSITS, Ch. 5
Burden of proof, 5.4.1
Forfeiture, parallel doctrine of, 5.3
Development of, 5.4.3
Donaghue v. Parkman, 5.3.1
Judicial scrutiny and, 5.4.4
Keefe v. Fairfield, 5.3.2
King v. Milliken, 5.3.4
Smith v. McMahon, 5.3.3
Overview, 5.1
Prospective versus retrospective analysis, 5.4.2
Retention pursuant to contract, 5.2
Dubinski v. Wells Bros. Co. of N.Y., 5.2.3
Garcin v. Pennsylvania Furnace Co., 5.2.1
Kaplan v. Gray, 5.2.2
Overview, 5.2.4

DIRECT DAMAGES
Single look rule and, 9.1.2

E

ECONOMIC BENEFITS OF SINGLE LOOK RULE, 11.2.2

ECONOMIC RAMIFICATIONS OF LIQUIDATED DAMAGES, 1.2.6

EFFICIENCY
As objective of liquidated damages, 1.3.3
Single look rule and, 9.1.4

EISENBERG, MELVIN, 13.3

ENGLISH LAW

COMPENSATORY PRINCIPLE IN, 3.1

PENAL BONDS IN, 2.1

F

FORFEITURE
Deposits, as parallel doctrine to, 5.3
Development of, 5.4.3
Donaghue v. Parkman, 5.3.1
Judicial scrutiny and, 5.4.4
Keefe v. Fairfield, 5.3.2
King v. Milliken, 5.3.4
Smith v. McMahon, 5.3.3
Single look rule and, 9.1.8

FREEDOM OF CONTRACT
As objective of liquidated damages, 1.3.1
Compensatory principle versus, 1.4
Single look rule and, 11.2.6

H

HOLMES, OLIVER WENDELL, 4.2

HUMAN COGNITION
Limits on, relevance to liquidated
damages, 13.3, 13.4

I

**INCAPABILITY OF
ESTIMATION OF ACTUAL
DAMAGES,** Ch. 6
Adoption of two-prong test in
Massachusetts, 6.4
Background of, 6.2
Overview, 6.1
Prospective versus retrospective
analysis, 6.3

J

JUDICIAL REVIEW
Prospective nature of, 1.2.1

**JURISPRUDENTIAL DEBATE
ON LIQUIDATED DAMAGES,**
Ch. 13
Eisenberg on, 13.3
Human cognition, relevance of limits
on, 13.3, 13.4
Overview, 13.1
Posner on, 13.2

**JUSTIFICATIONS FOR SINGLE
LOOK RULE,** 9.1
Bargaining abuse, preventing, 11.2.4
Compensation for buyer's option, 9.1.5
Consequential damages and, 9.1.3
Direct damages and, 9.1.2
Economic benefits of, 11.2.2
Efficiency of, 9.1.4
Facilitating efficient breaches, 9.1.9
Forfeiture and, 9.1.8
Freedom of contract and, 11.2.6
Overview, 9.1.10
Predictability of, 9.1.1, 11.2.3
Punishment versus windfall, 9.1.6
Security of, 11.2.3
Seller as risk-bearer, 9.1.7

L

LEASES
Acceleration clauses, limiting use of,
Ch. 12
Balancing equities, 12.3.3
Established norms, acceleration
clauses exceeding, 12.4
Establishing baseline, 12.3.2
Mitigation of damages, evidence
of, 12.2.2
Overview, 12.1
Sales distinguished, 12.3.1
Single look rule and, 12.2.1
Single look rule in, Ch. 10
Cummings Properties, LLC v.
Empire Technologies, Inc.,
10.2
Cummings Properties, LLC v.
National Communications
Corp., 10.3
NPS, LLC v. Minihane, 10.4

LICENSES
Acceleration clauses, limiting use of,
Ch. 12
Balancing equities, 12.3.3
Established norms, acceleration
clauses exceeding, 12.4
Establishing baseline, 12.3.2
Mitigation of damages, evidence
of, 12.2.2
Overview, 12.1
Sales distinguished, 12.3.1
Single look rule and, 12.2.1
Single look rule in, Ch. 10
Cummings Properties, LLC v.
Empire Technologies, Inc.,
10.2
Cummings Properties, LLC v.
National Communications
Corp., 10.3
NPS, LLC v. Minihane, 10.4

LIMITING PRINCIPLE
Acceleration clauses, danger of
overcompensation under,
11.3.1, 11.3.4
Argument for, 9.2
Need for, 11.3
Panagakos v. Collins, 11.3.5
Recommendations regarding, 14.2
Specific performance and, 11.3.2

M

MITIGATION OF DAMAGES
Evidence of, 1.2.5
Acceleration clauses in leases and
licenses, limiting use of,
12.2.2

N

NONCOMPETE AGREEMENTS,
3.2
Overview, 3.2.4
Perkins v. Lyman, 3.2.2
Pierce v. Fuller, 3.2.1
Stearns v. Barrett, 3.2.3

O

**OBJECTIVES OF LIQUIDATED
DAMAGES,** 1.3
Compensatory principle, 1.3.4
Efficiency, 1.3.3
Freedom of contract, 1.3.1
Predictability, 1.3.2

P

PENAL BONDS, Ch. 2
Compensatory principle and, 2.2
In English law, 2.1
In 19th Century Massachusetts law,
2.2

POSNER, RICHARD, 13.2

PREDICTABILITY
As objective of liquidated damages,
1.3.2
Single look rule and, 9.1.1, 11.2.3

**PROPORTIONALITY OF
LIQUIDATED DAMAGES**
Acceleration clauses and, 10.1
A-Z Servicecenter, Inc. v. Segall, 7.1.1
Cummings Properties, LLC v.
National Communications
Corp., 10.3
Kelly v. Marx, 8.1, 9.2
Lynch v. Andrew, 7.1.4
NPS, LLC v. Minihane, 10.4
Second look rule and, 9.3.3
Security Safety Corp. v. Kuznicki,
7.1.2
Shapiro v. Grinspoon, 7.1.7
Stipulated damages clauses and,
9.3.3
Two-prong test and, 6.2, 6.3
Warner v. Wilkey, 7.1.3

**PROSPECTIVE VERSUS
RETROSPECTIVE ANALYSIS**
Deposits, 5.4.2
Two-prong test, 6.3

R

REAL ESTATE
Acceleration clauses, 11.3.3
Second look rule in, Ch. 7
A-Z Servicecenter, Inc. v. Segall,
7.1.1
Colonial at Lynnfield, Inc. v.
Sloan, 7.1.5
Lynch v. Andrew, 7.1.4
Schrenko v. Regnante, 7.1.6
Security Safety Corp. v. Kuznicki,
7.1.2
Shapiro v. Grinspoon, 7.1.7
Reaction to, 7.2
Warner v. Wilkey, 7.1.3

REASONABILITY OF LIQUIDATED DAMAGES, Ch. 6
Adoption of two-prong test in Massachusetts, 6.4
Background of, 6.2
Overview, 6.1
Prospective versus retrospective analysis, 6.3

RECHARTING OF LIQUIDATED DAMAGES LAW, 14.2

RECOMMENDATIONS, 14.2

REFLECTIONS ON LIQUIDATED DAMAGES LAW, 14.1

RESTATEMENT (FIRST) OF CONTRACTS
Deposits and, 5.1, 5.4
Penal bonds and, 2.2
Second look rule under, 14.1
   A-Z Servicecenter, Inc. v. Segall, 7.1.1
   Colonial at Lynnfield, Inc. v. Sloan, 7.1.5
   Security Safety Corp. v. Kuznicki, 7.1.2
   Shapiro v. Grinspoon, 7.1.7
Stipulated damages clauses and, 5.4.5
Two-prong test
   Adoption in Massachusetts, 6.4
   Background of, 6.2
   Overview, 6.1
   Prospective versus retrospective analysis, 6.3

RESTATEMENT (SECOND) OF CONTRACTS
Compensatory principle and, 1.3.4, 8.1
Human cognition, relevance of limits on, 13.3
Penal bonds and, 2.1, 2.2

Second look rule and, 14.1
Shapiro v. Grinspoon, 7.1.7
Reaction to, 7.2
Single look rule under
   Bargaining abuse, preventing, 11.2.4
   Compensation for buyer's option, 9.1.5
   Kelly v. Marx
      Logical extensions of, 11.2.1
      Limiting principle, 9.2
   Stipulated damages clauses and, 9.3
      Acceleration clauses as, 10.1
      Proportionality of, 9.3.3

RESTATEMENT (THIRD) OF RESTITUTION AND UNJUST ENRICHMENT
Single look rule and, 9.2

RETROSPECTIVE VERSUS PROSPECTIVE ANALYSIS
Deposits, 5.4.2
Two-prong test, 6.3

S

SALES
Stipulated damages clauses (*See* STIPULATED DAMAGES CLAUSES)

SECOND LOOK RULE
Demise of, Ch. 8
   Kelly v. Marx, 8.1
      Logical extension of, 11.2.1
      Reaction to, 8.2
Real estate, Ch. 7
   A-Z Servicecenter, Inc. v. Segall, 7.1.1
   Colonial at Lynnfield, Inc. v. Sloan, 7.1.5
   Lynch v. Andrew, 7.1.4
   Reflections on, 14.1
   Schrenko v. Regnante, 7.1.6

SECOND LOOK RULE
Real estate *(cont'd)*
Security Safety Corp. v. Kuznicki,
7.1.2
Shapiro v. Grinspoon, 7.1.7
Reaction to, 7.2
Warner v. Wilkey, 7.1.3
Stipulated damages clauses and, 9.3
Actual economic loss, 9.3.2
Knowledge of agreement, 9.3.1
Proportionality of, 9.3.3

**SECURITY OF SINGLE LOOK
RULE,** 11.2.3

SERVICES
Stipulated damages clauses (*See*
STIPULATED DAMAGES
CLAUSES)

SINGLE LOOK RULE, Ch. 9
Acceleration clauses in leases and
licenses, limiting use of, 12.2.1
Burden of proof and, 8.3
In leases and licenses, Ch. 10
Cummings Properties, LLC v.
Empire Technologies, Inc.,
10.2
Cummings Properties, LLC v.
National Communications
Corp., 10.3
NPS, LLC v. Minihane, 10.4
Justifications for, 9.1
Bargaining abuse, preventing,
11.2.4
Compensation for buyer's option,
9.1.5
Consequential damages and, 9.1.3
Direct damages and, 9.1.2
Economic benefits of, 11.2.2
Efficiency of, 9.1.4
Facilitating efficient breaches,
9.1.9
Forfeiture and, 9.1.8
Freedom of contract and, 11.2.6

Overview, 9.1.10
Predictability of, 9.1.1, 11.2.3
Punishment versus windfall, 9.1.6
Security of, 11.2.3
Seller as risk-bearer, 9.1.7
Kelly v. Marx, 8.1
Logical extension of, 11.2.1
Reaction to, 8.2
Overview, 11.2.7
Reflections on, 14.1
Specific performance and, 8.3

SPECIFIC PERFORMANCE
Limiting principle and, 11.3.2
Overview, 1.2.3
Single look rule and, 8.3

**STIPULATED DAMAGES
CLAUSES,** Ch. 4
Acceleration clauses as, 10.1
Deference to contracting parties, 4.2
Garst v. Harris, 4.2.3
Guerin v. Stacey, 4.2.2
Morrison v. Richardson, 4.2.4
Overview, 4.2.5
Smith v. Brown, 4.2.1
Evaluation of, 5.4.5
Pre-Civil War cases, 4.1
Curtis v. Brewer, 4.1.1
Higginson v. Weld, 4.1.2
Lynde v. Thompson, 4.1.3
Second look rule and, 9.3
Actual economic loss, 9.3.2
Knowledge of agreement, 9.3.1
Proportionality of, 9.3.3

T

TWO-PRONG TEST, Ch. 6
Adoption in Massachusetts, 6.4
Background of, 6.2
Overview, 6.1
Prospective versus retrospective
analysis, 6.3